THE NEW AM
CRIME FI

THE NEW AMERICAN CRIME FILM

Matthew Sorrento

Foreword by Stuart Gordon

McFarland & Company, Inc., Publishers
Jefferson, North Carolina, and London

LIBRARY OF CONGRESS CATALOGUING-IN-PUBLICATION DATA

Sorrento, Matthew, 1976–
　　The new American crime film / Matthew Sorrento ; foreword
by Stuart Gordon.
　　　　p.　　cm.
　　Includes bibliographical references and index.

　　ISBN 978-0-7864-5920-9
　　softcover : acid free paper ∞

　　1. Crime films — United States — History and criticism.
I. Title.
PN1995.9.C66S57　2012
791.43' 655 — dc23　　　　　　　　　　　　　　2012026119

BRITISH LIBRARY CATALOGUING DATA ARE AVAILABLE

On the cover: Josh Brolin in *No Country for Old Men*, 2007
(Miramax Films/Photofest); background © 2012 Shutterstock

Manufactured in the United States of America

McFarland & Company, Inc., Publishers
　Box 611, Jefferson, North Carolina 28640
　www.mcfarlandpub.com

For my wife, Earlene
My mother, who loves work as much as fun
My father, whose cultural memory
I'm thrilled to have inherited
and
My sisters, Kate and Amy,
who share the love

Table of Contents

Acknowledgments

I'm fortunate to work in both post-secondary education and film criticism, a trying but rewarding balance that inspired the approach to this book. Of course, family and friends figure in greatly as well.

Special thanks go to Stuart Gordon, contemporary master of genre film who took time out to write the foreword. Many thanks to former *Film Threat* editors Chris Gore and Eric Campos, current publisher and editor Mark Bell, as well as Phil Hall, Don R. Lewis, Michael Ferraro, Amy R. Handler, and the rest of the staff; *Bright Lights Film Journal* founder/editor Gary Morris; Matt Borondy and the staff of *Identity Theory*; Daniel Lindvall, editor-in-chief of *Film International;* Fincina Hopgood of *Senses of Cinema*; Sarah Zupko, Karen Zarker, Marco Lanzagorta, Cynthia Fuchs, and Matt Mazur of *PopMatters*; David Hudson of MUBI.com; Molly Eichel, deputy Arts & Entertainment editor at the *Philadelphia City Paper*; Lou Gaul of Calkins Media; Kelly Roncace of the *Gloucester County Times*; Salwa Ghaly and Russell Prather of *PEHW*; Josh Goldbloom of the Philadelphia Cinema Alliance; Samuel Hughes and Peter Ivory of *The Pennsylvania Gazette*; Mark Rosman, managing editor at Greater Media Newspapers; and the Entertainment staff at the *Los Angeles Times* for (dis)honoring yours truly as one of "2007's crankiest movie critics" (at the expense of Disney's *Enchanted*).

Thanks to Janice Antczak, William J. Watkins (emeritus), Robert Mellert, and Jeffrey Ford (emeritus) of Brookdale Community College; Michael Robertson, David Venturo, Barry Novick (emeritus), Juda Bennett, Larry McCauley, Harriet Hustis, and Eugenia Shanklin (the anthropologist who taught a class on Vampires, Witches, and Werewolves and who, sadly and ironically, passed away on Halloween, 2007) of The College of New Jersey; Reynold Forman; Jean Martin; my colleagues, mentors, and friends at Rutgers University in Camden: Lisa Zeidner, Allen Woll, Robert A. Emmons, Jr., Howard Marchitello, Timothy Martin, Geoffrey Sill, Tyler Hoffman, Joe Bar-

barese, and M.A. Rafey Habib; and Donna Armstrong, Ellen Hernandez, Christine Webster, Julie Yankanich, Lesley Fredericks, Elena Bogardus, Jennifer Hoheisel, John Pesda, William Thompson, Marjorie Sokoloff, Robert Kaczorowski, Judith Rowlands, Margaret A. Hamilton, and Raymond Yannuzzi of Camden County College for being such supportive colleagues and administrators.

A final acknowledgment to Brian Putman (1975–2000), a dreamer taken too soon, and the Putman family, whose early-model VHS player helped shape my love for genre film.

Foreword
by Stuart Gordon

Why are we so fascinated with crime movies?

I think the reason is that we all wish we could be criminals.

Who hasn't dreamed of robbing a bank? And at some time or another we all wanted to kill someone. But we stifle these urges, and go on with our law-abiding lives. And then we flock to the movies to vicariously share in the mayhem and bloodletting. The ancient Greeks called this "catharsis."

Antonin Artaud, the crazed visionary playwright and director, created what he called The Theater of Cruelty. In his brilliant essay "The Theater and Its Double," he states that true theater must feature "the triumph of dark powers.... And that is why all the great Myths are dark, so that one cannot imagine, save in an atmosphere of carnage, torture, and bloodshed, all the magnificent Fables."

Artaud believed theater should enact crimes onstage — the more violent and disturbing, the better — and audiences needed to share in them and through them could expunge their dark desires in a socially acceptable way without actually harming their fellow man. In Artaud's words this kind of theater "is beneficial, for impelling men to see themselves as they are.... It causes the mask to fall, reveals the lie, the slackness, baseness, and hypocrisy of our world."

In other words: crime movies are good for us. And as Matthew Sorrento writes, the crime film is evolving and in many ways growing ever darker.

Crime films have existed since the very beginning of cinema, starting with 1903's *The Great Train Robbery*, which is viewed by many as the first narrative film. During the 1930s gangster films were king, with films like *Little Caesar* and *Scarface* loosely based on the real-life exploits of Al Capone and John Dillinger. But in these films the criminals always had to be punished, and each movie ended with the protagonist shot down. "Is this the end of Rico?" laments Edward G. Robinson, lying in a puddle of his own blood.

1

In 1992 Quentin Tarantino's *Reservoir Dogs* changed the crime movie for all time. In that film an undercover cop (Tim Roth) infiltrates a gang of armed robbers, but his hope of bringing them down ends in a bloodbath. So once again evildoers are punished. But in his next film, *Pulp Fiction*, there is not a policeman in sight. Samuel Jackson's Bible-quoting hitman lives to repent his many murders.

I met Quentin at the beginning of his amazing career. One night, during a vodka-fueled conversation in which I berated him for the too-easy-to-kill vampires in *From Dusk Till Dawn*, I promised him that I would never make a crime film if he would agree to stay away from horror. We shook on it, but in 2002 I broke my promise by directing *King of the Ants*, based on the 1992 novel by Charlie Higson.

In this story, a young drifter is hired to murder an accountant for a paltry $13,000. What drew me to the project was that the kid actually goes through with the killing and somehow we still care for him, even after he has murdered an innocent man in cold blood and gets away with it. But I had a hell of a time convincing the studios to finance the film. Shouldn't he be punished? One executive told me his company would make the film if the accountant had murdered our hero's brother or father and our guy was avenging his death.

But I stuck to my guns, knowing that the amorality of the character was the most interesting and most shocking thing about the story, and in fact the only reason to make the film. Eventually we found a little company called Asylum, who had the balls to produce it, although it was shot on a microbudget using leftover film, referred to in the business as "short ends."

So getting back to Artaud, if our desire is to be criminals, we sure as hell don't want to be caught or punished. And as Mr. Sorrento points out, neither do the characters presented by the filmmakers in this book. He has assembled an often unlikely but fascinating list of suspects, many directors you usually don't associate with the genre: Spike Lee, Sam Raimi, and Woody Allen, to name a few. But there are others who have built careers with their crime films, the Davids — Fincher, Cronenberg and Mamet — as well as the Coen brothers and, of course, the iconic Clint Eastwood. And somehow even I managed to sneak in, for which I am truly honored.

Let's just hope Quentin doesn't find out.

Stuart Gordon served as artistic director of The Organic Theater Company of Chicago from 1970 to 1985, before winning the Critics' Award at the Cannes Film Festival for his first feature film, Re-Animator *(1985). He has worked in a variety of genres, including horror (*From Beyond, *1986), comedy (*The Wonderful Ice Cream Suit, *1998), and crime (*King of the Ants, *2003;* Edmond, *2005; and* Stuck, *2007) and lives in Los Angeles.*

Preface

To many, there seems little reason to discuss crime in movies. Jean-Luc Godard's famous quip, "All you need to make a movie is a girl and a gun," implies the frequency of crime onscreen, alongside romance. An emeritus colleague of mine responded similarly when I told him about my interest in teaching and writing about the subject. "Don't all films contain crimes?" he asked me, before wishing me well in an avuncular manner.

Though my colleague sees — and Godard suggests — redundancy, the frequency of crime has grown into something unique in the current American cinema. Recent films use the crime genre to explore a variety of themes and create genre hybrids. In doing so, the crime film has become the most pervasive genre of the American cinema. By analyzing films in this genre for three archetypal characters — the criminal, victim, and avenger (first identified by Thomas Leitch in *Crime Films*) — we see broad thematic material created from limited motifs. The current crime film is often pessimistic, at times nihilist, drawing itself close to the distinctly American tradition of film noir. Since the contemporary crime film has so far been ignored in scholarship, this book serves as a critical introduction to these works and a study of contemporary genre.

While the films' resolutions are often dark, this study focuses on artists who pay tribute to tradition while inspiring it to grow. In the classical style, many of the films use the narrative patterns of myth and the fairy tale to reflect the universality of criminality and vengeance. Certainly, many films not featured in the book use genre as a shooting corral, a template for broad action and showy performances. The films and filmmakers discussed here employ historic and revised crime plots to connect high thought with popular taste, warranting this genre serious discussion. As the most widespread film genre today, the new American crime film has intermixed with other genres, most frequently the Western. With this genre's focus on bounty and threat, heroes and villains, recent crime films use Western motifs to investigate the

Border Patrol and soldiers returning home (Chapter 11), contemporary rogue avengers (Chapters 12 and 18), and drug trafficking (Chapter 16). While rethinking classic crime plots (the heist film, see Chapter 1; the erotic thriller, Chapter 13; and the gangster film, Chapter 15), the crime film has also made unique connections to the espionage thriller (Chapter 2), the "high-school-as-hell" film (Chapter 5), the horror film (Chapters 7 and 17), and surrealism (Chapter 10). This book's subject has also explored disparate themes, such as feminism (Chapter 3), rural poverty (Chapter 4), journalism-related topics of crime and reportage (Chapters 6 and 9) and food science (Chapter 8).

While a genre study, this book features the auteurs behind the crime film's recent rebirth. Each chapter focuses on a recent work, its narrative and archetypes, and the tradition it inherits and reworks. Visual style is an emphasis, though much of the book considers the films' narrative patterns, the mythical structures that have thrived throughout the history of crime stories. In this sense, the book may serve as a guide for screenwriting buffs and students in addition to the film enthusiast and specialist. I hope to inspire further discussion as the tradition continues.

Introduction
Why Genre, and Why the New Crime Film Has Arrived

A good tale takes us from the ordinary to the extraordinary. When we begin a story, we come into a character's ordinary world, in the Joseph Campbell sense, waiting for some new turn, for a quest to begin. Naturally, in realistic fiction, the new, special world is nothing more than a new situation or state of mind. In romance, it is the promise of love, which better serve up some problems for viewers to stay interested. In adventure, it is the journey, leaving home and security to travel outward, for new experiences on the road to maturation. In comedy, it is a series of unlikely misadventures, since the best kinds stem from the irony of situation. In horror, it is the threat descending upon our hero, who has to fight to the finish after all his friends (and sometimes neighbors) have hit the dirt, courtesy of a bogeyman or monster.

With crime stories, the character abandons the ordinary world once a crime casts its shadow, either before him (if he is a criminal) or upon him (if he is the victim). A crime is surefire storytelling fodder — it demands a change in the character, since it alters his universe in a flash. For the victim of a crime, he now fears the world he once thought to be safe, and may feel the urge to avenge the offense, or even ponder the nature of evil, should he have the down time to do so. The criminal will enter a new, thrilling world, one in which everything is within his reach, until the authorities, or rival criminals, advance upon him.

Like all storytelling modes, the theme of crime plays upon the psyche: it pulls events away from the superego's control, for the id to take over and thrill the viewer. Crime is storytelling at its most primal, demanding a quest be taken by those involved. At the same time, the genre calls for a classical narrative structure to unfold. We expect either an ending in the Shakespearean

5

comedic tradition, in which the criminal's opposition rights the offense and restores order, the audience leaving with a sense of security; or the tragic mold takes shape, in which an ordered universe collapses gradually into disorder, the crime revealing a universe much darker than the previously innocent characters expected.

The joy of seeing chaos resolve into stability, and a stable world descending into chaos, still thrives in our plot-driven fiction. It harks back to the warrior myth told through ancient oral narratives, with triumph and restoration the rule. Tribes had their heroes, a he-man or super-human who would face a trial. From these early myths, the classic hero has evolved, been reprocessed, and even diminished into crude forms, such as professional American football. In this contact sport, the suspense of action fiction is served without the distraction of characters, choices, desires — humanity has been boiled down into the execution of coaches' strategies. The battle plans are modeled on warfare, with a masculine display just as prevalent. American football gets some melodramatic drive from press conferences and media coverage, scandals outnumbering any noteworthy accomplishments. Professional wrestling includes more melodrama in its performance. The characters trash-talk in between matches, which revs up anticipation before athletic actors perform comic-book-character roles for a rehearsed few minutes of suspense. The superhero myth is similar, as wrestling presents a role-player facing larger-than-life obstacles: a villain, the tough main event, winning the title belt. Wrestling's champs are the classical heroes modified for our explain-it-all times. Viewers of this athletic theater desire rough physicality and action over the humanistic drive of good storytelling.

Suspense is the key: it's an objective of the football game and wrestling match as well as plot-driven narrative entertainment. Suspense is instant escapism: it knocks away the routine of our lives with its swift thrust of action. Fans of football and wrestling want the most immediate form of suspense, and thus they flip the channel to the gridiron or the mat. Crude as these forms of entertainment are, they are still fantasy, removed from realism and vaguely recalling the classical hero.

The crime film, with its inherent action, delivers suspense, along with the need for the characters involved to deal with the events. We exchange the faceless, masculine performers of football and the exaggerated wrestling figures for more relatable humans. Central characters in these films either commit the crime, fall victim to it, or avenge it, thus driving our need to witness the conflict's resolution.

But the action isn't enough: we want to know the criminal, the victim, or the avenger. Thomas Leitch identified these three archetypes of the crime-film tradition,[1] following suit from Foster Hirsch, who noted three similar types in his seminal work, *Film Noir: The Dark Side of the Screen*.[2] As one archetype becomes central in a given film, the work inherits a genre archetype, one that is distantly recognizable to us, since it is a mainstay of our unconscious. As the roots of the hero's quest remain within the Jungian unknown of our unconscious, through the crimes that would befall the hero, those he may commit, or ones he would avenge, creative sensibilities have refined his quest into new narratives. The universality of such figures makes the crime film the most dynamic of genres.

Our desire for crime tales, our repeated telling of them, have fashioned another journey for the hero. The film enthusiast who ignores this truth demeans what he loves; he who dismisses genre molds wanders in the shadows of the collective unconscious, never tapping into our universal desires. Genre is at the heart of popular storytelling: inventive traditional storytellers commit to it and spark fire into a template by revising it. This type of filmmaker uses a nuanced style of storytelling to revive and reconstruct a recognized form. Even the experimental storyteller, who seems to abandon the forms altogether, still works off our genre expectations. This writer or director uses genre as a springboard, as it guides his quest to fashion his or her own personalized tale. As the great artists have said, in order to break the rules, one must know them first. In some manner, and to various extents, all storytellers know and use the rules of genre. The crime genre deals with offense and vengeance, the most primal of generic forms. As this book shows, the genre materializes in various forms and commingles with other genres.

If I risk sounding like a "mythical" screenwriting guru, touting format to sell the idea that we all have great artists within us, I apologize. I stress the forms for the simple fact that they live on, especially through the narrative film tradition. Screenwriters and directors who revitalize genre forms have created a new rebirth of the crime theme in contemporary cinema. While crime movies have been departmentalized in criticism — down to gangster film, film noir, the heist picture, the erotic thriller — we will treat the crime film as a unified genre, in the tradition of Leitch's breakthrough (if less regarded) 2002 study. The subgenres of the crime film make varied use of the three character archetypes: the criminal, victim, and avenger. Here, we will see how contemporary films — specifically those spanning from the late 1990s to the present — have redefined this genre's style through new use of the classical archetypes. These new styles, by directors specializing in crime and journeymen who respect and reinvigorate the genre, show the range of material the genre can cover. Through this new, varied but unified style, we now have the most rewarding movement in contemporary cinema, satisfying in both narrative and theme.

This movement answers a problem in popular culture. We are currently in the nadir of formulaic crime-themed television. Countless television detective series follow a cryptic formula, in which we are given characters to either love or hate, and a point of view that stubbornly remains through each narrative. A problem appears — often in the form of a dead, beautiful woman (an unfortunate legacy of Edgar Allan Poe's essay "The Philosophy of Composition") — which mandates the detection of a super-wise person-of-the-law. We have the exception, such as the exciting drama of HBO's *The Wire* or David Mamet's *The Unit* (see Chapter 14 for more on his crime films). Yet, formulaic police thrillers dominate American networks as does reality programming. The police procedurals are so formulaic that viewers don't even receive the suspense they deserve. Instead, they are walked through a bland puzzle. Lacking the satisfaction from crime television, American viewers turn to the voyeurism of reality television, and lock themselves into the suspense of whether a contestant will be "America's" next best dancer, or the (pseudo) love of a Z-list celebrity. It's no wonder that viewers flock to the characterless suspense of football and wrestling.

While television calls for a new mainstreamed crime fiction, contemporary movies show another nadir. The rise of "torture porn" — a term credited to critic David Edelstein — is striving to take up a dictatorship over the horror genre. Compared to crime/suspense, horror has a distinct difference in its affect on the audience. An effective horror scene traps a viewer in dread, and when a horror film can serve up many moments of suspense, the film becomes most rewarding, as a duly dread-inducing and suspenseful experience. The genre of torture porn, serviced by director Eli Roth and the makers of the never-ending *Saw* franchise, works solely by entrapment (not even terror), into a state of gore-disgust. Not to suggest there aren't classics in the gore horror genre — including *Night of the Living Dead* (1968), *Re-Animator* (1985), Peter Jackson's 1992 *Braindead* (titled *Dead Alive* in the U.S.) — but these films sure-handedly entwine dread with wit (often humorously). Torture porn replaces the voyeurism of reality television and expose-all viral videos. All it aims to do is trap, and does so with auto-wreck sensationalism. For purer suspense, the multiplex serves slick, bland action, of which cynically shallow Michael Bay is the proclaimed leader.

Both popular movie styles — torture porn and spectacle-heavy suspense — are termed genre films, which is part of the greater misunderstanding. Genre stems back to the classical Hollywood style, long in the making and described by David Bordwell, Janet Staiger, and Kristin Thompson in *The Classical Hollywood Cinema*. They have shown the varied and nuanced approaches brought to classical forms. The old connotations of "genre" leaves many an enthusiast bemused and cranky. Yet, this point of view dismisses that genre forms are revitalized through careful invention.

The Archetypes of Crime: A Film Tradition

The contemporary crime films analyzed in this book reach back to earlier forms, some to the earliest filmmaking. Silent melodrama worked with accentuated characters types conceived for the stage — outright heroes, ladies in distress, and villains with the stigmas of leering eyes and large mustaches. With good folks wronged, those of strength and integrity would resolve the issues. Viewers enjoyed the villainy before the hero would conquer it, and through the darker characters, the beginnings of a tradition soon arose. In the silent films *The Musketeers of Pig Alley* (D.W. Griffith, 1912) and *Regeneration* (Raoul Walsh, 1915, made after the director worked on Griffith's *The Birth of a Nation*) we see early versions of the film gangster, a hazy but gelling archetype that would resonate with the early–20th-century movie-going public.

Its melodrama aside, the silent film gangster is rooted in a deep, American unease. Many examples, including Walsh's *Regeneration*, pinpoint poverty as the root of crime. Walsh's film, in fact, is a naturalistic take on how a poor orphan's childhood would logically develop into a life of crime. This melodrama redeems the criminal hero, thus redirecting the morally chaotic world into a sound one. (His means of redemption are a baby and a good woman, recurring factors that helped many silent heroes leave a bad road by celebrating family values.) Like the prototypical gangsters of the silent era, the icon of the early sound era is an emblem of social commentary. Evil isn't borne of religious denial or the loss of moral conscience; some just get run down by the big vehicles in society.

The movie gangster turned the American villain into an ironic hero. The figure was an assertive, self-made man to Depression-era audiences in the 1930s.[3] In trying times, he went against the law to make the world his own. After working under a mob boss, one who sold — or forced the sale of— contraband alcohol to speakeasies, the gangster figure rose to overtake his boss, becoming the kingpin. He had a right-hand man, one who usually betrays him at some point. And this standby must take the plunge, at the hands of our gangster-hero. The gangster usually possesses some kind of perversion — in the case of Tony Camonte in *Scarface* (1932) it is a desire for his sister; for Rico Bandello in *Little Caesar* (1930), it's his excessive fondness for the buddy who betrays him. All gangsters must fall by story's end. The growing influence of the Motion Picture Production Code — though not in full power until 1934, a version was introduced in 1930 — leaves the coppers as fabricated winners.

Yet, audiences loved the thrill ride of the gangster's ascent, as much as newspaper readers loved following the exploits of real-life gangsters, the inspiration for these early sound films. The joy of Howard Hawks's *Scarface* lies

Guino Rinaldo (George Raft) and Tony Camonte (Paul Muni) take down the boss in Howard Hawks' *Scarface* (1932, The Caddo Company).

in its flashy (for its time) violence, its gleeful if ape-like hero (a live-wire Paul Muni), and its soundtrack (only a few years old, sound on film was new to viewers). The early gangster films' ripping bullets, sirens, and squealing tires — screen action brought to our ears — made fine use of film's new dimension.

The gangster became an icon, continually returning in favor. He made a big comeback in the late '40s, with James Cagney's most powerful take on the figure in *White Heat* (1949), and the elegiac gangland tale on a remote island, John Huston's 1948 *Key Largo* (here Edward G. Robinson returning as the baddie opposite Humphrey Bogart). The gangster reemerged throughout the '50s and '60s. B-grade budget filmmaking used the classical archetype — based on real-life gangsters, as were the premier pictures — in films like Roger Corman's *Machine-Gun Kelly* (1959) and *The St. Valentine's Day Massacre* (1967). The figure made a large comeback in the late '60s–early '70s, through a film that would redefine cinema: *Bonnie and Clyde* (1967). Taking its cue from the style and genre-reprocessing of the French *Nouvelle Vague*, the film showed how *cineastes* from across the pond showed new appreciation for American cinema and helped us redefine it. The year 1972 saw the release of the hyper-iconic *The Godfather*, through which generations of viewers would honor and worship the gangster icon. Chapter 15 of this book will discuss the "new gangster."

As the gangster was reborn, circa early 1940s, another crime tradition took hold, one as powerful and enduring as the gangster film. Coined by the French, whose critics conceptualized American culture before they helped revise it in the late 1960s, film noir became a popular style with various plot forms. But one plot gained the most strength: that of a morally questionable man pulled into crime by a seductress, again named by the French as the "femme fatale." The most primal noir plot features a loner who's moved into crime by his desire for the fatale. *Double Indemnity* (1944; more powerful as a film than the source novel) and *The Postman Always Rings Twice* (1946; the novel more powerful than the film) both featured this plot, and both source novels were written by James M. Cain (though the dialog of the film version of *Double Indemnity* benefited from Raymond Chandler and Billy Wilder's scriptwriting[4]).

The film of *Double Indemnity*, directed by Wilder, benefits from a unified tone, realized through dark, portentous performances, visuals reflecting equal parts dread and solitude, and a trademark classical score (by Miklós Rózsa). The actions of Walter Neff (Fred MacMurray) and Phyllis Dietrichson (Barbara Stanwyck), who together plot the murder of Phyllis's husband, bring about a steady downfall. The film transforms the passion Walter feels for this black widow — here donning a blond wig — into a feeling of guilt. This narrative delivers a more powerful demise than the detective noirs, which remain objective and removed even if the style is just as moody.[5] The stylistic influences were the shadowy German Expressionist cinema of the Weimar era and French poetic realism; the socio-political sources for such anxiety were the post–World War II unease and the male population's collective anxiety concerning the assertive wartime woman, who took over the workplace in her husband's absence.

Along with its principal narrative archetype, the noir style worked into many plots: the stalker villain (*The Night of the Hunter*, 1955), fatale as outright black widow (*Sunset Blvd.*, 1950), lovers on the run (*Gun Crazy*, 1950), the boxing picture (*The Set-Up*, 1949). Noir presented an outlook that countless crime films would inherit, through the revisionist private-eye film *Kiss Me Deadly* (Robert Aldrich, 1955) and up through Orson Welles's Mexican border noir, 1958's *Touch of Evil* (both films suggesting more sex and violence). The consensus claims that the movement was ended by this time, with good reason. After these films, the trademark dark outlook was tributed more than adopted. Once filmmakers started consciously thinking in noir terms, the style became neo-noir. After the rebirth of the gangster, circa 1967, color films like Roman Polanski's *Chinatown* from 1974 (in which the investigator unveils political crime instead of smaller-scale offenses in the underworld) and Robert Altman's *The Long Goodbye* from 1974 (in which Chandler's revised private eye meets post-hippie Los Angeles) served as pastiches of the style but notable in their revisionary power.

In the post–Vietnam/Watergate decade of the 1970s, the crime film turned to surveillance and other motifs of paranoia. The obvious forerunner to the '70s paranoid thriller would be 1962's *The Manchurian Candidate*, one of a handful of American films to light the first sparks of the New Hollywood era (along with Hitchcock's *Psycho*, Kubrick's *Dr. Strangelove* and *Lolita*, and others). Yet, *The Manchurian Candidate*, featuring a Chinese conspiracy to infiltrate America by brainwashing, belongs more to the espionage/political thriller tradition, even if much of the film plays as a masked gothic.

The paranoid thriller proper began with Francis Ford Coppola's *The Conversation* (1974), in which an audio surveillance expert comes across another hidden crime, one that sets him to obsession and unease. Films in this movement of thrillers include *The Parallax View* (1974), *Three Days of the Condor* (1975) and, most effective with its sense of doom, *Marathon Man* (1976) which, like *The Manchurian Candidate*, doubles as a gothic, especially in its trademark dental-torture scene and the ex–Nazi/dentist's (Laurence Olivier) reckoning on location in Manhattan's Jewish diamond district. These films replaced the dark world view of neo-noir with a paranoia concerning watchful parties and their technologies. (Chapter 2 will discuss an updated version of this style.)

The early 1970s also saw the emergence of the renegade cop, the most popular entries being Don Siegel's *Dirty Harry*, starring Clint Eastwood (whose contemporary crimes films will be discussed in Chapter 12) and the *Death Wish* series, starring Charles Bronson. William Friedkin's *The French Connection* (1971) helped to launch the cycle, with its ruthless crime fighter Popeye Doyle (Gene Hackman) running down international crime, filmed on location in jittery, hand-held camera work. A popular offshoot to the renegade cop picture was what's now termed the "Blaxploitation" cycle, with beefed-up cops that soon grew cartoonish. Ironically, an independent surprise hit, *Sweet Sweetback's Baadasssss Song* (1971), launched the cycle as a victim film. A persecuted African American man (played by writer-director Melvin Van Peebles) kills a cop in self-defense and is on the run for the rest of the film. The 1970s-cycle moved far from Peebles ragged, furious film. Today, its relation to the often parodied "Blaxploitation" films is almost unrecognizable.

In the early 1980s, neo-noir returned, namely with two films that were remakes of classical noirs. Bob Rafelson directed Jack Nicholson and Jessica Lange in 1981's *The Postman Always Rings Twice* (scripted by David Mamet), for more heated-up results. Also more heated than its inspiration was *Body*

Heat (1981), loosely based on *Double Indemnity*. In both of these 1981 films, Leitch has noted the presence of a more dominant femme fatale, one who takes an upfront role instead of operating behind her lover *à la* Lady Macbeth. This new femme fatale's motivation inspired the female villains of the 1980s erotic thriller. The femme-most-fatale, reflecting the soft-core cable porn of the 1980s, responds to a married man's rejection of her (after their tryst). The new fatale archetype, crystallized by Glenn Close in *Fatal Attraction* (1987) and Sharon Stone in 1992's *Basic Instinct* (both of which were hits, while Madonna's attempt, *Body of Evidence* [1993], flopped), was perhaps a reaction to the liberated 1980s woman. While the mainstream erotic thriller became a sensation, a lesser-known but still notorious surreal neo-noir, *Blue Velvet* by David Lynch, was more profound and influential (see Chapter 10, on Lynch's "crime nightmares").

Through the late 1980s/early '90s, David Lynch continued working in the crime tradition, directing *Wild at Heart* (about lovers on the run) and creating the *Twin Peaks* television series (about an ongoing, curiously odd murder investigation). The decade's beginning also saw Martin Scorsese's new take on the gangster in *Goodfellas* (1990), which has its own epic, yet personal style, different from the filmmaker's gritty urban crime pictures in the 1970s. Though the 1990s soon came under the influence of a video store brat named Quentin Tarantino, whose cheeky postmodern crime obsession and sure-handed dialog and action drew droves of fans and the attention of critics. *Pulp Fiction* (1994) is the inventive film that veered American crime cinema in a new direction. Its cleverness and thrills are coupled with a vertiginous self-consciousness, the latter of which other filmmakers could co-opt, thus gaining the worst of a fine style. This post–Tarantino movement (which I'll call "post–*Pulp Fiction*," to be more specific and more correct) is where this book begins. The films that have broken free from the *Pulp Fiction* influence are the subjects of this study.

But like viral-video-fueled self-referencing and regurgitation of the current media age, Tartantino's work will continue — and thankfully, his most recent project as of this writing, a revisionist war film *Inglourious Basterds* (2009), is thrilling, inventive, and humorous (like his two-film action series, *Kill Bill* [2003–2004]), even if it suffers from the dizziness of an overly movie-conscious style. Many elements of the crime film could be pinpointed here: the eponymous gang (itself inspired by an 1978 Italian exploitation film of the same name), after all, are Jewish renegades who act as psychotic Robin Hoods against the Nazi army. But this book looks to purer examples of the contemporary crime film. In a reaction to the post–*Pulp Fiction* spate of films, the works of the new crime film return to tradition to draw all the power of the primal genre archetypes. While the *Pulp Fiction*-style alludes and at times just name-checks, it doesn't invoke and add to a tradition. The style, which collects scattered references, is more of a mash-up than a revision. The films in the new crime tradition, however, invigorate the classical motifs. This new tradition celebrates the humanity of the criminal, victim, and/or avenger while indulging in the primal pleasures of the crime story.

The chapters of this book approach each film from the viewpoints of the central three "crime" archetypes. The most iconoclastic crime films center on a criminal protagonist. Such films present a distorted reality, if told in his/her point of view. The victim film shows the story of hero who enters the world of crime unwillingly and must either transform into an avenger or, or occasion, turn criminal under duress. The avenger's tale is one in which a crime must be redeemed, in which, again, the hero may turn to criminal or victim. By touching on a variety of related genres and themes — horror films, the Western, mythical structures, the politics of war, teen crime, and food science — this study will present the wide range of crime films told with the classical archetypes. Films that spotlight more than one archetype — with avenger and criminal both dominant, unlike in the classical archetypal films — are frequent in this movement, while postmodern characters, which fill more than one role, are also common. These films often contain a network of criminals that reflects the depth of crime and its ramifications. A criminal network is nothing new in American crime stories. But the variety of criminal types, and their various roles and occasional dualities as victims, is a fresh trademark of this new movement.

Veteran critic Stanley Kauffmann breathlessly summarized the thematic objective of most crime films, that they "strip away greedy self interest to reveal nullity."[6] In this light, a recurring tradition of films seems reductive, as countless examples attest. But his thesis covers the crude run of routine entries, which make for a collective monkey that the thematically rich films in this book all shake off their backs. While assessing their themes, I return to the spirited quest of another crime-analyzing veteran critic, the late Manny Farber, who celebrated the rough feeling of what he called, in 1956, the "underground film"[7] — what we today would call the action-based genre film. Having to reclaim a style ignored in the arthouse-wild decade of movie-going, in his essay, Farber considered the thought behind the films profiled, but more so on their feeling. The new crime film is worthy of such discussion. It, essentially, honors a cinematic tradition.

1

Say Hello to the New Heist
Spike Lee's *Inside Man*

To begin our discussion of new crime films, we look to one of the most regimented traditions: the heist picture. It would be difficult to argue the tradition as archetypal for the crime style, since the gangster film conventions of the 1930s and early film noir (in the 1940s) preceded the heist tradition. The newer style developed somewhere in between the rule-bound structure of the onscreen gangster, living high by committing many crimes (robberies being only one of many forms), and the doomed world of noir, in which criminals spiral to a downfall. The heist film proper looks to only one crime: its plan, set-up, execution, and aftermath. Thus, the plot style works as a variant of one of the simplest: the goal-oriented narrative, in which a protagonist plans and achieves a goal, against the antagonist's power or lack thereof. Whether the heist comes off or falters creates the viewers interest, as we remain with the criminal's perspective during the in-depth depiction of a crime (the avenger's point of view becomes secondary). This story form results in a unified, efficient narrative. On film, the heist keeps images brisk and leading to the next scene.

In this style, the criminals ordered efficiency may seem iconoclastic, though still playing as a regulated system.[1] The anxiety of the heist plot comes when the criminal's system is threatened, and a breakdown is possible, often at the hands of the police. Procedural subplots often appear to jeopardize the robbery and make it worthy of our interest. While the film entertains with the suspense of the robbery, tension comes from the threat to the criminals' system. The classical heist, if it be effective, keeps the police threatening (if at times ineffective), though the crime force will remain strong. *The Taking of Pelham One Two Three* (1974) — a classically styled heist film, though it capitalized on the current hijacking anxiety following the Munich Olympics crisis—features criminals who almost make it, until the police eventually track them down. At the crisis point and aftermath of the classical heist, the police frequently succeed at catching the thieves. In this case, the heist's order is completed only for morality to win, often as a *deus ex machina*. As in *Pelham*, it can be a stroke of luck that puts morality back on top.[2]

The classical heist earns its title since it adheres to the tenets of the classical Hollywood narrative: goal-oriented characters, causal narration, clear resolutions.[3] When the heist narrative meets the noir tradition, the order dissolves into a breakdown. The noir heist features the same attention to order as the classical style: a detailed plan put into action by members who, for the most part, can execute. Yet, this tradition presents the same fate of other films noir: the criminals' plan is doomed, usually by fate more than chance (the flaw in the classical style).

In Stanley Kubrick's *The Killing* (1956), a gang pulls off an intricate race-track heist. While its order seems threatened at times, its downfall results from one tragic strain: a femme fatale named Sherry (Marie Windsor, nick-named the "Queen of the Bs"), the wife of a milquetoast gang member and racetrack employee, played by Elisha Cook, Jr. In the end, his cheating wife's move for her boyfriend to steal the cash becomes the gang's downfall. While their sharpshooter dies pulling off his end of the deal (by shooting a racehorse in action, to cause a disturbance), and gangleader Johnny Clay (Sterling Hayden) is spotted by a cop after hiding the money, the gang would get away if the boyfriend (and his cronies) didn't invade their meet-up spot, which forces Clay to run for an airport, where he checks a bag overstuffed with cash. By adapting the novel *Clean Break* by Lionel White, Kubrick and co-writer Jim Thompson revised the heist plot through narrative reflexivity. The tale shifts through time to reveal the motivations of each character, most of whom are ordinary men looking for a better life. (Clay is a jailbird with five years on his record.) The motivation and attention of each ensures success, though it takes only one weak link. The heist style is doomed and in kind with the noir tradition.

The 1955 heist film *Violent Saturday*, directed by Richard Fleischer, may seem to work in the classical tradition. The film pays equal attention to its gangmembers, who are planning to rob a small-town bank right before closing time on Saturday, and the victims of the heist: a bank manager, and an unlucky fellow (Victor Mature) whose car gets hijacked as part of the heist. The small town issues—infidelity, alcoholism, a peeping-tom bank manager—seem like cheap foil to the film's crime scheme, making the film one-half melodrama to fill out the down time. Yet Mature's everyman turns avenger against the robbers when they bring him to an Amish homestead, which the gang has infiltrated as a home base. Their violation of this pure example of family values proves to be their tragic downfall. The film's conscience urges the Amish father (an unusual role for Ernest Borgnine) to become an unwilling avenger assisting Mature. Violating the family results in the gang's doom, as their captives end the heist. Their plan is, essentially, foiled by itself.

The noir heist added irony to a tradition based on efficiency. The plan's flaw may seem the workings of a higher moral conscience in the Hollywood studio system — perhaps the same strain that assured the classical gangsters must fall, as do criminals in the James M. Cain–inspired films noir, *Double Indemnity* (1944) and *The Postman Always Rings Twice* (1946). Like any established tradition, inventive filmmakers have approached it with reflexivity, if not irony. The extreme, ironic treatment of the heist will lead to comedy, making its cops and/or criminals bumbling, as in *Ruthless People* (1986) and *How to Rob a Bank* (2007). The ironic-comic criminals may be ineffectual from the start or, as in the Coen brothers' *Fargo* (1996, see Chapter 16), deadly if bumbling.

If the noir heist posits an ordered system plagued by a fault with severe effects, then the New Hollywood era, ranging from 1967 to 1977, had little use for it. At this time the antihero became the main attraction, and a futile quest, his regular obstacle. The bank robberies in 1967's *Bonnie and Clyde* bank were far from stellar — one banker in that film swears his institution to be broke, so Clyde pulls him from the building to break the news to Bonnie. Admittedly, this film concerns a gang on the run, hardly planning out their moves. A heist in the hands of an iconoclast would feature rebellion more than efficiency. Thus came *Dog Day Afternoon* (1975), featuring a bank robber with unusual goals: to pay for his boyfriend's sex-change operation. Both the classical and noir heists take considerable time to detail the plan, while *Dog Day* begins *in medias res* of the heist scenario, as Al Pacino's Sonny walks right up to the bank with large flower box in hand (already part of heist iconography, since it was used in *The Killing*), and his doomed robbery commences. The unfocused urgency of Sonny's robbery proves he has no plan. His heist quickly becomes a hostage situation, with the film's setting almost completely restricted to the bank. The absurdist ordeal reveals the panic of the heist leader, a character given in-depth portrayal, even if clueless at his endeavor. In the meantime, Al Pacino helped to shatter the stereotype of gays on screen.

By extending the heist and eliminating its build-up, the film makes use of the hostage motif, a move that tapped into the post–Watergate/–Munich terrorist anxieties of the 1970s. The stakes are higher, as the robber now becomes a potential terrorist himself, as he holds a city in fear through police and media attention. At the same time, the heist becomes a city spectacle, with onlookers affected by and fueling the situation. By extending the crime to this severity, *Dog Day Afternoon* provides the conceit on which to model the Bush-era heist picture: Spike Lee's *Inside Man* (2006). This new take on the severe heist uses the strongest elements of both the classical and noir traditions.

The heist/hostage plot fashions an ideal ticking-clock scenario: the crime commences, step by step, while the authorities await, ready to strike. Written by Russell Gewirtz, *Inside Man* does not exploit media coverage like *Dog Day Afternoon*, but like the 1975 film, the former pulls viewers between two narrative expectations. If the police are to resolve the situation, the disorder would return to order, as in the Shakespearean tradition of comedy and the classical film. A dire situation growing worse would be more like tragedy — disorder leading to a downfall, as in the noir heist. Most of today's heist pictures tend to use the classical plot: an ordered plan (or spree) cracked by the police near the film's end. Thus, such films provide powerful roles for actors: as criminals mastering the plot or police hopefully working one step ahead of it. In *Reservoir Dogs* (1992), the film that made writer-director Quentin Tarantino into a name, we have a notable example of the doomed noir heist. By borrowing the robbers' names-as-color motif (Mr. Pink, Mr. Brown, etc.) from 1974's *The Taking of Pelham One Two Three*, the film references the ordered classical heist, while its multi-perspective narrative style invokes the structure of *The Killing*. Like Kubrick's film, its main influence, *Reservoir Dogs* presents a gang infiltrated by a policeman (Tim Roth) posing as a member; hence, a robbery doomed by its inception. Extremely ironic (though non-farcical) robbery films are common, such as the kidnapping film *Julia* (2008), but new versions of the classical heist feed the public's desire for on-the-mark robbers. Yet, with the memory of *Reservoir Dogs* and its noir treatment, the unique heist film tends to feature order with the threat of a tragic fault. Today, there is little excuse for a heist film not offering some complexity in its motifs.

To invoke the classical tradition, *Inside Man* presents a bank robbery inclined to order. At the moment the criminals enter the bank at the film's start, their intricate plan is obvious. They pull on overalls and masks, and take out the cameras through a vague means (the growing light appearing on surveillance footage is enough for viewers to dismiss plausibility). As the robbers bring their hostages — bank employees and customers — to a back room, we see details of their plot, though it remains unknown. Action appears but adds to a mystery, in lieu of the classical heist's clarity. The intricacies of the plan may seem overwrought, as if years of onscreen heists have led scenarists to become too smart in their efforts. But the hyper-order of this heist is part of a sheen.

Once the police, led by Detective Keith Frazier (Denzel Washington), reach the scene and attempt to interpret the details of the robbery/hostage scenario, the robbers, led by Dalton Russel (Clive Owen), create a performance for their opponents: a misleading appearance of an ordered plan that channels

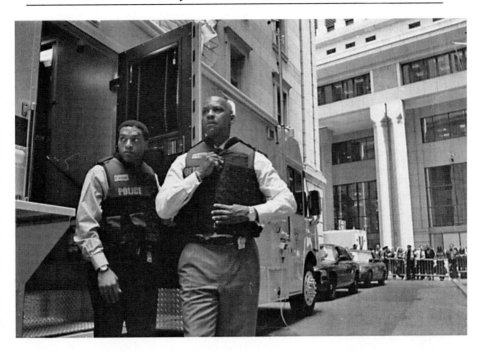

Detectives Bill Mitchell (Chiwetel Ejiofor) and Keith Frazier (Denzel Washington) gear up to crack the heist-turned-hostage situation in *Inside Man* (2006, Universal Pictures).

disorder to the onlookers. The "masked" heist is hardly new — see *Machine-Gun McCain*, which presents a robbery hidden behind the ruse of explosions. Yet, we don't expect the distraction to be part of the actual heist. To create an illusion of usual hostage scenario, in the film's first scene appears a direct address from Russell invoking the rule-bound nature of his heist.[4] This prelude seems to exist in a nether diegesis, with a vague backdrop, perhaps included for narrative clarity, as a way to set high stakes for the viewer. This moment positions Russell as an agent of control, in spite of the disordered illusion to come. Throughout the film, Russell repeats his intention to "walk right out the front door," in spite the police presence — a rule he sticks to, though it remains vague and in service to the film's decoys.

Inside Man continues to play on our expectation for order in the heist film. Director Spike Lee, in his later works, has looked to genre forms for an alternative to his character-based dramas. Recently, Lee looked to the war narrative in his film *Miracle at St. Anna* (2008), in which he critiques the tradition's myths of heroism and ignorance to race. His character study *The 25th Hour* (2002), based on a novel by David Benihoff, looks at the fall of a conscience-plagued drug dealer as he prepares to begin his prison sentence. Not much of a narrative arch appears, aside from the revelation of who ratted on him and the gradual acceptance of his sentence, by himself and his friends. Nonetheless, the anti-plotted film looks to the psychology of crime and guilt in his characters. In *Inside Man*, Lee directs attention to the mind of the crime film viewer: what we expect, view, but actually witness.

While opening with a multicultural song on the soundtrack, drawing from both tribal and urban hip-hop influences, the film mainly uses classical orchestration for its emotional pull. In the darker, portentous moments, the film recalls 1974's *Pelham* with the use of deep bass strings. The modern embellishments by film scorer Terence Blanchard has a celebratory feel to it — to the visages of New York, its peoples of various cultures. On the soundtrack, multiculturalism is joined with genre tradition by a filmmaker dedicated to both.

The film style needs an emotional charge, since it borrows much from *Dog Day Afternoon* which features a heist that becomes city spectacle. Like this earlier film, *Inside Man* does not ground us in one side of the heist, as do many pictures (*The Killing*, *Violent Saturday*, etc.). Lee's film undercuts the opening monologue by following it with near omniscience, which this version of the heist requires. Lee and cinematographer Matthew Libatique must reconcile the two perspectives: the open exteriors of the bank and it dark enclosures. Thus, in Lee's usual style, he and Libatique double-shot all the footage from two opposing positions.[5] The style looks for all possible angles of performance from its actors, yet also considers all the spaces as possible onscreen subject. For exterior scenes, Lee and Libatique use high-angle pans and crane shots to highlight the bank's enclosures. This technique pairs a lively urban setting, reflecting the curiosity of the onlookers, to the dark secrecy within. The interiors rely on grounded tracking shots that reflect the mystery, since Steadicam shots (often used in place of jerky handheld camerawork) would reflect too much confusion. While the visual style suggests that the images of the robbery reflect its order, the narrative highlights show how the system perceived by the police is regulated disorder.

The gang's operation is the police's mystery: hence, a "text" for the genre viewer's interpretation. The police rely on the fact that the system cannot be too intricate to jeopardize the plan. The classical and noir heists are built upon such a premise in the "text," for the interpretation of the police and interpretative enjoyment of the viewers. Speed and efficiency of the heist are usually what brings us pleasure. A red-herring-filled, seemingly faulty system is rarely the game. Even a surprise whodunit, like Sidney Lumet's *Murder on the Orient Express* (1974), offers one mysterious system working continually: the oddities of the surface just mask it. In fact, such mysteries are obsessed with discovering an order that must be present. The police's reliance on order in *Inside Man* leaves them susceptible to a sheen of a system. It begins with Dalton's communication with the police, and his demands for an airplane for escape. It doesn't fool Detective Frazier, who knows from referencing *Dog Day Afternoon*—a heist text existing within this filmic universe—that such a plan would never work. This purported escape plan invokes tradition, though ineffectual, since the plan put into effect in *Dog Day* just realizes suspense, and no hidden game on the part of Pacino's Sonny. In *Inside Man*, a dupe audio source also causes suspense, as it does, in fact, fool Frazier. When the cops bug the gang members, they play an audio of a former Albanian president into the hidden microphone. The police rush to find a translator, which requires an onlooker going to find his Albanian ex-wife. A true foil comes when we learn that the robbers have managed to bug the police through a metal case listing their demands. Ironically, the criminals work off the system of the police, not the other way around.

The counter-bugging helps the criminals to create their illusion of order. The police interpret the crime by analyzing Frazier's communication with the masked Dalton. Dalton has disguised all of his hostages to appear like his accomplices. Thus, victims are interchangeable with criminals to both the victims themselves and to Frazier, when he enters the bank. His codes for interpretation are blurred. As the victims, when left alone, discuss whether the robbers are terrorists, the disguises take on imagery of Islamic extremists, along with the film's other references to post–9-11 racial profiling. Consistently, the facial masking highlights the film's overall modification of the heist, as a sheen of order. Thus, Dalton continues his tête-á-tête with Frazier, which in a traditional heist would be means for suspense, but proves a decoy once we learn of Dalton's actual plans to pull off the heist.

When Frazier tries to unmask his opponent, during a meeting in the bank, Dalton reprimands him for "crossing the line." In the next scene, Dalton directs the police surveillance cameras to a high-level window, where they view a hostage's execution. The cold-blooded style of the image, plus its crude cinematography, recall extremists' video executions: the act of viewing them spreads as much terror as is seen on the film. The execution channels horror in its initial viewing, but repeat viewings reveal a delayed explosion of blood near the victim's covered head. It's apparently a sham long before the cops discover proof of it being one, when they eventually find fake guns and a vial to expel fake blood.

When Frazier learns that the criminals have bugged him, his team decides to raid the bank. At this point, Dalton casts the heist's central illusion: his release of disguised victims intermixed with most of the criminals. It is a moment embodying the police's futile grasp for order. Before the attempted raid, the police even play out the situation facing them to analyze the effectiveness of their own system. Captain John Darius (Willem Dafoe) describes the best- and worst-case scenarios while Lee presents both onscreen. They plan to take out all disguised parties with rubber bullets, thus addressing their lack of knowledge. But this plan is foiled once the criminals and victims, all wearing the same disguise, exit the building, when the police begin then cease their fire of the rubber bullets. This moment begins the third act and connects to the flash-forward interviews of the victims and criminals that appear throughout the film; these moments depict the power of the heist's central disguise. The victims' suffering takes precedence, while the criminals hide behind it. The police then enter to discover the evidence of the fake assassination. Further, the bank's holdings appear untouched, until we learn that something greater has been removed. When the police inspect a storage area, we know that the heist leader hides right behind a wall: the term "inside man," usually meaning a robber who works within the robbery spot (like George in *The Killing*), now refers to a man who exploits something from the bank that only an insider would know about. The term also relates to his method of stealing and escape, by hiding out behind a vault after the release of hostages and robbers. The release of the hostages — itself a performance — covers the actual robbery.

Much like a drawing-room mystery, everyone who escapes is a suspect. When the case proves unsolvable, Frazier's boss instructs him to bury evidence (a .357 pistol Frazier saw Russell using, but never recovered after the release). Also buried within the investigation is the effort's true aim: to blackmail the bank's president, Arthur Case (Christopher Plummer, playing the other "man [hidden] inside"), a sure method of completing their actual robbery of his diamond collection. Case holds odd sentimental value to his past connections to the Nazis, who helped him establish the bank. To him, this secret is worth more than all the bank's contents. The proof (an envelope with Nazi-related contents), along with the diamonds, is within one safe deposit box, the real target of the robbers. Thus, Case hires a fixer, Madeleine White (Jodie Foster), to cut a deal with the robbers, one that's refused. This fixer figure adds another avenger to the framework, on an elite/hidden level that also extends the criminal network. The threat is not just to wealth, or to the well-being of a group of citizens, but to a figurehead on the highest economic and political power — one who can sway the influence of New York's mayor. The fixer, in turn, works for the elite, the real vulnerable element within the heist, while Frazier works for the everyday citizens who are now held hostage. (Head-to-head verbal confrontations between Frazier and White, like those of Frazier and Russell, offer brief social commentary). Lee and Gewirtz's take on the heist is decidedly ironic: the narrative goes beneath a robbery to reveal political machinations.

Critic Roger Ebert complained of the implausibility that a man who played an important role in the Holocaust could survive to 2005 as an active presence.[6] Yet, the suspension of disbelief invokes another 1970s thriller, *Marathon Man*. Made in the post–Watergate age of paranoia in mainstream cinema, this film looks to our forefathers/leaders as the source of hidden evil. It presented another form of terrorism, the fear that our own foundation is corrupt, to an age still recalling the Munich Olympics terrorist crisis. Thus, *Inside Man*, through intertextuality beyond its association to the heist film, counters the fear and imagery of contemporary terrorism with a threat of three decades ago. The robbers' going after a corrupt authority taps into our fears while offering us satisfaction.

Inside Man relies mainly on associations to the classical heist, though the film aligns itself to the noir tradition, even if the crooks do not see such fatality. The noir style appears in the film's attention to the past — how it affects the actions of the main avenger (Frazier) and the film's two criminals. Frazier faces a check-fraud charge, a weakness that is exploited by his opponent (the fixer, White) once she learns of it. Since this will jeopardize his longtime desire for a promotion (and his security to get married), he is drawn to the fixer's promise for a raise in rank, through her connections to the mayor, if he protects Case. Of course, a more haunting attention to the past belongs to Case, whose secrets of Nazi involvement open him as a target for blackmail and persecution, should the information be revealed. As noted earlier, this film critiques post-terrorism New York policies: the hostages worrying if the robbers are terrorists, the casual racism of the foot-patrol officer who first reports the robbery, and a Sikh bank employee forced to remove his turban after his release. But these moments draw attention to the fear related to the heist, which is continually misread by the police. The paranoia grows into a fatalism, while faith in the avengers wanes. Yet, as the film wraps, Frazier continues his avenging against Case, who's shaken by the encroachment against him, but still at liberty. Frazier's aim may be sizable, with the multiple connections of his target, as well as the evidence of a traceable ring in his weapon. When on the hunt for Case at the film's end, Denzel Washington dons a 40s-style suit and fedora, recalling his noir detective role as Easy Rawlins in *Devil in a Blue Dress* (1995) — an avenger who, in fact, cracks the case. As player in a heist-turned-blackmail scheme, the avenger strives even in bleak, bemusing circumstances.

2

Paranoia Reemerging
Tony Gilroy's *Michael Clayton*

When crime narratives like *Inside Man* hinge on machinations of the powerful, we expect the emergence of the fixer. The film *Michael Clayton* (2007) takes this shadowy figure and gives it full life as a central character. *Inside Man*'s Madeleine White seems a picture of efficiency, as her screen time reveals only her most effective actions on the job. With a point of view withholding access to her private life, she remains a flat character, existing to drive the narrative. The fixer figure has thrived in this new paranoid style of crime and action films, in which culprits are powerful forces running government agencies or large corporations.[1] In reality, the fixture exits on the borderline of modern folklore — like the American Mafia, it has factual basis but is shaped through urban legend. In the new crime film, the modern myth takes life as an organ of corporate crime. He or she may be onscreen, or working just behind the scenes. Needless to say, their dirty deeds aren't done cheap.

Michael Clayton looks beneath the flatly drawn fixer in modern films. Likely once the picture of efficiency and effectiveness, the eponymous character, played by George Clooney, has begun his fall from it. It's likely to have been a gradual process, as his integral job for a large New York law firm's now swelling beyond his grasp. In the tradition of many ironic professionals in movies, the fixer cannot manage his personal issues, much less the fixes for his firm's high-priced clientele.

The film introduces him at a private gambling table. Writer-director Tony Gilroy's expository-friendly dialog, from another card player, reveals Michael's failure at the restaurant business (a side gig), when Michael receives a cell phone call assigning him to a seemingly ordinary, late-night job. Reaching the home of a valued client, Michael refuses to provide a "fix" for the client by covering up his hit-and-run of a pedestrian that night. On his ride back, Michael stops to look at a triad of horses on a hilltop, just before dawn — Gilroy has described the moment as an attempt for Michael to reconnect with life.[2] His workplace doesn't seem so threatening at first. The film opens with a taut series of scenes revealing a firm, which we will soon learn is his workplace, in a moment of routine crisis. Yet, scenes shown before we meet Michael at the table — in a room of lawyers trying to close a case with a firm called UNorth, and a woman in private, sweating bullets (seemingly due to the case) — foreshadow the actual crisis. Michael's meeting of the horses (potentially an overload of symbolism, should it run too long) is interrupted by his car exploding in the background. When Michael runs off, he appears shocked but knowing, before the image fades to white, and he transforms into a fugitive, likely an innocent man on the run. As the

In *Michael Clayton* the title character (George Clooney) learns the truth about UNorth (2007, Warner Bros. Pictures).

film flashes back, it will detail how this company-endorsed investigator becomes the hunted, a victim figure that Alfred Hitchcock refined before it reemerged in the post–Watergate 1970s thrillers (*The Parallax View* [1974], *Three Days of the Condor* [1975], *Marathon Man* [1976]) in which the villain(s) is a corporation that sends out its hyper-skilled assassins. Michael sees his life falling apart before he's threatened by his own corporation.

There's paranoia about what's to come: Michael is haunted by what's already happened. Hitchcock's fugitives move fast, eventually reaching the appointed time/location that will prove their innocence. Michael is plagued by debt, a failed marriage and bar business, lost friends, and all that may affect his young son, Henry (Austin Williams). He seems more affected by the past than what faces him. At the end of the car explosion scene, a title reveals the film to be moving back four days earlier. The extended flashback motif isn't uncommon in recent films (David Fincher's *Fight Club* [1999], for example). It can place the narrative's end up front, thus tempting viewers with what's to come. But in the noir style it redirects our attention to the overbearing backstory.[3] We are as curious about this title character as we are about the conspiracy after him.

Though now chased by a corporation's assassins, Michael social and spiritual isolation has been long in coming. His ex-wife and son now live with a sensitive middle-ager, while Michael moves through offices and gambling tables, and must make trips to his abandoned restaurant.[4] To his co-workers, save his boss, Marty Bach (Sydney Pollack, who directed *Condor*), Michael is a résumé. At one point a UNorth employee reads Michael's credentials as a voiceover, an example of the writer-director's ability to deliver exposition as legitimate dialog. It could be the type of miniature biography that scenarists use to build character and a narrative.[5] But here it reflects how this world regards Michael by what he's done and is able to do, without considering how it could affect him. While action reveals character in narratives, a man crumbles when reduced to just his actions.

Michael strives for intimacy with his son, Henry, a side character organic to the narrative, as his presence becomes integral to the plot. But Michael's relationship with Henry remains parental, one of responsibility more than a connection. In his car after a birthday party, Michael tries to be close with Henry, when Michael assures his boy that he will grow up strong. Yet, even in film's most intimate moment, Michael can't let down his guard. His aim for intimacy seems more of an act of desperation. Gilroy originally wrote and filmed a scene featuring Michael's casual, ongoing affair with an attorney co-worker.[6] While the filmmaker has made clear his intention for this deleted scene, that it was to show another personal failure for Michael, it plays as the most personal moment in the film, closer than his mainly professional existence. Michael's interactions with Bach seem real, reflecting an enduring professional relationship. Yet, their interactions are restricted to professional issues: namely, dealing with Arthur Edens (Tom Wilkinson).

Arthur Edens instigates the action of the film. He turns himself into a fugitive while looking for a release from his oppressive job, thus setting Michael into motion. Michael is summoned to retrieve Arthur in a Milwaukee jail, in a scene that clarifies the film's vague opening voiceover narration. Appearing over images of a lawyers' workroom, the opening voiceover serves as an ironic "voice of god" that has gone mad. Arthur's words urge for the truth to be revealed about the manufacturing of pesticides by a company called UNorth (whom the lawyers are defending in a billion-dollar lawsuit), and how "the time is now." While calling for action, the voiceover suggests a noirish obsession for the past. The latter style often uses voiceover to reveal the narrative's central conscience, frequently that of the investigator/avenger. Arthur wants to avenge the corporation's crimes, and hence Gilroy grants him the opening "words of truth," though Arthur will prove incapable to realize justice. He experiences a moral awakening during what appears to be a breakdown. It turns out to be a rebirth — his transition (psychological if not actual) from criminal (agent of the corrupt UNorth) to avenger against it. Unable to make the full change, Arthur remains a doomed noir investigator. He will not succeed, Michael will take up for him, though resisting at first. Arthur's instincts (though self-destructive), together with Michael's faith in him, create a network of avengers that complement the network of criminals (more on this later).

Incarcerated for his meltdown at a deposition, in which he strips down and rants (we see the video footage later in the film), Arthur has had a long, working relationship with Michael. Michael may have helped Arthur stay on his medication, but they speak to each other, even in heated moments, within a synched manner of familiarity. Now, Michael has a more pressing responsibility over Arthur, in that he has jeopardized the billion-dollar UNorth lawsuit.

To fix Arthur's problem, Michael must negotiate with him. At a hotel after Arthur is released, Michael tries to reestablish their bond proper, through adjoining hotel rooms away from the police office. The bond is broken when Arthur flees, which revs up the suspense after a quiet stretch of onscreen time. In his abandoned hotel room, Arthur has scrawled upon the walls, "Make believe it's not just madness" — his conviction that there is greater meaning behind the power negotiations of the lawsuit and his participation on the "dark side" of it. Arthur has learned of a fantasy novel, *Realm + Conquest*, being read by Michael's son, Henry. The novel, invented by Gilroy for the film, is an allegory to be interpreted. In its plot, various people dream a common dream (an example of what parapsychologists call "mutual dreaming") to assemble for a great undertaking. The communal nature reveals Arthur's need for belonging — the stress of his profession has left him as isolated as Michael. During his mania, Arthur sees meaning in the heroic allegory. It becomes his call to action, as he moves from villain to avenger against his own crime.

Hence, Arthur flees to his own Eden — New York City — where he will undertake his quest. It's a place where he can reveal his information and summon a UNorth victim, Anna (Merritt Weaver), to realize the "Summon to Conquest" motif from the novel. He walks through Times Square, seeing the colors of sundry ads and freedom of the populace walking about him. Thinking his previous work to have made him "Shiva, the god of death," Arthur finds new energy within the urban crowd, experiencing Walt Whitman's world en masse. When Arthur buys a whole bundle of bread loaves, we see his desire to surfeit. The Whitman connection is apt, since Times Square is built upon the former Long Acre Square, a point at which three rivers met to create the

Great Kill, a river running from what is today Times Square to the south end of Manhattan.[7] (The trinity reflects Gilroy's use of three horses, even if the filmmaker has been baffled by mythical interpretations of his film.[8]) Yet, the lights of the ads distract Arthur from the corporate power they represent, which screams true when a UNorth logo appears on a giant digital billboard. The open, special world is still under the villain's control.

When Michael finds Arthur, the latter establishes the upper hand in a power relationship. He reminds Michael of the law, and how Michael will be overstepping it if he demands that Arthur return and resolve the UNorth fiasco. Arthur affirms his nature, which earlier in the film Michael describes to Karen (Tilda Swinton), a higher up at UNorth: Arthur is a "killer" in court, which accentuates his villainous nature prior to his awakening. Though the putative "fixer," Michael relies on his legal skill to negotiate, though Arthur all but upends Michael with plain legal discourse. What would have been a battle in an old-time adventure becomes an exchange of sharp words.

Arthur doesn't know the extent of the greater villain's control of New York. He's being tailed by Mr. Verne (Robert Prescott), one of two blonde henchmen hired by UNorth to quell the threat of the company's evil deeds being revealed. Gilroy's choice of casting reflects the film's mythic narrative roots: the light-haired hitmen, in contrast to the graying shareholders of UNorth. The team of henchmen work like demonic angels sent by this tale's Lucifer, a mega-corporation. The assassins work with efficiency to clean away the path for UNorth's dark intentions. More covert, more severe form of fixers, they are able to take down Arthur, and nearly Michael.

A major force at UNorth, Karen is the parallel to Michael. While he "fixes" for the law firm and its clients, she takes on the same type of service for UNorth and its shareholders. She is new at providing this service, which is evident in her shaken manner of contacting Mr. Verne by phone. When she is interviewed in an early scene, we learn she has stepped into the vacated post of Don Jeffries (Ken Howard) while he's moved up to CEO. As an underling to Jeffries, and as such part of his criminal network, she executes the secret moves UNorth needs to remain profitable and free from legal trouble. UNorth's first step to clear themselves of trouble was to hire Michael's law firm. But this large deal proves to have its leaks, when Arthur turns from defender of the firm to avenger against it. This risk moves Karen to assign Mr. Verne as an accomplice to the case (in this film, even hitmen operate as a business: they instruct Karen to download an "email encryption package" to complete the transaction). When they kill Arthur, it's done with cold, scientific efficiency: a stun gun knocks him out, before they inject in him a lethal dose of a drug to make it appear to be a suicide. Upon Arthur's death, Karen reaches her ultimate villainy, perhaps unwilling but severe. When ordering the hit on Arthur, she's unable to verbalize what she needs. Mr. Verne speaks euphemisms to describe his procedure, and Karen wishes she could operate in such shielded talk. When she says, "Okay," Mr. Verne asks, "Okay, you understand — or okay, proceed?" The scene cuts before we get the response, though we know she's unprepared to cross the boundary, despite her experience with executive decisions.

Gilroy strengthens this (now *actual*) corporate killer by assuring that we sympathize with her. The first image of her, sweating in torment before she executes a major corporate decision, looms over all of her scenes. Actor Tilda Swinton's words are painstakingly delivered — we can see the tension in her facial muscles and in her throat. We may read this as tension common for English actors performing an American accent, seen at times in the work of other masters like Emma Thompson, Clive Owen, and Kate Winslet. But Swinton's tension highlights her character's predicament, as the voice of her firm and its agent of action. True to his goal, Gilroy refuses to chain his film to American politics[9]; yet, as one of the very few women with power at UNorth, Karen is an outsider who's found her way in — a woman who must continue to prove herself worthy. It's all the more daunting a task, as she must compete with dehumanized company men like Don Jeffries, willing to ignore morality and humanity for profits and their own private America dream. In Karen's interview, she describes her personal life as overshadowed by her career. Her description proves true when Gilroy cuts back to her, rehearsing her answers. She is her own fugitive, lost in the job that has consumed her.

The film's point of view remains objective, clarifying the actions of the various criminals, victims, and avengers. Gilroy hardly ever reveals Arthur in isolation: in most of his screen time he communicates with another party — speaking to Michael, delivering threats, or being watched. We get a fleeting moment of Arthur isolated when entering his apartment, just seconds before his brisk cover-up murder by Verne and an accomplice. His rebirth is a final bliss before death. The murder turns Michael from victim to avenger, as he begins investigating Arthur's purported suicide. The arrival of Anna to New York, which Michael discovers when calling her family in Iowa, becomes a clue. And yet Arthur avenges beyond his death — he has copied the secret UNorth document numerous times. The copies convince Michael of the cover-up and set him to his final move.

While blackmail is behind *Inside Man*'s heist, Michael uses blackmail to shield his vengeance. By presenting Karen with a copy of the UNorth document, with a red cover that bears the title "Realm + Conquest," Michael makes a high-priced demand for his silence, only to tape her confessing to Arthur's murder and Michael's attempted one, through blowing up his car. Before he confronts her in the final scene, we return to the film's opening moments, through the noirish flashback technique. We discover that his flashing GPS unit results from the Verne team planting a bomb beneath it. Into the burning car Michael throws his watch and wallet, as evidence of his death — and spiritual demise. The freedom of the horse triad is lost on him. When learning of the news, the shaken Marty silently wonders what kind of machinations work behind UNorth, which having indirectly hired Michael, now treats him as *homo sacer*, banished and suitable to murder.[10] His ghostly appearance to Karen shocks her, as he's been professionally and physically banished.

His choice to condemn Karen, Jeffries, and UNorth — all while the stockholders sit just a room away — may seem like the ultimate vengeance by an individual over a corporation. But we cannot forget the traction of Michael's final decision, that it fashions the film into a tragedy. By informing the police about UNorth, he has breached the confidentially agreement in his new contract. To take the $80,000 from the law firm to pay off his bar's bills, Michael had to sign away his rights to disclose information about his firm, which is susceptible to a major lawsuit by UNorth should he breach. The bad publicity for UNorth has but little weight in Michael's legal bind to his employer. While Michael's blackmail of Karen calls in the police (his brother, which like the use of Henry, shows the strong inter-connectivity of characters in Gilroy's script), the firm will undoubtedly sue Michael to the point that his bar debt would be trivial. In other words, though he tells Karen she's "so fucked," he has screwed himself permanently, financially if not spiritually. The final blackmail remains mostly in Michael's point of view, as Karen's panic attack appears in trailing background while Michael walks away. Gilroy highlights Michael's tragic move, as the vengeance comes at a major cost. Now Michael becomes the true *homo sacer*, one who cannot be redeemed. The film's final shot — Michael's long, destination-less ride in a taxi — reflects his permanent banishment, now that he's condemned the most powerful and is their prey (as we recall the existence of the likes of Mr. Verne). He cannot fight on, as will *Inside Man*'s Detective Frazier. But like Spike Lee's film, *Michael Clayton* reveals the corporation as potentially the most powerful criminal form — temporarily defeated, but forever defeating.

3

Scandalous Notes
The "Feminized" Crime of
Notes on a Scandal

The term "female noir" is something of a misnomer — anyone familiar with the style knows that women are essential to it. The classical Hollywood plot always included heterosexual romance, since the hero would have to win the ordeal and a lady.[1] The same is true for the classical crime narrative. This romantic interest is, naturally, the femme fatale, an archetype reflecting the male protagonists' anxieties of the "other sex." Aside from variations, like the subtextually homoerotic films of Alfred Hitchcock — the Leopold and Loeb–inspired *Rope* (1948) and the Patricia Highsmith adaptation, *Strangers on a Train* (1951) — a fatale will fuel much of the noir plot. Notably, in the plots of the noir style, a femme fatale lures the hero into a life of crime (for a loner who falls into trouble) or into an association with a criminal underworld (in the case of a detective-centered film).

While feeling passionate about the fatale at first, the hero will eventually feel an equal amount of sexual guilt. Once he ignores the warnings against fulfilling his desires, he sinks in deeper. Today, having deconstructed this classical mythos, we realize that the man is morally questionable before entering into the relationship.[2] For 1940s audiences used to a more phallocentric cinema, he was a victim of a bad seed with fine legs who'd turn heads for her benefit. In retrospect, we note that the femme fatale indicated the World War II era's collective distrust of the liberated woman, and hence, a standardized misogyny to fuel criminal sensationalism. The best femmes fatale made the archetype alluring if not always credible.

The prototypical femme fatale is Barbara Stanwyck, who practically solidified the archetype in 1944's *Double Indemnity* as Phyllis Dietrichson. First conceived by James M. Cain in the source novel under a different name

(Phyllis Nirdlinger), the character was refined by co-screenwriters Billy Wilder and Raymond Chandler. Stanwyck's throaty line reading accentuates her deadly attraction, as does her angular appearance, sexy yet sharp.[3] Her aggressive sexuality cloaks the male anxiety associated to her, and she appeals as a carnivalesque mix of the pleasing and terrifying. A victim of caricature or not, Stanwyck's role remains powerful at the far end of a tradition.

The distinct femininity of other female leads helped to define the fatale. While other contributions are noteworthy — such as Lana Turner, with her doeish-yet-diabolical eyes, in *The Postman Always Rings Twice* (1946), or Veronica Lake, with her ornamental hair — Stanwyck fulfilled the role with a range of physical and verbal traits. With Mary Astor in *The Maltese Falcon* (1941) as a predecessor, Stanwyck brought the black widow to noir, making the male lead's path one of descent.

Yet, to consider the feminized noir proper requires discussing another Golden Age starlet who, though not as iconic as Stanwyck to film genre style, is still an essential. Large eyed and intense, Joan Crawford was a stunning beauty of the silent- and early-sound eras. With age, she grew severe in appearance, the brow and cheekbones becoming witch-like, and the close-up-ready eyes now condemning. She became a gothic icon after launching the "crazy mama" film cycle in the 1960s with *What Ever Happened to Baby Jane?* (1962); posthumously, she became a caricature herself as the source material for *Mommie Dearest* (1981), her image forever hijacked by Faye Dunaway.

Earlier on, as she matured as a performer, she starred in the title role of the 1945 noir *Mildred Pierce*, a woman-as-hero film that essentially pits Mildred against another femme, her conniving daughter Veda (Ann Blyth). The film is a doom-laden tale of a woman working her way into entrepreneurship in a restaurant. The source novel, again by James M. Cain, showed the sweat and toil of the working world, whereas the film revised Mildred as noir with a opening flashback relating a crime, not appearing in the novel. Crawford's Mildred works and works, as if guilt as much as duty drives her to provide for and please her little girl. But Veda is the bad seed, pushing her mother over the edge. The female-centered noir explores Mildred's inspiring work ethic, even if she seems doomed. Noirish fatalism and her impending downfall drives the narrative, keeping it almost as consistent in tone as *Double Indemnity*. The villainous Veda's final move — Hollywood sensationalism at its best — is to steal away Mildred's man. The female battle destroys familial integrity and reveals an incestuous perversion, like an act of the Fates in a Greek tragedy.

Crawford has made other noirs into female-centered thrillers, including *Sudden Fear* (1952), in which her husband (early-career Jack Palance) tries to do her in; and *Possessed* (1947), in which her obsessive concern with her husband is explained away as a neurotic disorder. Yet, neither of those films subverted the fatale-reliant noir structure better than *Mildred Pierce*. The film is a woman's game, as Mildred's trial is never against a male character: Mildred battles Veda, while Mom's husband (and the girl's lover) is a MacGuffin. The rare woman-centered noir pits woman on woman to trump the male-centered nature of the classical Hollywood cinema. This female-only focus doesn't allow for many plots, since a man in the foreground will veer things back to the classical mold. Only certain set-ups can push men aside: mother/daughter battles, women friends turned enemies, and the lesbian thriller.[4] Our contemporary film, 2006's *Notes on a Scandal*, blends the latter two themes.

An important precursor to this film is the Wachowski Brothers' *Bound* (1996), a neo-noir centering on a duo of lesbian heroes (the brunette doppelgängers Gina Gershon and Jennifer Tilly). The lesbian attraction appears for sensational appeal, undoubtedly, yet is a natural development to this post–erotic thriller filmic universe where the women hold more interest. This thriller clears room for a new kind of subject matter: passion between two women and their resistance to men's subjugation of them. This film investigates a woman's actual place in the darker themes, beyond fueling an ordeal that a man must overcome.

Though putatively a British production, *Notes on a Scandal* picks up from this tradition. The film employs the urge of a lesbian-masking-as-friend to give the noir completely to women. We cannot think of the film as a realistic character study of a repressed lesbian — such a pursuit would be frustrating long before it proves unfruitful. Yet, the gay interest is more of a vehicle for a tale about betrayal in close relationships. This crime film delivers something strange and invigorating to the male normative style.

It's best to think of all types of film noir as examples of a wide style.[5] Indeed, critics and scholars have toiled to assert this. Approaching the story of Barbara's (Judi Dench) interest in Bathsheba (i.e., "Sheba," Cate Blanchett) with this concept of noir in mind is best. Based on Zoe Heller's 2003 novel *What Was She Thinking? Notes on a Scandal*, the film opens in the point of view of the 60-year-old Barbara. In the classical noir tradition, her voiceover serves as running commentary, though here the speaker ironically reveals the truth while delivering masked assertions. It is quite different than the prototypical, confessional narration of *Double Indemnity*, driven by guilt to serve the Motion Picture Production Code's agenda, even if it did lend its own sense of doom. This film also reveals story in retrospect, while *Notes'* voiceover commentary reveals the source of the film's menace, Barbara's disturbing behavior. It's the fuel behind this crime film's motifs and tension.

Barbara is a bitter, elderly history teacher, whose instruction and discipline serve the school, though her attitude does not. At night in her diary, she expresses her hatred of her students and coworkers. The mock-confessional

Sheba Hart (Cate Blanchett) gets ensnared by the conniving Barbara Covett (Judi Dench) in *Notes on a Scandal* (2006, Fox Searchlight Pictures).

entries in voiceover, which appear in nearly every scene featuring Barbara, consist of long, lyrical sentences — enough for Sheba, after she reads them, to mock Barbara for thinking herself a "Virginia Woolf." At first appearing like the stereotypical "spinster" schoolmarm, dutiful if resentful to policy, Barbara strikes back at her daily silenced existence through her "secret life," the existence within revealed in her diary. It is a long-running commentary, spanning rows of journal books that director Richard Eyre scans in the film's opening minutes. In one sense depicting obsessive behavior, the journals affirm Barbara, by serving as a canvas for the woman behind the "performance" as school teacher. Her notes show her affirmation as well as the obsessions that fuel the crime plot: her disgust as well as those who occasionally gain Barbara's interest. In this genre treatment, the narrative will not affirm Barbara's human worth, which is ignored by so many; this goal appears in the "spinster"-centered cinematic tradition, including *Now, Voyager* (1942).[6] Nor will *Notes* use the spinster archetype as a shortcut to hysteria, as does Robert Wise's otherwise vital 1963 film, *The Haunting*. The woman upfront in *Notes* isn't a party exploited by her creators, but a character finding her own disturbing path.

The film's other central woman, Sheba, occupies another kind of "secret world." Having wedded her former college professor while young, she had spent her adult life raising her two children, one with Down syndrome. She finds little freedom teaching art at a comprehensive school for working-class children. Here she wishes to employ her artistic skill, something she abandoned as a serious pursuit after marriage. Nonetheless, she keeps a private residence, a hovel behind her house that houses her pottery (the main interest) and memorabilia, notably a picture of herself dressed in punk garb — i.e., the purported inner-spirit of Sheba, with makeup that will reappear at the film's crisis point. Later in the film, after chaos has risen, her husband describes it as her "lair," implying that her secret life has grown out of control.

Sheba's spirit is part of what attracts Barbara. The former, even if over 40, has the high-profile stature as the new prof on the block. Thus, she appears to be "green" to her colleagues when she arrives to the school. Their suspicions aren't far off: Sheba is naïve about her job, jumping into it without a clear view of her new environs. This vulnerability especially attracts Barbara, since it will serve her personal gain.

Sheba's vulnerability also offers Barbara the opportunity to indulge in (not quite sexually) her new interest. It's deliberately unclear if Barbara understands her own sexuality. Otherwise a loner, she desires close female friendships. It's as if she unknowingly plays by the rules of the pre-modern literary tradition, in which homosexuality was, at best, an undercurrent. Her sister, who appears in only one scene, inquires to Barbara about her *different* personal life, at the mention of which Barbara tenses. The sister shares her concern in a hushed, quasi-repressed manner, likely trying not to scare her sister off. Flatly resisting the truth, Barbara acts like a confused youth finding her identity, even if looking the coot.

Sheba exposes herself to blackmail by having an affair with her student. The boy, 15-year-old Steven Connolly (Andrew Simpson), initiates the affair by going to his teacher for help with his art work. He makes advances to Sheba by asking her to continue her careless petting of his hair, and then lying to her about his having an abusive father; by making these moves, he plays the role of a trickster. Sheba falls into both traps, and soon the affair begins. Barbara discovers it during a school play, a festive show that leads the obsessive woman to uncover a performance of another kind. Barbara sees Sheba's fellating of the young boy as a seamy act (in how Ayre films it, lit low-key and framed through a slit in the wall). Fuel for Barbara's opportunistic impulse, the spectacle also seems to arouse her.

Barbara doesn't learn the full story of the affair until she confronts Sheba in the very next scene, via a curt phone call. Through Sheba's confession, we witness the scene of a crime told in voiceover and flashback, a swift mininarrative now using the style akin to the *Double Indemnity/Citizen Kane* tradition. Barbara gains more knowledge which she can exploit — the affair between Sheba and Steven is more than a night's assassination. Sheba's into the thing fairly deep, all the more guilt for Barbara to add in her blackmail scheme. Her "I'll never tell" promise just calms Sheba for the moment and grants Barbara enough leverage to bring their relationship beyond a casual work acquaintance.

The two attention-getting appeals of *Notes* are external to the film's true importance. On the one hand, the film possesses the high-concept promise of a female teacher-student affair. A favorite of the tabloids, this scenario has gotten special attention in recent years, with the random cases highlighted and seeming more prevalent than they really are. This situation counters the male teacher-female student stereotype that seems like a rule when a male character happens to be a college professor. Perhaps the female-teacher-as-predator may hit upon a new, larger cultural phobia of the assertive woman, now that female politicians have gained more power. The sexually assertive female rose in the cinema of the post-feminist era — her perverse, demanding nature reflecting a phallocentric phobia of her. The "predatory" female teachers are treated with more suspicion and have become magnets to national press, while the more common male offense slips by, or is limited to local news. The illegal affair of *Notes* provides the film with a high-concept lure, as a combo-punch of deception, denial, and condemnation.

On the other hand, the top-billing roles of this "arthouse" film promise an exercise in powerhouse acting. Judi Dench plays Barbara with controlled grace; energetic when need be but tunes herself down with ease. She's made even outsized roles seem personal. Blanchett has the grander presence, now associated with the *Lord of the Rings* mythos and as a high-energy Queen Elizabeth in two films to date. She knows subtlety but cannot deflate her strong poise. The trademark scenes in her films come when unleashing her backstock of energy, and in *Notes*, they don't come until the film's crisis point, when Sheba learns of Barbara's deception and confronts her. So enraged is Blanchett's performance that she nearly flies over the top. Prior to the film's release, fans anticipated what the match-up would bring.

As promising as both appeals are, this crime narrative succeeds through its characters. As adapted by playwright Patrick Marber (*Closer*), *Notes* shapes its lead characters first and then constructs the causal narrative around them. Hence, we get a character study of dramatic quality that doesn't spare the thrills and value of a genre-based crime narrative. The humanity of an (un)silenced, aging woman won't die away in her unlikely, thrilling tale. Instead, her character makes it all the more thrilling.

The pseudo-predator, Sheba should be the film's heart of darkness. Overwrought by her family life, she tries to escape it through a teaching job. Yet, the position brings another struggle for her. Her working-class students leave her looking harried in every scene; the film's brief moments in which she's on lunch or tea break are the exception. Heller, Marber, and Eyre deserve acclaim just for showing this truth about the profession, while most education-themed films use troubled students as fuel for mock-teachers who need just a little care to bring about success in the classroom. Sheba, at this point in her career, struggles just to manage the class. Her dual strife, at home and at work, leaves her vulnerable to a child's advances, which culminate into her sex offense.

The source of darkness in the film is the dominant viewpoint, Barbara, whose obsessive nature appears from the early minutes onward. Her effectiveness as a teacher appears in two brief scenes: one in which she commands a classroom at the period's end, and then halts a fistfight with ease; the other in which Sheba gets tossed when trying to break it up. These functional moments oppose Barbara's careless attitude towards school policies — she takes the old-guard stance against the youngbloods around her. But her teacherly duties fade when she's home, when living her real life in her diary. In it, she condemns education and her coworkers, shows disgust for the population she must teach, vents blatant disregard for all the things that add to her unhappiness. We understand that this anger stems from her loneliness and, more indirectly, repressed sexuality. Even if her consummation of it would make her content, this playout is a far cry, considering Barbara's kind of repression. Further, this goal would be better suited for a minimalist character study. In *Notes*, Barbara is committed to drawing nearer to the appealing Sheba, even if the approach is against the latter's will. Barbara is the ironic black widow of this modern noir.

The viewer is lured in by her destructive appeal. Barbara's happiness depends on subtle manipulation, and we root for each advance she maneuvers. When Sheba's weaknesses show, Barbara exploits them, and the latter's disturbing approach, which we love and hate, creates the tension and progression of a thriller. We await Barbara's next move, and how Sheba will reveal more or resist, only pushing Barbara further. Barbara's greatest opportunity comes in Sheba's tell-all about her affair with Steven, which takes place in Sheba's "lair" after Barbara has confronted her. The narrative of the film differs from the novel in that Barbara's sexual desires are sublimated in the latter. The film lets Barbara's sexual tension bubble in to fuel her manipulation and our interest in it.

Barbara is the latest entry in a long storytelling and film tradition: the spinster. Hardly trustful if noticed at all, the figure existed in novels and films as a side player, usually quirky if allowed to reveal any character. When the traditional spinster takes center-stage, as does Bette Davis's Charlotte Vale in *Now, Voyager*, she must prove her self worth with little reward, usually through a long, painstaking effort. And even at journey's end, she must live on in non-contentment. In *Now, Voyager*, Davis adheres to traditional family values by falling in love, albeit with a taken man, and proving her maternal instincts, by mentoring his daughter with low self esteem, a younger version of Charlotte. When he grants her custody of the young girl, Davis accepts her reward, even if her romantic yearning stays unrequited. "Don't let us ask for the moon," she says to him, and we'd guess she couldn't ask for much else, even if she wanted to.

The single, liberated woman came into her own in the New Hollywood era, and the post-feminist women of today's cinema have different struggles. The struggle closest to the classical spinster archetype may be in teen angst — like Dawn Weiner in *Welcome to the Dollhouse* (1995), rejected by family and deplored by schoolmates. The modern spinster would have to be trapped in values of an older era. The aging Barbara is nearing retirement, and likely was a woman on the job before the sexual revolution had begun.

Hardly hiding her vitriol, she's certainly not liked by her peers. It doesn't help her case that she manipulates her way into visiting Barbara's, on a frequent basis. The disgust that Sheba's husband and daughter have for Barbara is latent, until she, crying over the death of her cat, demands attention from Sheba. With a cat as a symbol of spinsterhood, and her crying over it all the more pathetic to unsympathetic parties, Barbara uses the "spinster's loss" to pressure Sheba and tighten the narrative tension. From a car full of restless children, Hubby screams, "Is this some kind of coven!" and "What kind of spell..." directly at Barbara, who keeps her weepy attention off them and on Barbara. At first, the family seems to welcome Barbara, as if the old-time spinster-scorn has died off. But under pressure of a boy with Down syndrome — who, rather insensitively, symbolizes the chaos of Sheba's life — and a hot-tempered teen daughter, the latent attitude towards the spinster rises in Sheba's family. After Sheba's affair comes out later in the film, the daughter is so disgusted with Barbara that it's as if the former blames the latter. Regretfully universal — and still alive, according to *Notes*— the term "spinster," like the word "witch" (as Molly Haskell notes), has served as a "scareword" to "isolate" a certain group of women of lifestyles opposing the traditional family.[7] Here a patriarch assigns witch-like attributes to the "spinster" figure, and both related stereotypes merge into an insult doubly odious.

Barbara's repressed life has made her "vampiric," as Sheba brands her later on, after Sheba discovers Barbara's grand scheme by reading her diary. In this fight scene — unbelievably the most suspenseful of the film, given how exaggerated it may sound — Sheba condemns Barbara as a bitter old virgin, thus adding more punishment to one who's never fulfilled personal needs. *Notes* deploys the "spinster" stereotype for dual commentary, in that Barbara must remain trapped in the prison of a word and, through its repression, resort to deviance for pleasure and vindication. The only "room of her own" she could find was a series of possessive platonic encounters (we learn of one before and, at the film's conclusion, possibly another). Barbara's choices are apathetic, making for a unique turn on the usually moral imperatives of crime cinema, and show one criminal exploiting another (i.e., a sex offender). Barbara unwittingly becomes part of the oppressive system.

Beside the film's clever use of the archetype and comment on stereotype, the plot progression offers a multi-tiered crime scenario. Barbara's journals indicate her history of similar manipulations, and when her principal urges her to retire, with the scandal wracking the school and community, he brings up an old restraining order against her, confirming the evidence in her journals. With this criminal instinct as the premise, Sheba's affair, a sizable crime on its own, opens up room for a more severe criminal reaction from Barbara. The suspense builds from Sheba's resistance, usually beyond her control, which angers Barbara — she reacts by tightening the blackmail with threats. When Sheba "abandons" Barbara, by not consoling her sorrow after her cat dies, Barbara retorts by letting Sheba's secret out to a Judas figure interested in Sheba, a pathetic male teacher — one who'd go to *Barbara* for assistance in committing adultery! This is Barbara's hamartia as it brings on her own condemnation, along with Sheba's. For Sheba must leave her household — her husband needs "time" — and she asks Barbara if she can stay for awhile. Thus, Barbara thinks her plan complete, only if the convergence didn't bring Sheba too near, i.e., getting close to the diary. Before she finds it, Sheba's already regressed, having applied her punk-rock makeup which turns into a kind of warpaint, her preparation for the film's most intense moment. After physically going after Barbara, Sheba accentuates her "mask" with a war cry as she runs outside into a sea of paparazzi, thrusting up the evidence she's found — a gothic flourish that embellishes the film's crisis point.

Sheba returns to her home, for a decidedly ambiguous reunion with Hubby. Barbara returns to her outlook over a London park — a wide open visage that, as Eyre notes in the DVD commentary,[8] spells out isolation. There she meets a lonely newcomer, and offers her an opera ticket. The cyclical motif, often overused as a tack-on, works here — we leave reminded that evil never dies, especially when borne at the hands of cold, exterior forces, and is 100 percent human.

4

Searching the Wasteland
Debra Granik's *Winter's Bone*

It's a debatable point in the world of noir: if the genre is limited to the city. Even the British setting of the female noir *Notes on a Scandal* is considered urban, and hence in kind with the usual style. Naturally, the urban underworld is essential to early–20th-century pulp novels and films inspired by them, the prototypical city being Los Angeles (though Dashiell Hammett used San Francisco, while other writers used New York or Chicago). Naturally, an urban population consists of a variety of types, from those in the high rise to the homeless. The social disparity allows plenty of room for organized crime and its networks.

Essentially, the city in noir is a version of the wasteland, though the over-populated variety instead of desolate. Any territory in question has always been a factor for the avenger figure. Whether he's patrolling the 19th-century American frontier or the modern city, his deep-rooted dream is to save the territory, bringing the wasteland to the idyllic "garden" for which the first set-tlers yearned. The Western genre presents expansive settings as either lands of promise or desolation. The noir city is overrun with corruption, by which an investigator is beleaguered and which he has little chance of redeeming (if he can even solve the current case).

When we take avenger's tale out of the city, the proceeds veer towards the territorial disputes of the Western, where land is in jeopardy. In exterior, this style remains exposed by light (as opposed to the dark saloons), with the possible rewards (i.e., the land) in the open. The sun can oppress the territory, making the "garden" resound as dry wasteland and protagonists more inter-ested in survival and personal gain than moral duty. Noir beyond the city seeks the shadowy areas (like those saloons in Westerns), thus retaining the style's expressionist production design and impressionist use of the camera.[1]

It abandons the concentration of urban turmoil, but offers its own kind of decay. While the city's congestion fuels the paranoia, films noir beyond the urban avoid claustrophobia to offer their own form of naturalism. In either style, the protagonist remains in isolation. Like its urban counterparts, stories of rural crime are similarly informed by place.

In the non-urban noir, fugitives run from the police or criminals. An encounter may tempt the protagonist with crime, leading him down a bad path. Even if the locales offer fewer hideout spots per square mile, the temptations in the non-urban noir are the same. James M. Cain's *The Postman Always Rings Twice* (see Chapter 16), the prototypical noir, occurs at a roadside. Arriving at a gas station–diner is Frank Chambers, who's likely looking for some trouble. His lust for the blonde Cora inspires him to kill her husband. His capture plays as the Fall of Man updated for the Depression-era setting, as he must account for his violation. He's purged from his ironic "garden"— life with Cora at the restaurant, a kind of asylum from jobless America— when he must face justice in the city. Though Frank may be inclined to crime, his solitude in the desert-wasteland shapes his actions.

In contemporary cinema, the Coen brothers have used specific locales to inform their crime plots. Their characters spring from a distinct, often sparsely populated region. The solitude forced upon Ray and Abby in the Coens' debut, *Blood Simple* (1984)—itself a spin on *Postman*, which had been remade three years earlier by director Bob Rafelson from a script by David Mamet—urges them to run from Abby's husband, leading him to hire a shady private investigator. In *Fargo* (1996), two crooks hired for the kidnapping of a woman work freely in the desolate Northern milieu. Their cold-blooded work, along with the immoral aloofness of a man who hires them to kidnap his own wife, lead to the twists and convolutions of the noir plot. They are lost, out in the open.

Like *Postman*, *Fargo* uses the travel motif, a marked difference from the urban noir. In the city, movement from each locale is immediate, the congestion having abutted everything. Walter Neff's reflections in the urban noir *Double Indemnity* happen not during long drives, but in brief flashes. He reflects on his infatuation and murderous plans during short trips to meet Phyllis Dietrichson, or during a visit to a burger drive-in or bowling alley— communal spots where he remains isolated. The non-urban noir, in contrast, leaves room for humanity to wander, temporarily or perhaps permanently. Some money in the pocket will place the wanderer in a car (as in *Detour*). The less fortunate will be a rootless hitchhiker, the pure loner spawned from the influence of Cain's *Postman*. In both situations, harsh environments lead to bad choices.

Such bad choices seem to multiply in contemporary cinema, which captures various locales in detail. In *Winter's Bone* (2010), the crime occurs far beyond the concentrated city, in the Ozark Mountain territory of Missouri. The film's protagonist, Ree (Jennifer Lawrence), discovers a criminal network, though one unique to her milieu. Her story is a quest (like many noir detective works) for her missing father. He had put up bond on his family's home after his arrest for crystal meth cooking. His flight is like an extreme form of paternal abandonment. With her mother in a catatonic state and her two younger siblings needing care, Ree must locate her father within a week's time to save her home. Despite her existential plight, Ree works with a positive attitude. Only her perseverance can bring meaning to her wasteland.

The film's setting is vivid and realistic, one rarely seen onscreen before *Bone*. The territory of the Ozark Mountains was originally a mining area until resources became depleted. Today, though poultry farming and trucking offer employment, this mountainous wooded area has left many in poverty. Like many in rural areas, the people of the Ozarks have maintained a folk tradition in storytelling and music. Communities are limited but strong, requiring the filmmakers of *Bone* to achieve verisimilitude. Hence, the filming was done completely on location. In the process, director Debra Granik and her collaborators present people living beyond the commodities that are routine to much of America. In *Bone*, people live in log cabins, and hanging laundry outside isn't a nostalgic choice for one fortunate enough to have access to a dryer. The homes are filled with items alien to big-box culture, such as wood carvings. Thus the houses, in their own way, seem timeless. The homes in the area where Megan and Little Arthur reside could be from any decade in the previous century — even the dismantled cars and parts aren't easy to place historically. When we spot a satellite for the "Dish Network" at one house, the object appears alien. What would appear "simple" to some is free of the grand-scale assimilation of chain-store America, though much of the detail indicates poverty. Ree must feed her family with hash, and she is thankful for a neighbor's offering of a meat and potato dinner and use of their wood-splitter for a source of heat. The trees outside, which reflect home and freedom to Ree, can become a commodity when she's urged to sell the wood before losing her home. Should Ree exercise this choice, it would signal the death of her family, and confirm her status as a wanderer. This would indicate tragedy — i.e., Ree's complete loss of family and her only community.

The members of the area's methamphetamine subculture maintain a tight, closed-off existence. And, like the rest of the local culture in *Bone*, the criminal network is a close but limited community. As in a Raymond Chandler yarn, a network of criminals will be exposed one by one. Yet in *Bone*, the working-class network seems to lurk like a team of ghosts ready to pounce on Ree should she cross the line. This group knows about, or may be responsible for, the disappearance of Jessup, Ree's father. For Ree, the communal tradition of her area is disintegrating. Just now 17 years of age, she has left high school, needing to care for her younger brother and sister now that her mother has become incapable of doing so. Ree brings her siblings to school, and in an early scene she looks longingly at the color-guard practice and observes a baby-rearing class with interest. To Ree, the baby-care class appears like a bizarre performance, since she had learned about child care through trial by fire. The color-guard practice seems especially ironic, since they carry fake wooden rifles, while Ree thinks back to the very real one she has at home, one for which she will soon find a use. The activities at school are key examples of her exclusion from community, a fact that will resonate when she receives limited acceptance from the many family members near her home.

When visiting her neighbors to inquire about her missing father, Ree enters a foreign territory that adds a fairy-tale undercurrent to the narrative.[2] If her neighbors have communities, they are hidden from Ree. A colorful but brief scene of a country band playing in a living room shows interaction, as if culture thrives within the home, even if the outside is exposed to decay. The meeting itself is initially pleasant, a feeling which disappears once Ree begins to discuss her missing father. The local folk would rather not summon the ghosts lurking around Ree. Instead, they give her limited information and urge her away.

Since the film is limited to Ree's point of view, she has limited knowledge. In her unofficial role of investigator she must suffer a rough trail with many impasses. Her ordeal is a bigger knot than she anticipated, as are the aims of the confused protagonists of the classical detective noir. The film relies on the strength of Jennifer Lawrence's performance, who previously starred in the mystery-melodrama *The Burning Plain* (2008), written and directed by Guillermo Arriaga. Director Granik immerses her film in its realistic locale, while Ree must uncover its mystery.

The "cookers" and dealers of crystal meth should be treated as members of a subculture in the film.[3] Yet, the remoteness and poverty of the area fosters the drug production. Crystal meth is predated by moonshining (especially as depicted in popular culture), though the practice of huffing became prominent before the creation of meth, with the former's quick (though brief) and more accessible fix. The most recent (and most dangerous), crystal meth, can thrive in rural areas, and hence is a product of the Ozarks as is Ree's state of mind. *Bone*'s remnants of folk culture are the antecedents of a corrupt drug subculture. The former is omnipresent (though crumbling) while the latter becomes Ree's counterforce.

Like her access to opportunity and community services, Ree's search is limited. Her family does not own a car, and Ree must give up her horse to a neighbor, since she can no longer care for it. She asks a friend, Gail (Lauren Sweetser), to borrow her car, though her husband refuses. Ree progresses on foot, first to the house of her uncle, Teardrop (John Hawkes). She presses him, which he resists verbally, until he grabs her face to caress her skin. The move is perverse, though essentially he is playing on her weakness as a young woman. At this point, his hot-tempered intimidation suggests criminal traits. Though he will prove more caring to Ree, he's soon revealed to be a member of the drug-dealing network that Ree will face. Her pattern is that of a noir investigator, though the threat is more immediate to her. One at a time, she will encounter the various parties in a criminal network. All will resist her questioning until she crosses a threshold, coming too close to the boss.

Her next trip, to the home of Megan (Casey MacLaren) and Little Arthur (Kevin Breznahan), yields results similar to those at Teardrop's, though Little Arther is visibly shaken at the sight of Ree, in one of the rare shots that are out of Ree's point of view. Megan directs Ree toward the house of her grandfather, Thump, likely just to get rid of her. When Ree goes there, the resistance grows stronger. Stopping Ree outside is Merab (Dale Dickey), Thump's daughter, who doubles as his guard. To deter and intimidate Ree, Merab refers to problems that Jessup had with her nephew, then poses other veiled threats to her. Without even appearing onscreen, Thump (note his fairytale name) is positioned as the crime boss. We see similar folkloric associations in the criminal boss Gutman of *The Maltese Falcon*—an oversized (as Thump will prove to be) troll with malicious little gnomes assisting him.

Ree's inquiries have sent distress signals through the network. When she returns from Thump's, her neighbor Blond forces her into his truck. He drives her to a burnt-out rancher home, where he says Jessup died while producing crystal meth. The blackened house, with walls blown out, infuses an apocalyptic tone into the withering milieu of the Ozarks, signaling personal and communal destruction. As Ree inspects the wrecked house, she pauses when realizing that her father's life has been such a burned-out existence. She has an investigator's eye, refuting to Blond his claim that her father recently died there. (High weeds indicate that the fire happened long before Jessup disappeared.) In his attempt to hush her, Blond also seems suspect, though he offers to take in her brother, a prospect that would signal defeat for Ree.

Just after Ree fears the loss of her siblings comes an ironic scene. Back home, Ree brings her little brother and sister to their yard, with her rifle. She discusses the gun before showing them how to shoot it. Veering away from crime motifs, this scene reflects a staple of the classical Western: the shooting lesson. In films like *Shane* (1953) and *The Tin Star* (1957), moments of mentorship appear in which a seasoned gunman shows a young novice how to shoot — in fact, how to inherit the quest of protecting the land. These moments fore-

Ree (Jennifer Lawrence) teaches survival to her younger siblings Ashlee (Ashlee Thompson) and Sonny (Isaiah Stone) in *Winter's Bone* (2010, Lions Gate Entertainment).

shadow the skill of the "teacher," and how either he or his pupil will show acumen in the narrative's final battle, a requisite for the genre. In *Bone*, the lesson depicts the mentor's determination, i.e., how she will maintain her wits and persistence as she resolves the issue concerning her missing father. Yet, she teaches the children to shoot not to avenge, but to eat. Due to their situation, the family is pushed beyond the contemporary marketplace, with its convenience in packaged meat and other products. Their hunting may seem like a return to the earthly life, that of a noble savage, but they are regressing due to social factors. They may need gun skills to defend themselves one day, but presently the gun represents their immediate unmet needs. Though she's very capable, Ree won't use the rifle in a final showdown.

Ree's immediate opponents come to her. With the local sheriff visiting her house with bad news, she's reminded of the ticking clock (she has only one week to find her father). Satterfield (Tate Taylor), a bail bondsman, comes to tell her that Teardrop must be dead, since someone left money to pay the remainder of the bond that the house could not cover. The bondsman reminds Ree that the home is now leashed to the law. Satterfield is a semi-legal presence, for Ree calls the sheriff "the law." The former is closer to a bounty hunter, highlighting that Jessup, alive or dead, is a fugitive who Ree, the avenger, must hunt down. With Satterfield seeking her father, Ree must also become a bounty hunter. Her motivation and status are clear. She seeks out Jessup not for familial duty, but to reclaim what is rightfully hers and her family's.

"The law" remains more menacing to Ree. Satterfield notifies her that Jessup's car was found burned, news that resounds the image of his burned home and, literally, is more evidence that he must be dead. Ree remains unconvinced; she perceives this latest information as a means to dissuade her from continuing her search. Teardrop tells her to sell the timber on her property to claim some of the home's value before she must leave it. His suggestion draws another image of destruction, one that haunts her. She has nightmares of the woods being torn away by an unseen party, rendering the wildlife homeless.

The threat urges her to confront Thump when he is away from his home/ sanctuary. The public location where she finds him highlights her disconnection from communities: an auction house, the largest gathering of people in the film. At first, we don't realize that Ree is looking for Thump — for all we know, she has come across this gathering for the narrative to stress her disassociation. At the auction people assemble to buy livestock, a commodity removed from Ree, for which she must hunt in the woods. Like the school and Army recruiting office that Ree briefly visits (she was thinking of enlisting before her father was reported lost), the auction house, like anything communal, is a world alien to Ree. When Ree leaves the auction area and goes "backstage," to the animals, they are framed by the camera behind gates, within pens. Their only movement is through pathways that lead them to be purchased, and eventually slaughtered. Granik's multiple shots stress Ree's association to penned livestock — a heavy-handed move, though an undeniable sentiment.

Thump's association to the auction house (which is never clarified) connects the legal commodity (livestock) with the illegal one (drug dealing). Like the classical mobster, Thump has aligned his crime work with a legal network, possibly as a front. When Ree spots him in the livestock pen area, she has reached the furthest realm in her fairy-tale journey; hence, her yelling of his name is muffled by the animal sounds. She cries for vindication, and thus crosses the threshold into the world of crime. She pays the price soon after.

When returning to Thump's house, she is attacked by his three daughters, who take her into a shed for a beating. When she wakes, Thump is present — in the manner of the group's "boss" — along with Megan, Little Arthur, and other members of the network. In this revelatory scene, all the parties of whom Ree has inquired have assembled. The group intimidates her, before Teardrop arrives at the shed, not quite welcomed by them nor is he an outsider.

He will take her away, but agrees to "answer for her." Now that she has crossed the line and reached the center of the network, Teardrop reveals to her that Jessup was informing to the police. As a criminal breaking the group's code, Jessup made himself a fugitive. With a name associated to "Joseph" (the father), Jessup also channels "Jesus," since he has been sacrificed; Teardrop, fittingly with his name, is the sufferer left behind. Now that Ree knows of Jessup's actual status, she has become disenfranchised, and a potential fugitive.

Now in her most vulnerable state (even if her uncle has taken her in), Ree lies in bed, beaten, dreaming of the trees she fears must be sold. After she awakes, Teardrop brings Ree to a convenience store at night to question a gang member. He reveals nothing, to which Teardrop reacts by going into a rage and smashing his windshield; now Teardrop is even closer to his own banishment. From there, Teardrop takes her to the "land of the dead," a graveyard, in a desperate attempt to settle the mystery of his lost brother. On the way back, the fugitives are pulled over by "the law." Teardrop scolds the sheriff for "squealing" to Thump about Jessup's informing. The sheriff's strained silence and countenance suggests that his involvement went further than ratting to Thump. As in the noir tradition, the police are ineffective, and in this

Ree (Jennifer Lawrence) and Teardrop (John Hawkes) search for Jessup in *Winter's Bone* (2010, Lions Gate Entertainment).

case corrupt, the network growing before Ree. Teardrop, when seeing a possible network member in front of him, goes for his rifle and stands off the
officer. This aborted shootout is the payoff to Ree's "faux" shooting lesson
earlier. "Is this how it's going to end for us?" Teardrop warns the officer,
regarding him as a traitor more than just an enemy. Though no one shoots,
Teardrop drives away, the victor for avoiding the law. Yet, as the syndicate
may include the sheriff, Ree's (and Teardrop's) fugitive status intensifies.

Then, the third reveal appears. Merab approaches Ree, saying that she
knows where her father's "bones" are. Now the title takes its full meaning,
after other connections strewn in the text (i.e., Ree's dog is fed only bones).
In the final season of the year — the season of death — Jessup exists merely as
crude remains. Effectively, Ree knows he is gone. Merab and her sisters blind-
fold Ree and bring her to a stream. Like the mythical river of Lethe, where
souls forget their previous lives, this body of water borders a Land of the
Dead. Merab tells Ree that even if she recognizes the location, she must *forget*
it. They will let her retrieve her father's hands by cutting through his bones
with a chainsaw. The hands are the minimal remains that Ree needs to prove
his death. They suggest Jessup to be clinging to life,[4] at least for Ree's sake,
for her freedom. Pulled just above the water, her father's body is a submerged
memory, barely freeing Ree, but also about to haunt her. Granik holds the
camera on a patch of gas on the water, like a waft of smoke, after they retrieve
the evidence.

As soon as Ree seems relieved, able to prove her father's death and save
her family, we recall the sheriff's words from earlier: the home will be safe *if
the DNA of the remains matches his*. Now that the sheriff is part of the network,
we cannot trust his treatment of the remains, since Ree must bring them to
him. Additionally, the sisters may have taken Ree to another body.

The next morning, Teardrop gives Ree a bag of money, left over from
the bounty. He then tells her, "I know *who*." A mystery is solved, but means
little. The family is benighted, regardless, and Teardrop doesn't bother to tell
Ree the name of the killer. Teardrop's gift of baby chicks to the younger sister
and brother are faint touches of rebirth, and the sounds of a banjo played by
the boy are without structure, empty rings. With her ironic elixir/reward —
finding her father, (possibly) saving her house, receiving some leftover cash —
Ree stares into the distance, not seeing her trees or any possible communities.
The classical whodunit would reveal and punish the moral deviation and
restore order. Ree's investigation clarifies the mess in which she's found herself.
Her search does not break down the ordeal step by step, but grows more con-
voluted until an insurmountable problem is revealed. Ree's drive to establish
order and closure has darkened the pitch of her life, which has become as cold
and lifeless as a bone left out in the dead of winter.

5

Teen Crime and Redemption
Gus Van Sant's *Elephant* and *Paranoid Park*

With few exceptions — see William Wyler's *The Children's Hour* (1961) — teachers' crimes have become popular only after 1990s tabloid scandals; teen crimes have existed much longer. Since its milieu is so distinct — with oppressive teachers, relentless bullies, oppressed teen misfits — the "high school as hell" film resists association to the crime genre, even if the two are kinsmen. Outsiders or rebels fall victim to jocks, yet the conflict often results in a coming-of-age tale. The underdog protagonists assert themselves, grow confident as they reach maturation, and eventually defeat their oppressors. These rebels accept and justify their individuality, unless they take things too far — as does Carrie (Sissy Spacek) in her 1976 eponymous film, or the psychopathic J.D. (Christian Slater) in 1988's *Heathers* (two examples that veer toward the horror film). Yet, bullying teens or careless, abusive authority figures lead to crime narratives, with the central players as victims who must avenge themselves. In Keith Gordon's *The Chocolate War* (1988), Jerry (Ian Michael Smith) fights the oppression of both teachers and a secret student organization. His resistance to conformity results in oppression from the latter and violent bullying from the former. The final conflict plays out in a surreal, late-night boxing match.[1]

In this genre, the perspective is of a higher authority, one ready to reward the strong and condemn ignorant youths. An unconscious inclination on the part of the filmmakers, the moralistic point of view leads viewers to pass judgment on the characters and react to a "simplified social structure."[2] Even the best-made "high school as hell" films veer towards this classical mindset. The closest they come to the teens' sensibility is a giddy tone, as in *Heathers*, with the style reflecting yet condemning the oppressive teens. A true teen perspective remains absent from the oppressive high school film, with a notable exception being Gus Van Sant's *Elephant*, a 2003 film that re-imagines the Columbine High School killings of April 20, 1999. The premise benefits from the built-in suspense of a known tragedy. Viewers have little choice but to become engrossed while awaiting a horrifying event, as we are when watching Paul Greengrass's *United 93* (2006), about the September 11, 2001, terrorist attacks. Yet, *Elephant* leaves its sensationalism in the background to bring its teen characters upfront. The filmmaker doesn't condemn his teenage criminals, but listens to their experiences and to those who will become their victims. Through this perspective, Van Sant moves away from both the torn-from-the-headlines sensationalism and the issue-of-the-week after school movie (too often at the root of teen films). Interestingly, Van Sant's reactionary style uses crime motifs (also used in his early works[3]) to study innocence veering toward damnation. In *Elephant*, a tragic, suspenseful crime spree becomes a flowering character piece; in the similarly ironic *Paranoid Park*, Van Sant's 2007 film, noir is transformed into a euphoric coming-of-age tale.

The irreverent fan base of Van Sant, like that of many indie filmmakers, would resist genre classification. In his commitment to youthful perspectives, viewers and fans want him safe within the realm of innovative drama. The fact that his narratives resist classical narrative structure makes the argument seem stronger. Leery of making "exploitation," he doesn't want to reflect the shape of the "high-school-as-hell" film, with its growing showdown, or the noir tale, with the moralistic order bearing down on the criminals. Yet, by considering Van Sant's application of these styles, we realize the narrative structure beneath his distinct characterizations. He uses tradition as a frame on which to layer his style, one that investigates his young characters' perspectives.

Van Sant used subjective approaches in his early work, and the style became a rule for him (with the exception being his melodramas *Good Will Hunting* [1997] and *Finding Forrester* [2000], and his 2008 biopic of Harvey Milk). His debut 1982 short film, *The Discipline of D.E.* (i.e., "Do Easy," "a way of doing"), is a hilarious mock-instructional piece on how to avoid obstructions in a shifting reality. As an adaptation of a William S. Burroughs short story, drug references are extant; add to this the fact that the film's setting remains limited to an apartment household. The tale and its narrator assume that the described universe — where everyday objects seem "alive and hostile, trying to twist out of your fingers" — belongs to everyone. This ironic narrative, posing as objective reality, remains all the more subjective.

The filmmaker's breakthrough feature, *Drugstore Cowboy* (1989), plays more so as realism. Concerning addicts who rob drugstores, the film refashions the lovers-on-the-run motif. Their milieu isn't the western road, with random stops along the highways as crime scenes, but modern retail shops, in which they appear as immediate misfits upon entering. Recalling the old-time drugstore/soda fountains, these bland interiors seem as otherworldly as the seedy motel rooms to which they flee afterward. Together, the two settings compose a wasteland within a realistic portrayal of Portland, Oregon — Van Sant's home town that has become a career-long inspiration. His next feature, *My Own Private Idaho* (1991) — about criminal refugees of another kind — returns to the city. Two male prostitutes (River Phoenix and Keanu Reeves) wander from hitchhikes, johns' places, and coffeehouses in a dreamy narrative, reflecting Phoenix's narcolepsy. The director's next film, an adaptation of Tom Robbin's *Even Cowgirls Get the Blues* (1993), takes its misfit character to the actual road to find bizarre locales in another warped universe.

After the mainstream success of 1995's *To Die For* (based on the Pamela Smart case), about teenage rebels-turned-contract killers directly associated with the tabloids (though the filmmaker looked deeper), Van Sant shifted to *Good Will Hunting* and *Finding Forrester*— both objective-style crowd-pleasers and examples of the filmmakers' technical mastery more than style. Afterward, his collaborator in the earlier film, star/co-writer Matt Damon, helped Van Sant to return to his style and toward a breakthrough in it. The script for *Gerry* (2002), co-written by Van Sant, Matt Damon, and Casey Affleck and starring the latter two, is an absurdist journey into the desert. If the film's narrative calls for an acquired taste — better know Samuel Beckett's work and like it, should you watch — *Gerry* uses a telescoped realism, a style to which Van Sant has since committed himself. *Last Days* (2005), Van Sant's ethereal retelling of Kurt Cobain's demise, distills such absurdism into the hyperreal — as unpleasing a viewing experience as it is (we never lose sight of the main player's pain), the film is noteworthy for its blend of styles. Having discovered a new form of subjective verity, the filmmaker makes compelling the descent of his characters, something greater than the removed perspectives on pity to which we have become accustomed in youth-turmoil tales. *Gerry* and *Last Days* ponder the characters' isolation and unavoidable demise. *Elephant* and *Paranoid Park* highlight the traction of crime: the need for it, in the former example, and the effects of the accidental in the latter. The crimes of these characters transform their perspective, in Van Sant's portrayal of adolescent confusion.

If *Elephant* and *Paranoid Park* look to isolated teens, *Last Days* depicts life after the teen years as apocalypse. Blake (Michael Pitt) has returned to a woodlands home, which is something of a commune. Though people loaf around — some try to communicate with Blake, others seem to avoid him — he wanders as if removed. Save for the occasional burst of relief, such as a scene by a waterfall, his world might as well be the barren desert of *Gerry*.

Van Sant's long takes (with the cinematography by Harris Savides) show the world as it appears to, yet it falls away from, Blake. Outside of this view, the woods could be a sanctuary. This transformation makes *Last Days* particularly disarming.

The films that bookend *Last Days* in Van Sant's career — *Elephant* before and *Paranoid* after — use such an immersion into character perspective. *Elephant* is an ensemble piece that realizes a dreamy milieu for both the youths about to kill (outcasts turned vigilantes), and those about to die (essentially all the teenage characters). Van Sant singles out a few of these teenagers. John (John Robinson), a golden-blonde son of a drunk, is late for school due to his father (Timothy Bottoms). John's late arrival saves his life — he sees the two soon-to-be gunmen, Alex and Eric (Alex Frost and Eric Deulen — Van Sant has an uncanny approach of naming characters after the actors playing them), entering the building dressed in fatigues and carrying weighty duffel bags. The film also lets us into the killers' worlds, to depict their latent resolution, a product of their alienation — evidently a result of their getting bullied at school and ignored by staff. Van Sant's camera brushes against some of the victims, whom the filmmaker treats with the same curious, objective intimacy as the gunmen. By relating the eventual victims' issues — isolation, bulimia, alcoholic parents — Van Sant shows the alienation of Alex and Eric as a similar byproduct of growing up in the American nightmare. Even if actually more severe, in Van Sant's style the crimes are nothing stranger than the abuse some kids receive.

The school massacre must become the crisis point: to place it at the beginning, or even in the middle, would submerge the film in tragedy. (Greengrass's *United 93* avoids this issue: the bombed buildings are an early narrative beat, while the final conflict involves the passengers overtaking the plane.) But to avoid the "high-school-as-hell" narrative trap, Van Sant frames the attack as an undercurrent, an event occurring in continuum: it has already happened, it is occurring, it will continue. Fate seems to be at work, as the film reflects a hallway interaction from three different perspectives. Offering the varied lives of teenagers associated to one disastrous event, this technique recalls the framing device of Stanley Kubrick's heist-puzzle film, *The Killing* (1956), and its descendant, Tarantino's *Reservoir Dogs* (1992). These films bring out the human factor in a plot-driven heist — by fracturing the plot, we learn of the different lives and various motivations. Van Sant uses that technique to account for all of his characters and how the central crime will affect them; and yet, he grants them more life than would realism. While Kubrick and Tarantino's works play as clever genre revisions, in which motivation leads to crime, Van Sant shows how life's constant beyond it.

Outside, John encounters a dog, with a slow-motion jump that signifies the last taste of innocence before experience comes crashing down. Just after, he sees the two armed boys, one of whom spares him with a warning: the matter-of-factness makes the moment especially disturbing. If we weren't listening for it — already warned by the boys' appearance, even from a distant approach — we'd miss their words. Yet, the Columbine tragedy has trained us to reduce "misfits" clad in black as dark portents — their casual entry reflects continual judgment. Later on, in scenes at the gunmen's homes interweaving with events at the school, we enter their lives. One boy plays the piano while the other plays a shootout video game on the computer. Van Sant holds the game onscreen to show how, for these boys, clicks of a button — movement as little as the pull of a trigger — will change their lives. The flowery score over this image continues an approach throughout this film as well as *Paranoid Park*: music as emotional reference, correlating to character and not to moralistic viewer's judgment. Hearing "highbrow" music — far from the styles usually associated with teenagers in films — seems an offputting choice at first, but is telling in retrospect. So is a gunman quoting *Macbeth*—"So foul and fair a day I have not seen" — which also recalls the soon-to-be-convicted-murderer Damien Echols (in Joe Berlinger and Bruce Sinofsky's documentary *Paradise Lost* [1996]), who in the film is questioned by the D.A. about his interest in *Macbeth*'s "Out, Out" quote (misquoted by Echols as taken from *A Midsummer Night's Dream*).[4]

The gunmen's button-click visit to a gun-buying website in Texas is hardly commentary on technology, but reflects a means for these teens to fulfill their desires, to realize their fantasy of claiming control. The control, of course, will be temporary: "Today's the day we die," one tells another, as they step into the shower together, on the morning of the massacre. The two murderers/suiciders bond with a kiss, one of them never having had the chance beforehand. Their approach to the school, a little time after, from John's point of view is a sudden burst of terror, colliding with the film's gliding images of teens walking the hallways. When the narrative returns to the two gunmen, as they prepare for their last day, our disgust at the imminent crime is shattered. It's a fatal event charged by fate — a summation of how these teens had lived, shaped by their psychological response to some tough social factors.

Earlier in the film, a gunman-to-be gets whipped with wet toilet paper during class. It's one of a few scenes occurring on a day prior to the killings. In this early scene, the bullying motif is overly familiar — a jock playing the good student when the teacher is looking, then aiming at the outsider, who's drawing in a notebook at the back of the class. One future killer finds understanding in the other, and as the film depicts them together, we come to realize that isolation/depression-turning-nihilism may be their only common ground. One boy tries to show his "plan" to a random female student (occurring prior to the last day), a potentially shocking moment that's snuffed when the girl ignores him. It's another warning sign familiar in the culture of bully identification, but often ignored. Van Sant lets these events swim within other breezy snapshots of youth. A better-adjusted teen, Elias (Elias McConnell) finds a means of expressing himself, and relief from teen life, through photography. His art allows him to mingle with others: talking about it, exposing photos alongside friends, asking students to serve as models. Another colorful piece in Van Sant's style, he fits directly into *Elephant*'s plot at the moment of tragedy. When a gunman enters a library to begin his killings, Elias snaps a picture, saving the moment on impulse, also reflecting his own disassociation from violence as danger, but eventful. The moment is something *not to be missed*, even if no one else in the room notices a camouflaged kid, wielding a gun. While the object of his photo is still ignored by some, this photographer mirrors Van Sant: the event/experience must be documented. The photographer/director surrogate records the crime and how it came about, leaving it to us to imagine the aftereffects.

The eponymous conceit could refer to the "elephantine" tragedy swirling into existence, for the victims as much as the gunmen. It could reflect the latters' sizable problems not addressed, i.e., the "elephant in the room," and the culpability on the part of authority for not intervening. The lucidity of Van Sant's style reflects a looming elephant ride; the events mimic a fall from such heights, as crime becomes an option and a cause of tragedy.

If *Elephant* is Van Sant's multiple teen tone poem, then *Paranoid Park* is his return to the purely subjective, into one character's perspective. In describing the latter film thus, we return to *Last Days*, though this film's ultra-subjective feel produces a detached tone, reflecting the young musician's falling away from himself. In this sense, *Paranoid Park* is an inversion of *Last Days*: the former film has its character come of age. If crime threatens him, his reaction to it results in an unlikely education.

The film begins as a noir that, like many, has a mythical framework. We meet a teenager, Alex (Gabe Nevins), preoccupied with the past. He obsesses over a vague recent event in a journal, to create an unusual noirish confessional style. He relates the details soon enough.

Alex has committed an accidental crime, and an investigation follows. In flashback, the murder happens near Eastside Park, what the local kids call "Paranoid Park," an illegally built skateboard area. The concrete pillars beneath a roadway have morphed into swimming-pool style curves. The skateboards rolling over them reflect youthful delirium, with an onscreen kinesis of the skaters flying just above the built-in swirls and swoops. The park's unofficial title, given by the skaters, reflects its ironic grandeur: "Park," implying fun, and "Paranoid" reflecting its alluring dangers, its promise to break them away from normality. The landscape has the texture of the L.A. River, noteworthy as an ironic netherworld within urban territory and, thus, the setting of many movie scenes. Skaters gravitate to the well-lit nightspot of Paranoid: an escape from the mundane urban life of Portland, the park seems able to trap them once they arrive. Alex comes to Paranoid Park as an outsider, one scared to take the "dive" on his skateboard into the waves. He visits right before he steps too far against the law.

One night at Paranoid, Alex sits on his board, overlooking a skate-pike's edge. Older kids, who say they live there, approach him, seemingly to borrow his board. When Alex agrees to lend it to Scratch (Scott Green), he returns it right after some riding, and asks Alex if he wants to see some freight-trains. Thus, we learn that Scratch is a modern-day cave-dweller/gatekeeper. He will lead Alex to the scene of the crime: the freight train tracks. The trains transfer materials to construct conventional society, from which Alex, by coming to Paranoid, has found an escape. While not openly angry at it, he has little interest in the establishment. His parents' marriage is ending, and we eventually learn that Dad will be moving in with an "Uncle Tommy." As such, the implied gay element "disrupts" the ordered, (hetero)normal world — as a fear to Alex, and in *Elephant*, as a final moment of rebellion (the gunmen's

Alex (Gabe Nevins) hangs out at the threshold of a new world in ***Paranoid Park*** (2007, HBO Films).

kiss in the shower). Likewise, we can read the park as a homosocial getaway, with its continual action pushing the imagery toward the homoerotic (the girls appear to be there just to watch). It's a communal territory well lit, while the nearby trains pull along in shadows. The train tracks are a gateway for Alex, and the train-riding an ordeal he must undertake to officially enter the new world.

Yet, an authority figure, in the form of a security guard, protects this piece of formal society. The slow-motion run of the portly, middle-aged guard seems out of control, and he impulsively swings upward at Alex, who hangs onto the freight car. The guard's lack of stability doesn't meet well with Alex's defensive swing of his skateboard at a better vantage point. Taking a blow, the guard falls backward, onto the tracks of an oncoming train. Moments later, Alex sees the guard, his arms pulling his torso far from his waist, a gristly string of organs connecting the two parts. He looks up to Alex, as if more disgusted than frightened by impending death. This moment takes stylized realism to the surreal, like the ending of *Last Days*, when the dead musician's soul climbs up ethereal ladder rungs. Told in retrospect, from a teen enamored with the gliding movements of the skatepark, this butchered guard seems to be Alex's invention, a waking dream image reflecting the moment's importance. From here, we understand our narrator to be unreliable, fuel to Van Sant's dreamlike imagery. Upon Alex's attempted entry into a new world, this ordeal's been thrown upon him, the results of which are filtered through his perspective. The manslaughter will certainly complicate his new interest. Likewise, his severing of the authority figure sets him on his flight from authority.

The nature of the investigation exists in the scope of the skate park. A detective's visit to the high school comes before we see the murder. The narrative depicts the one-on-one interview with Alex before we see the detective's group interview with all the "skater kids" at the school, while the real "cave dwellers" are out of authority's reach. Alex's one-on-one interview with the detective shows the former's state of mind. From the outside, we suspect he's merely keeping a poker face, as the cop tries to break his confidence with jokes about the sandwich he says he ordered the night of the crime. But actor Gabe Nevins shows the confusion of adolescence behind what appears to be a confident façade. It's as if the delirious feeling of Paranoid Park alters the boy's appearance. Like *Elephant*, Van Sant cast the film with unknown amateurs; Gabe Nevins originally auditioned as an extra. His newbie innocence shows through in his eyes, but the young actor's controlled face makes Alex's inner-confusion/outer-confidence work in closeup. In him, Van Sant found *Paranoid*'s ideal teen presence.

Similarly, the surreal nature of the guard's death reflects the illogic of the investigation. We learn that the police found a skateboard, though Alex had tossed his away after the incident. Further, he buys a new board at a skate shop, an event easily traceable by investigators. Yet, his status as a suspect never develops, and the narrative hardly implies that it will be undertaken. We are left with a subjective-surreal crime film, one limited to — and likely distorted by — Alex's perspective. And, hence, Van Sant clears the way to develop an (accidental) criminal's psychology. The tone reflects less the dark, conventional motifs of noir than the criminal protagonist's confusion, a feeling akin to his delirium.

After his rite of passage — entering Paranoid Park, proper — he reaches sexual maturation. His girlfriend, the bubbly airhead Jennifer (Taylor Momsen), describes herself as a virgin before they have sex, though Alex's actions afterward suggest that he was, too. The experience moves him to dump her, while he maintains a friendship with Macy (played by Lauren McKinney, especially credible among the strong, mostly amateur cast). She urges him to write about what is bothering him (the crime is unknown to her), as something he would say to someone close to him, but that no one will ever read. This suggestion, obviously, reflects the first-person narrative that frames the source novel (as it does for S.E. Hinton's *The Outsiders*, in novel and film form — another tale of accidental death). In the film of *Paranoid Park*, the first-person narrative frames the noirish retelling of the events. What's happened stays with him, until he unloads the truth, and sets it afire. His maturation now commences, while *Elephant*'s ends.

With plenty of skateboard footage filmed in the style common to skater videos (with a wide-angle lens and, at times, in Super 8), this film would qualify for that genre. This trend features rebels but, in the end, presents conventional characters in service of putting the sport onscreen (see *Wassup Rockers* [2005] and *Street Dreams* [2009]). Van Sant uses the footage to reflect Alex's mindset as he leaves innocence: confusion without a park in which to let it fly. The skate park is an escapist, special world, one of beauty and destruction — essentially, the kind of place to which *Elephant*'s killers transform their school. Van Sant's recent crime films show the apocalypse of "mature" order. Rebellion leads to fantasy through the glorious disorder of crime.

6

Night of the Hunters
David Fincher's *Zodiac*
and the New Serial Killer Film

The presence of the serial killer as a featured movie villain was a natural evolution. Such a secret menace with large-scale effects serves as an ultimate counterforce in a narrative, the extreme driving force of a crime story. Similarly, in the horror genre, science fiction/horror emerged in the 1950s to deliver a wider threat beyond the localized superhuman monster of previous horror films.[1] The alien monsters are still used in science fiction/invasion films as the super-sized monstrous bodies (see *Cloverfield* [2008], *Skyline* [2010], *Battle Los Angeles* [2011], etc.). Furthermore, in supercop films like *Die Hard* [1988], a terrorist villain can similarly jeopardize a large group. With more at stake, the heroics become urgent and stronger. The serial killer has similar effects in a narrative. In real life, he can put a populace in terror through press attention to his repeated crimes. While victims and their families experience the worst, the lurking killer's effects will spread through press coverage, police action, word of mouth. The best serial-killer films don't exploit such realities, but embody such a disturbance and, hopefully, reflect humanity's reactions to the menace (an aim rarely achieved).

As their crimes continue, real-life serial killers replicate their brutal actions while the threat grows with each murder. The effect differs from the crime spree of a gang like Bonnie and Clyde's, from which murders may result, though the side effects of robbery. In tracking a serial killer, the homicide investigator's job seems endless — in movies, it's far from the crime-investigation pattern of Conan Doyle/Agatha Christie–style whodunits. Raymond Chandler–style noir detective novels, which revised the classical British whodunit, could yield a string of bodies, causing the private detective's job to extend beyond his reach. Yet, the serial killer works toward the horrifying aftereffects of killings, and in the process, terrorism. Profits within a criminal underworld hardly concern him. He has wider-reaching aims.

While the bulk of early cinematic cops fought cut-out, melodramatic villains, the police onscreen would eventually have to trace the serial murderer. In a few cases, the treatment occurred in the silent and early-sound eras. In Hitchcock's silent British film *The Lodger: A Story of the London Fog* (1927), the police hunt for a murderer[2] named "The Avenger," whose notoriety amplifies threats to blonde women. (Hitchcock would later use a serial murderer in *Shadow of a Doubt* [1943], in which the noir style emerges as the return of the repressed: a beloved uncle proving to be something other than what he appears to be.) Like Fritz Lang's early sound film *M*, the 1931 Weimar German production in which a child murder is likely a rapist, Hitchcock's *The Lodger* mirrors the notoriety of Jack the Ripper, likely the world's prototypical serial murderer.[3] Edward Dmytryk's noir film *The Sniper* (1952), about a sexually impeded woman-killer, uses flatly photographed San Francisco locations to ground the study in realism, well researched by scenarists Edna and Edward Anhalt,[4] if over simplified in its conclusion. As a Stanley Kramer production (by a producer always ready to tackle "social problems"), the film positions itself as a credible report on a growing menace. Thus, Dmytryk and his screenwriters could use the risky, rewarding point of view of a psychopath, a breakthrough soon forgotten.

In 1968, director Richard Fleischer adapted the true case of the "Boston Strangler," Albert deSalvo (fascinatingly played by a cast-against-type Tony Curtis), revealing the subject to be a psychological enigma — even with detective John S. Bottomly (who obtained the killer's confession in real life) played by timeless moral authority Henry Fonda.[5] The film's first half focuses solely on the reactions of the police and population, with the killer introduced, at midpoint, as a quiet family man. The authorities apprehend him by luck; hence, the film putative ultimate hunt proves to be a red herring. Not so with the next entry. With the help of Fleischer's film, the serial-killer-narrative style reached the mainstream. In 1971's *Dirty Harry*, directed by Don Siegel, the eponymous character (played by Clint Eastwood) is assigned to hunt the "Scorpio" assassin, a sniper modeled after the Zodiac killer (still in his first wave when the film was released). (For more on Eastwood, see Chapter 12.) Dirty Harry has the noir detective's pessimism as he hunts a new kind of cinematic phantom. The "Scorpio," who eventually hijacks a school bus (something the real Zodiac threatened to do), urges Harry's rogue sensibility to grow, going to extreme measures in his hunt. Official procedures and due process only hold him back. After shooting the killer dead into a lake at the conclusion, Dirty Harry tosses his badge in after him. As in the classical noirs, the ethos of *official* police are of little help, since Harry abandons that status.

Setting a trend of rogue cops and avengers, Harry's actions were extremism borne from extreme situations: the post–Vietnam rejection of liberal policies toward crime[6] (policies that backfire in John G. Alvidson's 1970 film, *Joe*, about a working-class character [Peter Boyle] whose anti-hippie sentiments consume him and his acquaintance: a man who ends up killing his own daughter). The other counterforces to create the 1970s rogue cop were drug dealing/trafficking, which drives Popeye Doyle of *The French Connection* and *Shaft* in their respective films (both 1971), while the rape attack moves a civilian to more personal vengeance in *Death Wish* (1974), a film that uses Western associations to conceive its avenger.

In *The French Connection*, drug trafficking works through a wide network of criminals, while rape-vengeance urges Paul Kersey (Charles Bronson) of *Death Wish* to rid the city of lowlifes in the process. Serial killers embody ultimate human threat but, like their cousins the slasher-killers, supersede apparent human capabilities — in other words, they are human monsters. Their nature reaches out beyond crime conventions to the horror film. As a phantom, the serial killer is a new, if more realistic, version of the bogeyman archetype. In times of growing media influence, the monster now walks among us. The enduring monster archetypes — the vampire (solidified in *Dracula*), the mad scientist's child (Frankenstein's monster), the beast within (*Jekyll and Hyde*, the werewolf mythos), and the living dead (zombie culture) all point back to human anxieties — respectively, sexual anxieties/desires, God complex/forsaken children, breakdown of civilized man, and the failure of the body. In 1880s London, Jack the Ripper, a human monster, gained enough attention that he became a celebrity as much as a threat, and something of a legend, as he was never caught. The imaginary haunts, initially encountered in the shadows of a bedroom, became a real menace in the alleyways. Hunting the original was the job of Scotland Yard, even if it had the ultimate criminal on their hands.

The dual association of the serial killer film — crime story meets horror — added double strength to the narratives, until it seemed overtaxed, and problematic, by the mid–1970s to the 1980s. In the 1950s, tales of psychokillers ran through the underground, though Charles Laughton's *The Night of the Hunter* (1955) becoming a unique, well-known example (featuring a religious fanatic played by Robert Mitchum, who's equal parts mythical monster and psychopath). By the early 1960s, two films brought psycho-killers to the fore by psychoanalyzing them. *Psycho* (1960) features a nebbish psychopath (not far from a real-life serial killer) who hijacks the film by going from unknown antagonist to protagonist. Hitchcock thought it a joke to trick viewers into rooting for madness, even if he reversed horror expectations. The investigation reveals the killer, and makes way for his psychoanalysis, even if the verdict cannot help him. Then, science can take on a human monster, after a decade of mainstream American atomic-age haunts starring giant beasts and bugs.

Across the pond, the very highbrow Michael Powell had similar intentions for his psycho-killer film. In *Peeping Tom* (also 1960), his take was more analytical, not from a removed scientist's perspective, but more human, as the film's central character — a murderous scopophiliac (Carl Boehm) — turns the analysis toward himself. His obsession with killing is really an obsession with seeing fear. Far from a manifestation of the death instinct, his compulsive practice feeds on itself. It climaxes in a final vision — the image of his own death, as he turns a blade, and mirror, toward himself. Beyond just making the monster realistic, Powell positions him as a sympathetic figure, a bogeyman demystified and humanized. The killer in *The Boston Strangler* also becomes a case for such analysis. While revealed to be powerless to his own urges, deSalvo remains an enigma.

By 1971, such a real-life monster became demonized, the target to fuel Eastwood's Dirty Harry. The lovers/killers-on-the-run inspiration of *Bonnie and Clyde* (1967) led to Malick's *Badlands* (1973), also based on a real couple that goes beyond robbery to serial murder (later echoed by Oliver Stone's *Natural Born Killers* [1994], co-written by Quentin Tarantino). *Badlands* intrigues as an exercise in point of view (in lieu of the overused killer's point-of-view shot), while soon the serial killer would not see such careful treatment. The serial killer's bogeyman origins returned by the mid–1970s through the 1980s, with the slasher monsters of *Halloween* (1978), *Friday the 13th* (1980), and *Nightmare on Elm Street* (1984). In these films and their sequels the threat of murder sprees regresses to the cop-out duality: overly monstrous humans that grow semi-supernatural (Wes Craven's clever-premised dream haunt, Freddy Krueger, is an stronger device: a psycho-killer, now dead, but working as a ghost in dreams). These killers served the conservative, hero-needy American cinema of the 1980s, as they inspired especially super-hero–like avengers (or strong last-girls-standing in slasher films).

Like their maturation in the early 1970s, most film serial killers of today aim to interpret real-life criminals. We can trace this development back to a mid–1980s/early 1990s interest. Author Thomas Harris's Hannibal Lecter novels helped to bring the serial killer away from slasher-film formulas and toward analysis. The author's 1981 novel *Red Dragon* came to the screen as 1986's *Manhunter*, about an imprisoned killer who's mentoring an investigator, on his own hunt for another killer. Investigator Will Graham (William Petersen), about to retire (like many cinematic cops), remains obsessed with catching criminals, since he can think just like one. As in a game of chess, his reading of evidence helps him plot out his opponent's next steps. Though the investigator's imperative seems strong, with such a talent he fears his own stability.

His unwilling mentor, the imprisoned psychopathic therapist Dr. Hannibal Lecter (Brian Cox), threatens Graham further. The film balances the interplay between its investigator (who's jeopardized) and its killer, Francis Dolarhyde (who, like *The Sniper*'s protagonist, is humanized through his need for interaction). Dolarhyde's obsession with looking (he develops photography as a job, and note the connection to *Peeping Tom*) leads to his obsession with death.

   The Silence of the Lambs (1991), the Lecter follow-up film to *Manhunter*, develops the investigator-mentor relationship further, to help make it the first horror-themed entry to win the Best Picture Academy Award. Student/F.B.I. investigator, Clarise Starling (Jodie Foster), is unable to think like a criminal, and hence makes full use of Lecter's mentorship (now played by Academy Award–winner Anthony Hopkins). Their relationship becomes a layered game of "quid-pro-quo" (as Lecter describes it), which reveals content about both the case and Clarise. Like the series' first entry, Lecter's assistance leads to the killer, also with a built-in diagnosis (suffering from a psychotic gender identity crisis, he skins victims to build a female suit for himself).

   While *Silence* builds Lecter's character — having escaped by the end of the film, he transforms from mentor to criminal — a film released close to *Silence* (in 1990), but actually made closer to *Manhunter* (in 1986), immerses itself in the killer's experience. *Henry: Portrait of a Serial Killer*, directed by John McNaughton, proves to be one of the most disturbing films ever made. With a lead capable of embodying (and humanizing) a serial killer, Henry (Michael Rooker) becomes a mundane study of the routine that fills the "rest of the time." Though we see some murders, or their disastrous effects, the film's most powerful scene features Henry and partner Otis (Tom Towles) watching a video of their murder of a family. Their replay of the footage, with its chilling screams from the victim, reflects their obsessive fantasizing about their crimes. By realizing he can replay the image, Henry finds a means of duplicating his pre-murder fantasies, the countless ones he had before realizing his obsession. (His story changes when he recounts how he murdered his mother.) Henry shows the serial killer as an unstoppable force — no avenger can reach him, and none shall approach. The threat in this film, based on real-life killer Henry Lee Lucas (who confessed to hundreds of murders, exaggerating the actual number), would inspire an evolved serial killer treatment, namely, the films of David Fincher. Henry is a realistic threat, not a ghastly fabrication or fodder to fuel extreme justice. Far from bait to support "conservative criminal justice policies,"[7] Fincher's serial killers are objects for analysis in cinema that investigates its subject matter instead of exploiting it.

   Though Fincher's first foray into the style was not inspired by real life, his distilled statement on the genre and serial killer culture, *Zodiac*, would be. The narrative of Fincher's first serial killer film, *Se7en* (1995), is contrivance, though introspective of its tradition. The cryptic images of the opening credit sequence suggest the film to be in the exploitation strain, more aligned to charnel house gore films. But Fincher's high profile 1995 film brings the criminal within our understanding. The film constructs its killer's calculating process to present, as in *Dirty Harry*, the obsession of the avenger. John Doe (Kevin Spacey) commits murders to reflect each putative sin, and the final two will lead to the murder of an investigator's wife (also pregnant), and then Doe's own death. By following the seven deadly sins motif, this serial killer has a clear motivation, in opposition to the elusive ciphers of the Zodiac. While the future path of Doe is at first unclear to the investigators, the case, with palpable clues, is all the more pressing to crack. The motive of the film's killer plays like a direct reaction to the motiveless *Henry*, continually on the move and far from the police's reach. From the start, we realize *Se7en*'s killer wants to offer a statement on human sin and execute the unworthy because of it. Additionally, after cracking the killer's code, the investigators know exactly how many deaths face them. Promising a trail of bodies, the motif also incorporates a ticking clock.

Like the lead detectives in many procedural films, the job will be Detective Lt. William Somerset's (Morgan Freeman) last, and his first with cocky newbie, Detective David Mills (Brad Pitt[8]). In a style usual to David Fincher, the detectives work in the most noirish of modern cinematic cities. Though the production design details an unnamed city, the dank, seedy apartments and worn-out police headquarters could situate the events of either Fincher's *Fight Club* (1999) or, at its most nightmarish, the director's *Alien 3* (1992). The exceptions are Freeman's bachelor pad and Pitt's apartment with his wife, even if these are little more than respites in the film's dark universe.

The film's visual style is expressionistic, with the surroundings reflecting the threat of the John Doe killer. As the detectives trace him, Somerset remains logical, representing the objective conscious, while Mills grows more impulsive and hard-edged in his work. The latter describes the clues related to Dante as "goddamn poetry-rhyming" and also acts homophobic, afraid that his partner sitting next to him may suggest a gay relationship. After a scene in which they chase the man who proves to be John Doe, Mills becomes ruthless by entering the killer's room without a warrant. He describes the killer as an irrational madman, while Somerset suggests they take him more seriously. The counterforce (i.e., the killer) turns Mills into a renegade cop while Somerset remains restrained, cultured, like an evolved hunter working aside this new Dirty Harry. The conclusion will make the younger punishable for his approach.

The film acknowledges Mills as a renegade, when he becomes "wrath,"

Detectives William Somerset (Morgan Freeman) and David Mills (Brad Pitt) search for clues in *Seven* (1995, New Line Cinema).

the final deadly sin. His murder of Doe fits him into the seven sins motif, a killing he commits after learning that Doe has killed his wife (serving as Envy, in that Doe envies Pitt's life). *Se7en* suggests that personal romantic relationships have no place in the world of crime: as associated to Mills, his wife ends up a target for the killer. The film also notes that the power of renegade cops of old will no longer suffice: their wrath, at one time powerful, now fuels self destruction. Ending up arrested for his murder of Doe, Mills sacrifices himself and condemns his actions. Somerset, originally ready to retire, remains free and on the job.

During the mid-narrative chase, which occurs after they approach Doe's apartment, Doe has caught Mills, with a gun to his head. And yet he lets him go, later noting that he admired the investigative team, but more likely luring them to the final murder (his own, by Mills). Doe's sparing of Pitt recalls a moment in "The Most Dangerous Game," Richard Connell's adventure story about a hunter who prefers to hunt humans (also adapted into a 1932 film). Early in Connell's story, General Zaroff (the hunter) finds his prey, a ship-wrecked Rainsford, hiding in a tree, but spares him, allowing the chase to continue. In turn, Doe spares Mills to continue the game, and allowing Doe to complete his seven sins murder spree.

As a cultural prototype, Connell's story (and the film adaptation) allegedly inspired a real-life serial killing spree. The referenced moment in *Se7en* points to Fincher's later serial killer film *Zodiac* (2007), this one faithfully based on true events. While also reflexive of the genre, *Zodiac* does not compartmentalize its killer within discrete understanding. In the first letter that the serial killer sends to the *San Francisco Chronicle*, he includes a cipher that, when decoded, speaks of "man as more fun than killing wild game" because "man is the most dangerou[s] an[ima]l of all,"[9] which staff cartoonist (and future *Zodiac* author) Robert Graysmith connects to the Connell story/film. By dismissing the serial killer genre's need to sensationalize, Fincher's *Zodiac* concentrates on historical accuracy and the effects that a massive threat of a minimal power can inflict.

Titling itself thus, the film is obliged to show the killer in action. Never caught, the Zodiac remains one of the most enigmatic (and threatening) in the nation's history. Yet, the filmmakers decided to restrict his depiction to those who saw him in action: the surviving victims. With more focus given to the investigation, one could argue that *Zodiac* is not a serial killer film, but a police procedural, a claim also applicable to *Dirty Harry*. Yet, as both investigations are so influenced by the type of criminal, each film comments on how the police's actions are shaped by the crimes. Fincher focuses on the realism of the killings. Hardly filmed to thrill, the slow-motion shootings reflect the fervor stirred up in the film's populace, as influenced by the press reportage. The Zodiac's double stabbing at Lake Berryessa is especially painful in its realistic, unfiltered depiction (without slow motion). All the murders lack the point-of-view camera trickery in many slasher films, in which objective viewpoints suddenly collide with a killer's point-of-view shot. We never see through the Zodiac's eyes, since the authorities never found him or received his testimony.

The killing footage allows for the requisite attention to the procedural/reportage scenes. If Fincher chose to shoot the former scenes to thrill, the main focus would lag, as it would require equal parts sensationalism. Fincher's approach shows kinship to the "true crime" nonfiction genre, to which Graysmith's book belongs, even if many are potboilers not conceived for readers to ponder. The film's source material, however, is overly concerned with the details of the case — the clues, traces, and when they appear, the suspects. Hence, Graysmith in the film (portrayed as a young overachiever by Jake Gyllenhaal) eventually analyzes the case to the bones. The result is his thorough, engrossing nonfiction book, which can only point to a suspect, Arthur Leigh Allen, indicting him in print in lieu of it happening in court. The film acts similarly, tantalizing serial killer film fans with a highly likely suspect, even if doubt wins out. *Zodiac* plays on our insecurity about justice, which is

Detective David Mills (Brad Pitt) learns too much in *Seven* (1995, New Line Cinema).

obscured by a path of confusion. The tireless work of unofficial investigator Graysmith appears to cover enough grounds to condemn a movie villain many times over. In fact, the detectives — Dave Toschi (Mark Ruffalo), Bill Armstrong (Anthony Edwards), and Jack Mulanax (Elias Koteas) — seeing that handwriting and fingerprint analysis has proven inconclusive, have dismissed the case.

In *Zodiac*, Paul Avery (Robert Downey, Jr.) and Robert Graysmith (Jake Gyllenhaal) search a cypher for clues about the Zodiac Killer (2007, Paramount Pictures).

This film also complicates the criminal-investigator chain. As it has worked off handwriting analysis mainly — only one fingerprint was found, and possibly not the killer's — the investigation was filtered through the media, creating a complicated network in the avenging process. By writing the letters, the Zodiac communicates to the police but also to the populace, likely inspired by Jack the Ripper, the first serial murderer to terrorize through the media. (In the Zodiac-killer-inspired *Dirty Harry*, the Scorpio's letters appear minimally, just enough to connect the film to its inspiration.) In the process, the Zodiac targets journalists and detectives who, in turn, motivate the next murder. By spreading his threat, he achieves the effect of a terrorist and out of the hands of justice.

While *Henry* ignores the avengers, assuming the omnipotence of its criminal, *Zodiac* shows how such a force, by using the intricacies of public communication and policy, can defeat justice.

Don Siegel's 1971 film is more than a cross-reference for Fincher. In *Zodiac*, Graysmith and Toschi first meet at a screening of *Dirty Harry*, to which Toschi comments, "So much for due process." Fincher, naturally, works in opposition to this benchmark serial killer film, one that helped solidify a new, Vietnam-era American avenger. *Zodiac* portrays the actual police of the time, ironic to Eastwood's bemused but effective hero. The last investigator standing in *Zodiac*, Graysmith, doesn't arm himself with a magnum, but with research as a means of publishing the killer's story, hoping that it will aid in

Reporter Paul Avery (Robert Downey, Jr.) hears of new leads from Robert Graysmith (Jake Gyllenhaal) in *Zodiac* (2007, Paramount Pictures).

his capture. When Graysmith oversteps, Toschi says to him, "Easy, Dirty Harry"—this from a detective who, himself, had entered popular culture (as a short-lived character in Armisted Maupin's "Tales of the City" column for the *San Francisco Chronicle*, and even an inspiration to Steve McQueen's character in *Bullitt* (1968), who used Toschi's inverted gun holster). Graysmith's work amounts to the knowledge of the killer and the procedure's best attempts, in lieu of the *Dirty Harry*'s "just" ending. Like a revisionist Western, *Zodiac* brings the myth down to reality. The serial killer of cinematic realism may inspire a rogue's rage, but not his effectiveness.

7

Crime and Suffering
Stuart Gordon's *Edmond* and *Stuck*

While classification is more liberating than limiting, as I argue in this book's introduction, filmmaker Stuart Gordon is restrained by the concept of genre. Due to his reputation as a "horror director," he undeservedly remains a minor name in film circles. Gordon entered filmmaking by reaching to the horror genre's roots to maximize its potential and has recently brought such ingenuity to the crime film. Working against the slasher film motif prevalent in the early– to mid–1980s, he returned to the classical mythos of Frankenstein with Grand Guignol treatment of horror and comedy.[1] He entered the horror field as a workman, as a stage director having scoped out the territory as one ripe for success — as did George A. Romero, who fashioned *Night of the Living Dead*, a tale of dread geared to the late '60s, and even Hitchcock in 1960's *Psycho*, with its clever narrative tropes and tricks (leading lady killed off; point of view switched from traditional hero to offbeat killer). Both of these film-makers helped launch the New Hollywood movement through an unlikely genre. The predecessors to the horrors of Hitchcock and Romero were buried in low-rent grindhouses, far from the critical eye.

In Gordon's case, he created a cornerstone of what's now described as the 1980s horror-comedy sub-genre.[2] By this time, the slasher-bogeyman was the haunt, and while the human monsters offered some psychological depth to a genre usually reserved to the supernatural, many of the slasher films created a cutout for a motiveless madman. (See the countless *Friday the 13th* sequels.) The psychotics in Wes Craven's *Last House on the Left* (1972), on the other hand, make for a nifty if perverse entry, as it borrows equally from the drive-in sleaze and Bergman's *The Virgin Spring*. (A young Craven seemed versed in both arthouse and stoned-out trash cinema.) What the film lacks in substance it makes up for in economy (in, that is, delivering shocking moments of horrific realism). With *Last House* having appeared before the slasher boom, the psycho-killers to follow required little wit to fill out the kill-em-all-to-the-final-showdown structure. Soon enough, an everyday-bogeyman like Jason Voorhees could kill without motive and rise whenever he would feel like it.

Before Gordon, New York filmmakers Frank Henenlotter (*Basket Case*, 1982) and Abel Ferrara (*Driller Killer*, 1979) used wit in their exploitation horrors. By taking cue from directors like Herschell Gordon Lewis, whose 1960s brand of horror captured an ironic sensibility, Henenlotter and Ferrara knew that horror fans were always ready for a laugh. (Though, in the latter's case, we wonder if much of the humor is accidental.) Henenlotter's film *Basket Case* worked from a semi-supernatural premise, goofy enough for *Cracked* magazine yet akin to EC Comics. His Siamese-twin characters are separated in the film's backstory, one brother a small pile of flesh originally attached to the side of his full-sized brother. Hence, the little monster fits into the titular basket carried by his brother, for the film's extended pun and the odd(er) half to continue a murderous spree. Looney as the premise is, Henenlotter's film remains suspenseful amid the shocks and laughs. Ferrara, on the other hand, delivered a "hip" New York malcontent who slowly grows murderous, using the unlikely weapon of the title. The film tries to channel angst, that of an artist living in not-so-quiet desperation, until he grabs the drill for some random revenge against the world.

With Henenlotter and Ferrara emerging from the grindhouse (a milieu of regular mayhem), they were more attuned to the carnivalesque need for a laugh than were their mainstream counterparts. As the 1980s progressed, Stuart Gordon and producer (and future director) Brian Yuzna made a horror film *Re-Animator* (1985) with equal parts comedy. They adapted "Herbert West: Re-Animator," a Frankenstein/mad scientist story by gothic writer H.P. Lovecraft. The order of the day wasn't so much pieced-together humans (à la Mary Shelley and James Whale), but reanimated corpses: essentially a zombie film with their creator on the loose in a campus town. The obsession of Herbert West (Jeffrey Combs) makes him a dangerous human monster: the mad scientist who shall replicate many threatening beings. West delivers some curious actions and trademark lines that stand as some of the funniest of the 1980s. Even more rewarding are the film's clever, humorous horror tropes — a zombie throwing its own head, a headless one who leads an army rising at his perverse call, and — of course — the famous floating head scene, which capitalizes on a sexual pun. If these moments sound like parts of an average late-night shocker, the shocks of horror and humor make the film a fine hybrid.

The film thrilled critics Roger Ebert and Pauline Kael,[3] and its reputation grew strong and remains so, regardless of its less-satisfying sequels. Over the years, Gordon returned to Lovecraft (*Castle Freak*, 1995; *Dagon*, 2001) and adapted Poe (*The Pit and the Pendulum*, 1991; *The Masters of Horror* entry *The Black Cat*, 2007) while trying, with less success, to juice up science fiction (*Robot Jox*, 1990; *Fortress*, 1992). It was hard to be the father of *Re-Animator* and continue to please horror fans ready for a laugh. Coming off a genre built on dire scenarios for victims, Gordon in his newer work uses suffering to fashion a new, visceral form of the victim film. His victims become the prisoners of their own crimes, unlike the classical American tradition in which a victim must combat a powerful, external force. As in the filmic universes of Stanley Kubrick, the obstacles before Gordon's protagonists seem insurmountable. Hence, Gordon uses the victim motif to study suffering. His earlier films deployed torment to play with our expectations for shocks and jests. His later films use a similar approach to detail the psychology of suffering.

Gordon's first endeavor in crime turned to an odd novel, *The King of the Ants* (1992) by Charlie Higson. In Gordon's film adaptation (2003), Sean Crowley (Chris McKenna), a house painter, becomes an unlikely prisoner and victim of torture after killing for hire. The Hitchcockian twist likely intrigued Gordon, and his next entry, an adaptation of David Mamet's stage play, *Edmond*,[4] further explored the psychology of suffering. In retrospect, the play would have been an ideal debut film for Gordon, had he not banked on the reliability of the horror market. Having already directed the premiere of Mamet's play *Sexual Perversity in Chicago*, Gordon had also attracted the interest of actor William H. Macy (also a Mamet veteran) for the film of *Edmond* (2005), best know for his disturbing role as a spineless criminal in the Coen brothers' *Fargo* (see Chapter 16). The actor never shies away from victim roles, falling to either a greater force outside themselves, or their own faults. As the title character of *Edmond*, Macy falls to the latter influence which has the power of the former.

Mamet's stageplay transitions from the discontent of domesticity into the chaos of urban nightlife. The screenplay (also by Mamet) begins with Edmond ready to abandon his marriage and white-collar lifestyle and ends with his childish contentment as a prisoner, both literally (incarcerated) and sexually (as a boytoy for his cellmate). The plot progresses as Edmond resists his complicated, mature world. His resistance turns to violence, murder, and then incarceration, the state that will realize a contentment he's long desired. The narrative develops as a nihilistic tragedy, right up to the final crime — this one against Edmond. The crime motifs serve a broader, ironic narrative, which structurally and tonally recalls Dante's *Inferno* yet is steeped in classical tragedy. Ironically, the film wraps in the classical comic tradition, though Edmond's contentment is certainly subjective. In one of Gordon's blackest jokes ever, Edmond finds an ironic "marriage" in a prison cell.

This downward journey begins as a mock adventure, with the eponymous everyman breaking from the threshold of normalcy. His ironic call to adventure comes from a fortune teller, who, after revealing grim Tarot cards, tells him, "You are not where you belong." Edmond reads this as a sign to leave his wife and, likely, his white-collar job. He acts on the impulse when returning home in the next scene, to flatly inform his wife, "I'm leaving," and that he's not coming back; for his wife doesn't interest him "sexually or spiritually." His cold logic masks his lack of an emotional and physical connection to anyone.

This simplified world of prison provides routine, through regular meals, visitation, lights out, and even a sexual companion. The tone of the story — in both the language of Mamet's script and the dark urban realism of Gordon's film direction — suggests that Edmond's unease leads to his imprisonment (his content). His flight from middle-class discontent, into a mock adventure tale, brings seamy opportunities. Edmond ventures into the nighttime city streets looking for sex. He's willing to pay for it, but ends up becoming a loser even in the cathouse. He wants square deals from the prostitutes and gamblers/pimps. Yet, he feels as if everyone takes unfair advantage: to him, the prostitutes/sex workers overcharge, but Edmond is just ignorant of the suspect pimps and the card sharps living not far from his highrise.[5] Both types of street dwellers become tricksters on this journey, deceiving Edmond to instigate him. Two card sharps in one scene mug him when he spots their scam and foolishly calls them on it. After they beat him, Edmond pawns his ring to get a survival knife, with built-in brass knuckles, an emblem of domination and murder. In the film's mock-adventure motif, this weapon serves as a city-dweller's Excalibur — to Edmond, a means for salvation. The power the knife grants Edmond also seals his fate.

Now armed with a blade, Edmond defeats a pimp who has falsely led him to an alley, promising a hooker. The action he takes against this pimp (who becomes something like a gatekeeper) leads to a new, pseudo-philosophical confidence in Edmond. In a restaurant, he delivers frenzied chatter to a waitress, the kind of talk common in Mamet's sales-/con-men. (It is prominent in his 1975 stageplay, *American Buffalo*, and in 1984's *Glengarry Glen Ross* becomes the means of tragicomedy [see Chapter 14]). We hear it during Edmond's first stop out on the town: a slick bargoer waxes philosophical about the ability for sex and violence to assert us, in a talk steeped in bigotry and racism. Interestingly enough, this role is played by Mamet veteran Joe Mantegna, who won a Tony award as the persuasive/deceptive Ricky Roma in the United States' premiere of *Glengarry Glen Ross*.

Edmond adopts this kind of speech after defeating the pimp and straightforwardly picking up a waitress. She brings him home, after he declares his

The title character (William H. Macy) near the beginning of his descent in *Edmond* (2005, First Independent Pictures).

new happiness and a desire to bed her. In his post-coital fervor at the girl's apartment, he spouts his racism — "In the moment, thirty years of prejudice came out of me," he claims he felt during his attack on the pimp — when the woman shares her own bigotry against homosexuals. (It appears that Mamet was writing long before the discovery of the omnipotent urban gay gal-pal.)

Edmond then urges her to drop her pretensions about being an actress, since she has yet to perform a full play; like Holden Caulfield, he feels himself to be on a quest against phoniness, though to greater measures. When performed on the stage, Mamet's dialog and the cumulating murder may have been a little black joke on actors by the playwright for theater buffs — like meta-play ironic moments in the text of *Hamlet*. In the greater narrative, Edmond's newfound sense of control fuels his antisocial and domineering nature. Just having asserted himself through violence (against the pimp) and having met his need for sex, Edmond now wants the same control over the young waitress/actress. His domineering approach fuels her resistance, to which Edmond responds with rage, wielding his knife. In directing this scene, Gordon — who's always ready to shock — didn't want to soften the darkest moment: blood casts upon Edmond as the waitress (offscreen) gurgles in a violent death. Like a child, he passes blame to the girl: "Now look what you've done. Look what you've blood fucking done" (the final two adjectives showing the writer's Pinteresque mastery of curt phrasing). Whether he wants to pass the blame or not, Edmond knows his new self-reliance — based in violence (i.e., "blood") and "fucking" — has come to an end.

At this moment the narrative drops its mock adventure to align itself to the crime film. With his previous crime undetected, Edmond has committed the violence that will transform him. He is now a noir villain who, in his warped mindset, fashions himself as some kind of avenger.

After the killing, he continues his perverted sense of vengeance. He verbally assaults a woman on the subway: when she resists his small talk, he acts crazed and threatens actual violence.[6] At first, he stresses that he just wants conversation. Yet, before Edmond threatens to "slash her face," the woman thinks him a rapist: considering the context of their meeting, we cannot blame her. Edmond has no ability to communicate with the city dwellers, a white-collar executive far out of his element. Yet, the disconnection stems from his lacking of discrete closure: interaction without the ambiguities and different perspectives common to adult conversation. Edmond has regressed to a pre-adult state that has not mastered such maturity. Hence, he's best suited for a structured, limited environment: the prison awaiting him.

The woman on the subway points him out to the police. When he's called in for questioning, the investigator suddenly has him tapped for the murder of the waitress. Since Mamet and Gordon restrict the narrative to Edmond's perspective, the lack of investigation and evidence appearing onscreen seems sensible. By abandoning the narrative clarity common in a procedural, the filmmakers instead show fate running the film's course. When the investigator asks, "Why did you kill that girl?" Edmond briefly asks, "What girl?" The response of the interrogator (chillingly played by Dylan

Walsh) is the most fatalistic line in the film: "That girl you killed." The reply has calm insistence in lieu of interrogation-room urgency. Mamet and Gordon care little for such heated moments in the police-thriller formula. Like many characters in this journey, the interrogator is symbolic: he is a moral voice, a *deus ex machina* having descended to deliver Edmond, a false avenger/criminal, to his rightful judgment. What will come is the final counteraction to Edmond's futile rebellion. The investigator is another gatekeeper, bringing Edmond to the home he always desired. There, one more gatekeeper awaits the antihero.

The final gatekeeper is Edmond's cellmate (Bokeem Woodbine), a black man who's racially aligned to the source of the former's "thirty years of prejudice," but also his means of reaching salvation. It's as if imprisoning Edmond isn't enough: he must submit to the ultimate violation of his machismo masculinity. After Edmond is raped by his large cellmate, he turns hardened, bald and mustachioed, turning away visitors to the facility. His appearance shells the contentment he has found in his submissive, simplified life. He trades light-philosophical talk with his cellmate, then lies next to him after a goodnight kiss. Edmond finds peace through an ironic marriage and regimented world. *Edmond's* resolution ends his crimes by restricting him to the bleak house he sees as bliss.

Edmond leaves the safety of the highrise — the location of his work and his home — to find the city streets far below, a realm in which, as we have seen, he has little chance of surviving. With *Edmond*, Gordon borrows from nihilistic stage drama. As written by Mamet, the play's language and bleak situations allow viewers (and readers) to envision a subjective urban hell. Gordon succeeds in visualizing this without veering toward nightmarish clichés. Edmond's journey appears as random moments, with the greater "adventure" landscape obscured by a dense city. Like its source play, the film is fragmented, comprised of brief stops on a pseudo–Dantean journey. The futility and minimalism connects *Edmond* to the absurdist theater tradition, from which Mamet borrows often (from the origins, Samuel Beckett, but more so through Mamet's primary influence, Harold Pinter). Gordon's follow-up to *Edmond*, *Stuck* (2007), borrows from the headlines by adapting a bizarre Texas event in which a female driver hit a pedestrian and then drove him back to her garage, still impaled on her windshield.[7] The premise recalls Stephen King's *Misery*, in which a psychopathic female fan of a writer detains him at her home, though in lieu of a stalker-ish obsession, *Stuck* features (seriously) misguided desperation. Gordon uses the widespread media fodder to create a tale of isolated torment that is, like *Edmond*, minimalistic and absurdist.

From the outset, *Edmond* continues through a night-long trek down the wrong path, looking for something more. And Brandi (Mena Suvari, who appears briefly as a prostitute in *Edmond*), the accidental criminal in *Stuck*, wants as much — a new opportunity. Edmond enters the city streets, desiring what's out there; Brandi gets caught in an ordeal while trying to return home. Edmond feels his only hope is beyond his home and profession, while Brandi looks within her economic homebase for an answer, i.e., a possible promotion. She works as a medical assistant, a role traditionally requiring minimal training, and usually undertaken by women of lower socioeconomic status. Both Gordon protagonists are "stuck" and feeling lost when looking at their surroundings.[8]

Brandi's existence, however, is much more trying. Dealing with not-unusual irritations on the job (needy patients, a pesky boss), she receives some of Gordon's grue when she has to clean a bed sheet covered in excrement. Such work is familiar to medical assistants but unacknowledged by the citizens within and without the institution who rely on it. Gordon sticks to his credo — shock when necessary — while presenting an everyday victim (with some hope for a promotion) becoming a criminal. While Edmond's victimization is more internal and subjective, Brandi's exists indefinitely lest she move upward. Though he may feel as trapped as her, her crisis stems from social pressures, the discontent of the working class. Essentially, she is one from whom Edmond would feel isolated.

Going out after work is her release, as is her choice to "drop acid" there. During her ride home her ordeal begins, as the accident will leave her job and promotion threatened. The film intercuts Brandi's day (on the job) with that of Thomas (Stephen Rea), who has been fired and is getting evicted from his apartment. Sent to an unemployment office, he realizes that the office's computer system has lost his file. Hence, as a victim to bureaucracy, Thomas finds circumstances more dire than Brandi's. The two victims depart from their issues — Brandi, under the influence and away from that of her professional life, and Thomas, as a homeless streetwalker. Thus, Gordon has them collide in the accident.

Stuck plays as a character drama of the downtrodden, until Brandi hits Thomas, the victim coming face to face with the offender. Yet, Gordon presents both as victims, albeit Brandi less sympathetic than the other. Brandi drives off in a panic, her inexperience with crisis getting the best of her. When she leaves Thomas in the windshield, his flesh still caught in the broken glass, Gordon has a potential human monster on his hands. Though her indifference to him is despicable, Gordon directs the film sympathetically to Brandi. Her confusion of action comes down to youthful ignorance, something that many parents or family members tolerate in less severe situations. Brandi is at the center of this swelling instance of amorality, in a panicked situation reaching the darkest realms of offense against one individual.

As dire as it may be, the film delights as Gordon fashions a showdown

Brandi Boski (Mena Suvari) faces her victim, Thomas Bardo (Stephen Rea), in *Stuck* (2007, Image Entertainment).

between the confused woman and the injured man. He absurdly tries to free himself in minor (and painful) progressions that eventually become strides. It amounts to a battle of the wills, and we know early who will stay stronger. More importantly, like *Edmond*, the film moves beneath moral judgment to depict the humanity of those caught in tough spots, though karma shows by the conclusions. Much of the criticism, we must note, is against the systems that hold both down. Gordon proves that no line exists to separate the evil and the victimized.

8

In a "World of Shit"
Crime Motifs in Richard Linklater's *Fast Food Nation*

Recent films, detailing another kind of evil, have been swarming around Eric Schlosser's investigative text, *Fast Food Nation: The Dark Side of the All-American Meal* (2001). Beginning life as a series of articles for *Rolling Stone* in 1998, this book of investigative journalism confirmed many fears — vague, but persistent — that Americans have had for years. McDonald's French fries, for example, sported such a "beefy" taste that it was no surprise to learn that, according to Schlosser, until 1990 they were fried in 93 percent beef tallow.[1] Stories of young workers spitting on food are universal, and through interviews Schlosser confirmed it as true in many locations. In this regard, the book is equally eye-opening and devastating. It also reaches our latent fears which are, of course, the objective of the most effective crime and horror films.

And yet the films inspired by this text are far from what many would describe to be "genre" movies. Schlosser initially helped create a new movement in the documentary genre: the food science film, or should we say, the food science "terror" film. I won't use the more familiar word "scare" in this title, as it reflects a mid-century budget tradition that, for the most part, seeded as many fears as it worked off, and served up paranoia. Before we look at these new documentaries, the tradition of scare films is worth discussing, since opponents to the former style like to present them as the latter (i.e., Kyle Smith, the cantankerous right-wing film critic of the *New York Post*, called the new food documentary movement the "Your Hamburger Will Kill You" genre.[2])

With the familiar example of *Reefer Madness* (which, upon its original release in 1936, had the title *The Burning Question*, then the more educational-friendly *Tell Your Children*), the "school scare film" now falls under the cult film category, as the entries are oddities borne under an age of paranoia.[3] The best-known "school scare films" worked by presenting a threat to children as a straw man, with moral order as a vague hero. With the right framing, food science exposés may seem to promote a bogeyman type of threat, especially when aligned to forms of paranoia.

Yet, the food science film works in line with the tradition that Schlosser established: sound, well-supported journalism. And while the "school scare film" often posed solutions to their threats (scare the kids, but *kill the commies!*), food science documentaries end with a call for activism, as do the works of Michael Moore. The problems, it seems, are too massive for simple solutions. As we will see later in this chapter, this is suitable territory for the modern crime film. When this nonfiction style was synthesized into narrative in the film *Fast Food Nation* (released in 2006; hereafter *FFN*), a strong tradition in the documentary film had arrived.

Super Size Me (2004), the first widely viewed film inspired by Schlosser, is as outrageous as it is effective. Filmmaker/film subject Morgan Spurlock aims to prove, on camera, the detriments of the fast food industry by eating only McDonald's food for a month and, as part of his eponymous gimmick, "supersizing" his meal whenever an employee "up-sells" it to him.[4] His approach makes the project equal parts exposé and stunt film: his visits to the doctor show that his body can barely stand the maltreatment of a fast-food-only diet. Thus, Spurlock positions his film as a polar to Schlosser's argument — steer clear of the poison — though on the same side of the issue. The former briefly jumps the fence by interviewing subjects and addressing issues of the fast food industry, as does Schlosser, though Spurlock remains on the receiving end of the industry, not as a removed journalist investigating it. His film turns into an enjoyable blend of intellectual and mainstream entertainment. As entertaining as *Super Size Me* is, the narrative plays more on our fear factor than as an investigation of the subject matter. He proves his point about the unhealthy side effects of fast food early in his film. *Super Size Me* then plays like a reality-TV–style game show, a visceral race to finish a gruesome stunt. It condemns the target but overheats the proceedings. (Ironically, some of the project's best elements appear as extras on the 2007 DVD release: an interview by Spurlock with Schlosser that offers a nice summary of *FFN*, the book and some helpful updates, and a see-it-to-believe-it acid test of how fast food breaks down and gathers mold — or *fails* to. The latter, which shows different fast food meals under bell jars filmed over months, has become a viral video.)

The 2007 documentary *King Corn* investigates the unlikely base product behind fast food, and food processing in general. Similar to Spurlock's approach, two of the filmmakers participate in an on-camera experiment, while not risking their health. Ian Cheney and Curtis Ellis, two recent Ivy-league college graduates, experience the American corn industry by moving to Iowa and becoming small-time farmers. They learn of the technology that comes with corn farming — how it relies on ammonia fertilizer, how most of the product is grown into inedible raw materials, how the product's often processed into corn syrup (a process they try to replicate onscreen, in an amateur chemistry experiment, since plants processing the product won't allow them in), and how corn fattens cattle while their bodies aren't used to it, resulting in massive waste and a three-month life span if they stay on the diet. One of the filmmakers body-surfs on a mountain of corn, and they play "pepper" softball games with all the leisure time modern farming gives them. Meanwhile, the processing of their harvest reveals how corn is managed for high production and low quality. They provide visual examples that the book *FFN* briefly reports. Michael Pollan, a food-science writer of Schlosser's importance with more texts to his credit, appears as a talking head, filling in more disturbing truths.

Food, Inc., directed by Robert Kenner and first released in 2008 (two years after the film adaptation of *FFN*), is the most comprehensive of the documentary exposés, powerful if somewhat repetitive. While *Supersize Me* and *King Corn* feature outsiders looking in, *Food, Inc.* is the more traditional documentary in style. It gathers information on various aspects of the food industry, showing all the areas affected by mass production. The omniscient point of view brings viewers to mass-producing chicken farms, which abandon coops for containment drawers, along with different types of food engineering. Along with featuring Schlosser and Pollan, the film shows a ray a hope on the inside by featuring noble traditional farmer Joe Saladin, who stays aware of the over-institutionalized food system as he farms and slaughters by hand. Like hard journalism, *Food, Inc.* is committed to reporting facts and showing the evidence. In many ways, it's the capstone to the entries before it. While the talking heads' personalities are prominent, the viewer becomes the central party. Kenner wants us to consider how we will implement the information. Will things change when price will always trump consideration to our well-being? Objective as it is, the film is made to terrify, with a back-door attack on capitalism. Instead of the effect building to a climax, the film continues to provide examples and shock our sensibilities.

The devastating information traps us in fear, and thus we cannot avoid associations to the horror film.[5] Both enlightening and horrifying, the film veers toward the latter, if we take H.P. Lovecraft's assessment of fear being the strongest emotion.[6] The nonfiction assessments in *Food, Inc.* terrify because they relate to a culture affected en masse. While the perspectives of *Supersize Me* and *King Corn* personalize the films via the respective filmmaker experience (even if the effects are intended as universal), *Food, Inc.*'s objective point of view best reflects the massive effects. To feature individuals in this large framework would take another type of film, focusing on multiple-personalized points of view. Filmmaker Richard Linklater saw it as an occasion for a narrative (i.e., fictional) film.

The food science documentary will put off many, though resilient viewers come away enlightened. Each film leaves us with a moral question: Has the open market allowed for perversions of science, namely food science? And should we consider such actions *crimes*? Filmmaker Richard Linklater, whose early works *Slacker* (1991) and *Dazed and Confused* (1993) are documentary-style fictions, opted to adapt *FFN* as a fictionalized narrative, at Schlosser's suggestion (with the latter becoming Linklater's co-screenwriter). Schlosser was hesitant to make the obvious film adaptation of *FFN*, a documentary film. He was afraid the talking heads and other documentary techniques would water down the material.[7] While *Food, Inc.* (and even the book of *FFN*) works with terror and intrigue, a narrative film would relate the material to individual characters — the lives of those affected — and benefit from suspense, pathos, catharsis. The unfortunate truths can terrify, but they can also be read as crimes. Hence, Linklater and Schlosser fashioned much of *FFN* as a criminal investigation piece, an aspect that critics have largely ignored.[8] A quasi-mystery appears before Don Anderson (Greg Kinnear), an executive charged by the fast food corporation employing him, to look into his company's meat contamination while promoting their new sandwich, an item conceived and delivered like any other corporate product. The worlds that he investigates — i.e., the lives of those affected by the industry — show the wide effects of fast food. By structuring the narrative as a crime investigation featuring the victims, Linklater and Schlosser position the industry as one of the most powerful and unlikely criminal bodies of recent American cinema. Operating in the wide open but hiding its machinations, the situation falls in the darkest territories of the genre.

While Linklater and Schlosser agreed to "set aside" the book's tone and structure when adapting the issues into a narrative, they ironically gain "documentary"-like veracity by filming almost completely on location (even in a slaughterhouse, as we'll see later). As a rule, Linklater always begins his screenwriting with character, not plot,[9] and hence narrative style is essential to a journalism-based project like this. Since many devotees of the book have read the film as a misrepresentation,[10] a discussion of the film's techniques, or its structure as a genre work, may be taken as further defamation to a celebrated text. As a narrative with dynamic characters, the film of *FFN* creates a combative tone without relying on the conventional fish-out-of-water journalism techniques in *Supersize Me* and *King Corn*. Additionally, *FFN* rejects satire and ignores distorted or comic depictions that can come in tandem. While recalling Robert Altman and his descendent, P.T. Anderson, the ensemble narrative uses crime film motifs — with Don as an unlikely criminal investigator, the immigrants as victims, and teenaged victims turning avengers. With such character relationships, we cannot ignore the film's associations to the genre, even if dressed as a dramatized food science investigation. *FFN*'s crime/investigation techniques, which tie the content to humanity by revealing it in jeopardy, elevate the film over the documentary form.

The prominence of crime techniques or food science does not crowd out room for other genre motifs. *FFN* also works as a melodrama-cum-social documentary,[11] since the narrative develops actions and events more than character. Like many responses to the food science documentaries, critic Kristin Jones saw *FFN* channeling the dread of a horror film,[12] thus suggesting that the shocks trump the intrigue. While pointing to a general approach of melodrama, Gregory Stephens cuts to a deeper truth by revealing the film's cultural theme (with a term of incisive irony): the "poetics of shit."[13] The fast food industry treats its employees like shit, while we all end up eating it. Stephens's reading hews close to associations with the crime film. While effectively addressing the theme in relation to genre, he doesn't investigate genre in relation to the film's structure.

When constructing the narrative, Linklater invoked the ensemble tradition, citing Sherwood Anderson's *Winesburg, Ohio* — not far from Altman or P.T. Anderson — as an inspiration.[14] This approach accounts for the various persons committing, and being affected by, crimes. One narrative strand features Don, an insider, and in a sense a part of the film's criminal network. By investigating his own organization, he is a criminal uncomfortably turning avenger. Even if he exits the film early, he becomes a less-sympathetic victim while discovering the truth behind his privileged job. His character is more dynamic than his screen time would suggest. The next narrative strand features Mexicans illegally immigrating to work at a slaughterhouse. This strand begins as an immigration narrative, a large tradition that mimics origins of 20th-century American culture; in *FFN*, this quest for a better life turns horrifying and tragic. Their illegal transport, aided by parties in cahoots with meat packing management, correlates to the mainstreamed production of fast food and its machine-like delivery to customers. The hidden delivery also aligns to mass farming of cows, crammed together in a pen (an image that disturbs Don early in his investigation). While oppressed by American industry, the immigrants become victims of more overt crimes: rape, drug use encouraged by the management, and corporate blackmail of employees injured on the job. The last strand features teenaged employees of a fast food restaurant near the meat plant, in the fictional city of Cody, Colorado. This narrative represents the "other half" of the fast food workforce, on the customer-service end.

Finding themselves in an industry greatly relying on young, untrained workers, the teen employees move towards rebellion. They plan an unrealized robbery and engage in unlawful political activism: releasing penned-up cattle.

As an introduction to all three strands, the film opens with a bright, near-surreal scene in a hardly disguised fast food chain location called Mickey's. The bright, glossy production design and slow-motion cinematography present the milieu as a false reality that masks its machinations. The cheap, good-tasting but "shitty" end-product fosters a Soma-like happiness: alive throughout the joint's "dining room," it extends to the large road signs and billboards. The camera approaches a burger patty looking tasty from afar, but in close-up becoming a greasy, sickly landscape. (This bright scene cuts to the darkness of a rural Mexican street, which introduces the second narrative strand.)

To begin the first strand, the film presents a corporate committee discussing advertising for Mickey's. With higher-ups assembled around a boardroom table, the scene represents any number of corporate situations in American film. The board, a number of fortysomethings headed by a sixtysomething, discuss slogans, joking with double-entendres for their new sandwich, "The Big One." While their discussions are hardly criminal, their crimes are discussed under wraps. After the meeting, the boss informs Don about meat contamination revealed through research by graduate students, the academy positioned as an opposition to big industry. The boss first explains the contamination in scientific terms, then delivers the most popular line from Schlosser's text, to clarify the food science bureaucratese to Don: "There's shit in the meat." In retrospect, when considering the board's hidden agenda, it reflects a gangster meeting, their company a revised nationwide syndicate, which first extended its reach throughout America in the early 20th century.

This charge deploys Don from California to Cody, to begin his investigation. This town of big box stores lining the highways is the home to a branch of UMP (United Meat Packers), a large firm processing high amounts of meat at a fast pace. The city is also home to Mexican immigrants, the plant's main workforce, and teenagers who run the restaurants. Don's series of interviews reflects the variety of persons tied to the industry, a workforce panorama. Brought together in the narrative, these groups represent a new take on the "ship of fools" tradition, in which a diverse group must unify under crisis. Likewise, they reflect the varied characters encountered in Raymond Chandler's Philip Marlowe novels, the odd trail of witnesses leading to the detective's goal. Chandler and those following his tradition used these encounters to color the city's underbelly, the criminals and victims operating therein. Linklater and Schlosser employ the style to reveal the varied universe under fast food's influence.

Don visits the meat plant for an "official tour." He sees a clean, efficient system that shoots raw burgers through the freezing process and packaging, while the darker side of the system — the "kill floor" — is hidden away. The "kill floor" is where actual crimes occur: dangerous practices of mass slaughter and workplace injuries. At this moment, Don comes closest to the Mexican victims, though they are "behind the wall." While investigating the issue of meat contamination, Don doesn't reach the other equally serious issue. The sterile assembly system pleases him enough to settle doubts. This short scene, and his comments on what he sees in the one following, reflect the industry's powerful use of façade. This pleasing exterior, which Linklater depicts with documentary-like clarity, coincides with the mainstreamed process of food service in the restaurants: teenagers reciting scripts and following simplified food preparation. The excessive order assures profit, but hides the crimes of the system.

Don visits the local Mickey's restaurant and speaks with the manager, Tony (Esai Morales). When Don asks him about the conditions of the local plant, Tony says he's heard of some "nasty things" going on there, at once implying much but suggesting it could be hearsay. As a gatekeeper, the party who will direct the investigator to his next stop, Tony remains guarded. He has just told Don about his location's success selling the new sandwich, The Big One, acknowledging the power of head office marketing in fast food. Tony wants to keep the conversation near camaraderie by acknowledging the upper management's suspicions (issues at the meat plant) and not urging more problems. To keep minimal involvement, Tony tells Don about a mutual acquaintance who knows more about the meat plant, handing him a phone number to conclude the meeting.

This lead sends Don to a local rancher, Rudy (Kris Kristofferson), who's seeing his way of life being stripped away. With developments now abutting his property and dead bodies showing up on his land (more direct "gang" activity), Rudy is a disenfranchised frontiersman who's lost his lifeways. While the classical rancher-victims of the big screen had a chance to save their land, Rudy has been quietly vanquished and made powerless against the villainous meatpackers whom he describes as criminals. He also describes meatpacking and the fast food industry as part of a machine destroying small business. Played by Kristofferson (see Sam Peckinpah's *Pat Garrett and Billy the Kid*, 1973), Rudy invokes the rugged battler now weakened by forces far greater than those of the old-time "land war" in the Western film tradition (for an example, see George Stevens's *Shane*, 1953). To bring Don closer to evidence, Rudy introduces him to his housekeeper, whose brother works for UMP. She talks of the meat producing system — essentially an assembly line that dismembers carcasses — which moves too fast, causing the intestinal waste to spill into the meat. The dissembling is done by untrained immigrants using knives. With the real proof "behind the wall," Don has to settle for anecdotal evidence. All he will reach is a cover-up.

His last interview is with Harry Rydell (Bruce Willis), a beef supplier for Mickey's. A hardened man chomping on a burger, he is a Westerner happy for profits and proud of his blissful ignorance — the counterpoint to Rudy. When questioned by Don, Harry says that people need to be tough when faced with issues, implying that determination can overcome fear. While casually delivering a series of arguments, Harry says that Mexican laborers should be thankful for their opportunities in America, which are better than what their homeland offers. Essentially, a capitalist system works as long as each level is staffed. When pressed by Don, Harry tells him to just "cook the meat": the restaurant's system is calibrated to kill dangerous ingredients. He addresses the crime by showing how it can be covered up. His perspective, a shaky moral relativism, suggests that infractions are legitimate if they serve and please many. A crime boss initially deploys Don on his journey, but Harry becomes the more sinister gang boss, who acknowledges the dangers but is committed to his own benefit. He personifies profit over quality, happiness at the cost of hidden crimes.

With this defeat, Don "disappears" from the film, before casually recommending further testing and shifting responsibility to others. He won't appear again until the film's coda during the final credits, promoting the new BBQ Big One with a regretful look; the machine has reclaimed him as a cog. Linklater has said that the film pushes responsibility back on the audience,[15] making *FFN* a call to activism. Yet, as a revised investigator, Don has been defeated by the criminal network and its vast power. Though motivated to move from criminal status during his search, the culmination returns him to that status. To Linklater, Don is "no Erin Brockovich,"[16] the hero of a conventional, contemporary avenger's tale. Naturally, there's no solution to the crime Don discovers. It's the work of an industry as beloved as it is powerful. After Don's exit, the film focuses on the immigrant victims (the next narrative strand, discussed below), and the teenaged employees' unsuccessful, counteractive crimes against the industry (the final narrative strand discussed in this chapter): plans of a cash-register heist that never develop, and a socially conscious act of anarchy (releasing of cattle), the results of which are left ambiguous (possibly failing).

The second strand, concerning the Mexican meat factory workers, begins with irony. A group crosses the border for work, though their aim for something better immediately turns for the worse. Their walk through the nighttime desert is interrupted by a speeding vehicle — whether Border Patrol or kidnappers,[17] the immigrants are fugitives. The theme continues when they are picked up by a cargo van driver, Benny (Luis Guzmán), an opportunist from the East. He flashes his gun and threatens his human "cargo," thus verbalizing their captive status. Sylvia, one of the immigrants, is played by Catalina Sandino Moreno, who starred as the eponymous Colombian "drug mule" in *Maria Full of Grace* (2004). This casting choice in *FFN* connects the character to another captive forced into a criminal enterprise.

At first restricted to the van, the immigrants are then locked down in a hotel room, where they are passed off to meat facility manager Mike (Bobby Cannavale). He also uses intimidation to keep his illegal workforce in check. After assigning them jobs, he doubles in the roles of gangster and pimp: he marginalizes his female captives by demanding sexual favors. The effects of his sexual abuse spread to the women workers who aren't directly victim to it, through intimidation: they know that Mike sleeps with all the pretty girls, then gives them drugs. The voice of an older worker — when telling Coco (a friend of Sylvia, played by Ana Claudia Talancón) about Mike's actions — has an eerie threat about it, as if any girl could be next. Likewise, his "drug dealing" maintains his power, which also spreads to the male workforce. Sylvia's husband, Raul (Vilmer Valderrama), at one point tells her about the widespread drug use that, for some, makes work at the facility manageable. The management uses drugs to dull the workforce and marginalize them to near-slave status.[18] To continue a pimp-like control, Mike tricks the women into thinking there's more to their sexual relationship with him. When Coco, who has become Mike's victim, sees him with another girl, she gets his attention with spontaneous, violent sex, thus feeding into his manipulation. During their encounter he tells her that the other girl has nothing to do with her, hence maintaining his pimp framework.

Later, the meat plant's upper management exploits the presence of drug use in the employees. After Raul's back is injured in a fall — while helping a co-worker after his macabre leg injury — UMP's director of human resources accuses him of using methamphetamines on the job (a drug likely injected in his body when hospitalized). By committing another crime, the company shirks financial culpability for the injury. The abuse to the men, like the women, completes the spectrum of what Stephens calls "the poetics of shit,"[19] which connects the crap that America eats (fast food) to the way the industry treats its workers. Among other meanings, "shit" represents the multiple crimes enacted upon them. With no avengers in sight, their suffering is a testament.

Not that the narrative thread rests on this beat. The injury cover-up precedes a hellish conclusion on the kill floor. With Raul injured and Sylvia locked out of hotel work due to policy, she begs for a job at UMP, which Mike wastes no time to exploit. After demanding (and receiving) sex from Sylvia for the job, he brings her to the kill floor, where she will "pull kidneys."

After the film shows devastating images of animals turning into carcasses, Mike places Sylvia at the end of a conveyor belt where piles of guts spill along. "Look, breathe through your mouth," he tells her with a stiff face after pulling down his mask. When ready to begin the work, she looks down as if in near paralysis, until a tear streams down her cheek. The gruesomeness of this final scene, following the equally gruesome leg injury, could certify *FFN* as a horror film, as it traps us in the dread these people face. Honing back to its source material, and in kind with the documentary tradition of the food science "terror" film, Linklater filmed this scene on a real kill floor (in Mexico, due to restrictions in the U.S.). The film teases us with a moment of contentment, when Sylvia and Raul, pre-injury, eat at a restaurant chain. (The comforts of the American dream abound, even if she wonders whether the chicken in her meal was frozen.) Though the final scene, a macabre flourish, realizes the nadir of the crimes committed upon these victims. They remain in such a state.

The teen restaurant employees, as American citizens, don't know such a hell. But as Schlosser makes clear in his book, they experience another type of exploitation. The film introduces them when Don arrives to the Cody restaurant location. There he's waited on by Amber (Ashley Johnson), a high school student with aspirations who does her job well. She serves with a smile

Sylvia (Catalina Sandino Moreno) prepares herself for the "kill floor" in *Fast Food Nation* (2006, Twentieth Century–Fox Film Corporation).

while following the company's "script." Her friendliness works well with the customers, while the less friendly work the grill and fryer. Brian (Paul Dano) doesn't comply — when overhearing Don describing his job as he orders a burger, Brian spits on one before wrapping it for him. This moment can distance viewers through disgust and, as an early scene in the film, convince them that the film intends to horrify, further supported by the final scenes. Linklater presents it as resistance to exploitation, which Schlosser has confirmed by interviewing teen employees. Similarly, Brian's urge to defy the company results in criminal aims. His plan to rob the restaurant appears throughout his scenes in the film. Though only a desire, Brian's co-worker confirms one at a nearby McDonald's.

Amber, a character more developed than Brian, comes home to a single, overworked mother (Patricia Arquette) who microwaves her breakfast, another form of the processed meal. Though connecting with her mother, Amber's mentor is her uncle Pete (Ethan Hawke). He teases her about her Mickey's uniform, for joining what the rancher Rudy, in another scene, calls "the machine." By discussing his protest of Apartheid in college, he inspires her to protest the industry, what she feels to be "unreal." At a college party she gravitates toward a socially aware group. Back at a dorm room, the group decides in favor of active, over passive, protest against the meat industry. The industry's crime inspires the unlawful act of freeing cattle. Unlike Brian's vague plan, they pull off theirs by sawing part of a cattle gate. The irony, obvious from the start, is that the cattle don't exit, even if Amber urges them to freedom. Even more ironic is this moment juxtaposed to the confined Mexicans, who do not have even a tiny gate toward freedom (though fast food customers certainly do). The immigrants are trapped, incapable of even the American teenagers' aim toward justice.

After all, the investigator has long been defeated, already returning to his criminal network. If he's more enlightened, any evidence of it in his character remains latent, at best. The teenaged avengers remain confused as to whether their active resistance was more effective than other means. The kill-floor climax completes the commentary of injustice. We leave as concerned over the parties as we are angered by the abusive machine. *FFN*, like many recent crime films, shows the criminal bodies as insurmountable. Even the activism that Linklater aimed to inspire in the audience seems a far cry.

9

Noir and True Crime
Andrew Jarecki's *All Good Things*

As up-to-date as Linklater's narrative, the films of Andrew Jarecki have a contemporary sensibility, as they address current issues in an age of need-to-know, mass information. These headline-ready films are also steeped in the noir style. Jarecki is inclined toward full disclosure of disturbing content, which grants viewers exposure that may feel progressive or overwhelming. And yet the films are obsessed with the past, how protagonists look back to the events that have doomed them. As in the noir tradition, a reading of past events, which are puzzling on their own, becomes a narrative to be interpreted.

Jarecki's 2003 documentary, *Capturing the Friedmans*, looks to a notorious child molestation case in Long Island, New York. In 1988, Arnold Friedman, along with his teenaged son Jesse, pled guilty to numerous molestation counts allegedly occurring in the Friedman's basement, the site of Arnold's computer-training program. Jarecki discovered the story while making a documentary, *Just a Clown*, about professional jester David Friedman, another of Arnold's sons. *Capturing* includes numerous home videos, shot by David, that offer a rare, "insider's" point of view as the case (and the family) unravel. Steeped in David's perspective of his troubled family, *Capturing* works as a quasi-victim-cum-criminal-centered piece. The film becomes dynamic and ambiguous in that the truth of the crime is never revealed.

In early 2000s talking-head interviews, David supports his father during the trial and protests against his arrest. The path to truth was blocked by what most would describe as a witch hunt. When a U.S. customs agent discovered child pornography mailed to Arnold's house from overseas, federal agents soon recovered from his home several magazines of that nature, along with a list of students who attended his computer-training school there. The

90

recovery led to an investigation by the Nassau County Police of possible child sexual abuse. As the news spread, parents of Arnold's computer-school students started amassing numerous counts against him. Many accusations were so violent that physical proof must have been observed by the parents, though none was previously reported. One parent who appears onscreen (but whose identity is withheld) believed his son was not abused, and describes getting pressured by other parents to testify. In a milieu of an American victim culture, the film presents a target who's become commonplace: a middle-aged "pervert" who may or may not have gone too far. When Arnold and Jesse pled guilty in 1988, it may have been under pressure and the result of false testimony. Likewise, Jesse's later (and shocking) testimony—that his father's abuse of him when younger brought about the alleged crime spree—appears as a desperate attempt by both men to save one by condemning the other. The events to follow reveals the cold blows of fate. The hope of recent news, that the case may be reopened,[2] comes long after Arnold had committed suicide in prison, in 1995.

Capturing portrays the hypercritical present by *attempting* to read the past, even if the latter leaves any interpretations null. Jarecki's film delivers analysis as sterile confusion. The crime film archetypes take on a full, disturbing presence in light of noir: character is reduced to one's innocent or (putative) guilt, while the evidence exists in a swirl of confusion.

Such a powerful debut project must have shaped its director's sensibility. Hardly an industry outsider, Jarecki broke into feature filmmaking after directing for the stage then co-creating the service Moviefone (which he later sold to AOL). In passing, he wrote music for television (*Felicity*) when he attempted to make his first feature film on clowns, a life-long passion. That idea led him to David (as the initial feature project became a short film), and to the beginning of Jarecki's career and style.

As seen throughout this book, recent filmmakers have turned to journalistic inspiration. The true-crime nonfiction genre has taken a place in thoughtful cinema, far beyond the style's prominence in reality television cop shows. Notably, director David Fincher and screenwriter James Vanderbilt reorient the notorious case of the Zodiac—a serial killer so celebrated he's become deified — by using cinema to depict Robert Graysmith's original true-crime text (see Chapter 6). To rethink the gangster film tradition, Michael Mann (in *Public Enemies*) and Ridley Scott (in *American Gangster*) look to two real-life "bandits" who helped inspire legends of the American crime figures, circa 1930s and 1960s, respectively. Coming post-myth, these films show how the classical gangster grew (*Enemies*) and how the Vietnam-era drug kingpin came to prominence (*Gangster*) (see Chapter 15). Both films show how myth grows and recycles itself, and how truth seeps in to construct a new tradition. The legend has become fact, though both intermingle instead of one replacing the other. Similarly, Tommy Lee Jones, in two films — Paul Haggis's *In the Valley of Elah*, and *The Three Burials of Melquiades Estrada*, directed by Jones — used true cases to investigate the problem of crime and realizing its justice (see Chapter 11).

Before Jarecki's documentary, *Paradise Lost* used the enigma of alleged child murderers, three teenagers now known as the "West Memphis Three." As in the case outlined in *Capturing*, the local community pressured the law to condemn three local misfits (ironically, precursors to the Columbine shooters, in the public eye); guilty or not, their case seems to have been compromised. After Jarecki's film came *The Killer Within*, in which filmmaker Mackie Alston looks into the past of a college psychology professor who, in 1955, shot and killed his sleeping college dorm mate at Swarthmore (he had planned to kill everyone in the dorm, before halting after the first shot and confessing to the police). Found unfit to stand trial, Bob Bechtel was institutionalized and freed four years and eight months later, when he was found not guilty by reason of insanity. Again, we have the accused presented as a victim: the professor of almost 30 years revealed the secret to his family, friends, and the college community by saying that his premeditated murder — he drove to his mother's home to retrieve guns and ammunition before returning to his dorm — resulted from years of being bullied. In this case the victim-criminal admits guilt, but with an explanation. With his status, the film's subject has reached the power and influence as an academic and pioneering scholar of environmental psychology.

In *All Good Things*, Jarecki's 2010 narrative debut, he taps into the assumption that any stained soul can collapse into crime. The belief that a psycho-killer lurks on every city block comes from our culture of fear, and a misconception of criminality.[3] Like other mundane killer narratives (see *American Psycho* [2000] and *Mr. Brooks* [2007]), *All Good Things* suggests that a normative existence can transform into the extreme disorder of homicide. The witch hunt in *Capturing* also works off such a belief: Great Neck, New York, found its haunts and rushed to dispose of them. The conclusion of *All Good Things* reverses expectation, when plenty of evidence appears to try David Marks (Ryan Gosling) for the disappearance of his wife, though he remains uncharged. As in Woody Allen's *Match Point* (see Chapter 13), social status helps to protect the guilty. Societal pressures also instigated the crime.

All Good Things, foremost, belongs in the new style of filmed true crime. Jarecki's earlier feature used the documentary format, while his new film uses the style for narrative film. Inspired by the case of Robert Durst, the film depicts an unsolved crime that frustrates law enforcement and angers the populace. The film doesn't suggest it will offer a clear resolution, as do many contemporary crime films. Like *Zodiac* (though obviously smaller in scope), *All Good Things* looks to the *how* and *why* of the crime more than the justice for it.

Along with the new true crime film, *All Good Things* takes visual cues from the family melodrama that turns tragic. The great predecessor of the style is Douglas Sirk, who framed his 1950s works as kitchen sink melodramas, the familiar milieu to investigate women's troubles. Sirk's style has become territory for pastiche, most directly in Todd Haynes's powerful-in-its-own-right *Far from Heaven* (a film inspired by Sirk's *All That Heaven Allows* [1955] and, in turn, Rainer Werner Fassbinder's retelling of the original film, *Ali: Fear Eats the Soul* [1974]). The Sirk (anti-)melodramatic style has reappeared in independently produced family dramas, including *Little Children*, *Revolutionary Road* (set in the same time period as Sirk's films), *We Don't Live Here Anymore*, and *In the Bedroom* (the latter two adapted from short stories by Andre Dubus). Notable for our discussion is the latter film, which concerns a father's vengeance-murder for the killing of his son. Like the others discussed, this recent film uses nostalgia through glowing visuals and softened cinematography to suggest a storybook past (even if relatively recent) that has fallen from its ideal.

Such visual cues — a home looking brighter onscreen than it actually is — reveal family life veering towards the tragic. *All Good Things* uses such hazy nostalgia to evoke its inherent tragedy and to place viewers in the protagonist's dark past. A noir style suits this crime-story-meets-family-anti-melodrama.

Jarecki fashions this approach through his attention to personal history. In this sense, *All Good Things* connects most strongly to his previous effort, in which the personal story of David Friedman frames his family's crime story. Perspective is key here, since Jarecki turns from the point of view of caught-in-the-middle David Friedman to that of *All Good Thing*'s David Marks. In the latter film, Jarecki uses a formulaic framing device of the biopic: the free David of the present, speaking to an unseen interviewer about his shady past. The film isn't completely subjective — occasionally the point of view turns to David's wife, Katie (Kirsten Dunst), so viewers can sympathize with this victim. In a few scenes, David doesn't even appear, thus loosening the restricted perspective suggested by the framing device. By leaving David's subjectivity, the film loses the unity as it departs from investigating the criminal's psychology. Foster Hirsch notes that the strongest (and most psychologically unique) noir is restricted to the criminal's point of view.[4] Yet, Jarecki breaks his perspective while trying to capture the mind of a killer. To leave David's guilt questionable, Jarecki broadens from subjectivity to true-crime reportage, detailing the sundry facts more than the intricacies of the killer's mind. *All*

A troubling legacy: David Marks (Ryan Gosling) in *All Good Things* (2010, Magnolia Pictures).

Good Things depicts the social pressures that influence crime — how oppressive events lead to a severe action — while breaking its commitment to the noir style.

The film begins with Super-8 camera footage, another device of the biopic. Presenting David in his youth, this camera stock which gives the feeling of a home movie suggests fondness as much as suspicious distance. Aside from an aged David speaking to an interviewer, these images are the only ones to represent his early life, before he's entered employment for his father, Sanford Marks (Frank Langella). Sanford owns a large property-management firm, for which David runs errands. The firm has properties throughout the old Times Square in Manhattan, which Jarecki doesn't capture with nostalgia. To Sanford, the buildings are merely sinister remnants that need to be removed. Fittingly, the tone assigned to the old Times Square reflects David dark's oppressions, soon to be revealed. Measuring up to the family name will add more stress to the compromised protagonist.

When David meets Katie, his minor stresses that mask the greater one are relieved. Here, Jarecki uses melodrama/romance to reflect hope. The couple's chance meeting creates two developments in the narrative: David's marriage and his leaving the family business. He and Katie move to Vermont to open a business that rebels against his father's corporate sensibility. Though it offers temporary freedom, in retrospect the couple's health food shop called "All Good Things" represents the innocence lost to David. In this perspective, it was damned from the beginning, since his father tells him, upon meeting Katie, that she "will never be one of us." The business fails and David returns to his father's corporation. Hence, the latter character becomes the serpent who damns his son's attempt at an idyllic life.

David and Katie return to the New York area, where life is so ready-made for them that it leaves David confused. By destroying paradise, Sanford creates a Faustian deal for his son that goes sour right away. Sanford condemns the less fortunate and offers them little sympathy or help: he forces Katie's mother to split a dinner, to which he invited her. As a cog in Sanford's machine by day, David feels his family life at night oppresses him further. An argument between him and Katie leaves her so scared that she crawls out a high-rise window. Jarecki counters our condemnation for David by revealing that, in his youth, he saw his mother jump to her death at their estate. David struggles through therapy, letting out a barrage of profanity as if it were an acting class conceived for Nicolas Cage. When David moves to rage in everyday life, Jarecki uses flights of impressionism to show the stifled anger growing.

Katie's pregnancy doesn't bring hope. Her abortion, at David's urging, doesn't open them up to more opportunities. It shuts down something they are trying to build. The father's influence weighs upon the act. Katie and David discuss the abortion in coded language similar to that in Ernest Hemingway's "Hills Like White Elephants." The event begins the official breakdown of their relationship, as she moves to Westchester, New York, while Marks remains in Manhattan. In her new freedom, and perhaps to cope with her martial issues, Katie attends college. When she eventually graduates, David has a fit of rage at her family's party when she refuses to leave early. He pulls her away by the hair, an act showing the power of his status and family, since many men in her family watch without stopping it. Katie has as little power over the Marks family when she attempts to file for divorce. Sanford has solidified control over his son's finances, since the estate legally cannot be divided for her share, leaving her trapped in the marriage. In anger, she mails Sanford's cooked books to the Feds — they return them, preferring not to get involved.

When David murders the family dog, we learn of what he is capable, and when Katie disappears, the film repeatedly implicates David. Sanford takes a phone call afterward as if receiving another difficult bit of news. When meeting with David, Sanford learns of the lasting effects of his wife's suicide on his son. The narrative pairs father and son since both have lost their wives. The enigma is in David's remark to his father: "I'm just like you," leaving it vague as to whether David meant he's lost his wife or has gotten rid of her. Yet, the film repeats evidence that indicates David to be culpable. Sanford opens a portentous car trunk. A woman dumps bags into a river. With Katie's husband the obvious suspect in her "disappearance" in 1982, David goes free from scrutiny, his father helping him disappear. In a bizarre twist, Marks reappears in 2000 in Galvaston, Texas as a "mute" crossdresser, at the same time the investigation is reopened by Westchester District Attorney Janice Rizzo (Diane Venora). At this time, Deborah Lehrman (Lily Rabe) leaves messages on David's machine, asking for help and implying that she has something on him. Rizzo reopens the case based on an unpublished manuscript by Deborah, which resembles David's situation. In the film's final section, David's contemporary account to the unseen biographer proves to be his testimony in court for the murder of Malvern Bump (Philip Baker Hall). With the setting of his testimony revealed, David's accounts consistently contradict the events as dramatized. By depicting the kind of perjury that surely happened in the Friedman trial, Jarecki comments on the disparity between the truth and the record.

Jarecki also withholds revealing information until the end of the film to deliver surprise: David's relationship to Lehrman, and his brutal murder of Bump, which he says was in self-defense. (We learn that Bump killed Lehrman *apparently* as a part of deal with David.) Jarecki pulls the same trick at the end of *Capturing*: the news of Jesse's testimony against his father, and not learning until the very end of the film that Howard Friedman, brother to Arnold whom the latter has said that he molested, is a now an openly gay man. Appropriately, *Capturing* never reveals the truth about Arnold's original investigation, since it is not available. *All Good Things* reads beyond the testimony of the Lehrman and Bump murders to implicate David, but remains distant from the central crime that defined him. Since *All Good Things* ends by partially aligning itself to David's psychology, Jarecki dissolves the noir treatment to which the narrative was committed. Jarecki aimed to fuse two elements — character psychology and social commentary — that work well together in *Capturing*. Noir commits to the personal in lieu of the social, and hence *All Good Things* finishes at odds with itself.

10

"Now It's Dark"
David Lynch's Crime Nightmares

A beloved *suis generis* of the film world, David Lynch has a following which can be broken down into two camps: cineastes who admire his technical mastery, and cultists who love his sensibility. Lynch has delivered plenty of late-night freak-out films, in a career widely regarded to be full of modern classics. Loved for his shocking moments — as cultists will revere Coens' *Fargo* (1996) for its gunshot to the jaw of Steve Buscemi's character and his demise in a wood chipper — Lynch's tangible-yet-dreamlike visual style catches the eye of the highbrow viewer. Controlled compositions appear in both his trademark works of surrealism and his more traditional narratives (*The Elephant Man*, *The Straight Story*). Witness a cornfield in the latter film: just when it appears to be an element of static realism, the image seems to melt as Lynch and cinematographer Freddie Francis capture its movements with a moving aerial shot.

Lynch's visual sense never falters. Even if a narrative beat or performance in a scene misfires, his images suggest some deeper truth. He works intuitively, often discussing the importance of mediation to his work.[1] Thus he discovers images for the screen, or reaches a clarity of mind to prepare them for the camera. Intuition also helps him develop his narrative content, as cast members of *Blue Velvet* have attested[2]; hence, this approach remains a guiding principle behind the alluring illogic of his work. Distinct as it is, Lynch's narrative style isn't all that foreign: he structures his films like symphonies. In his works, emotions rise and fall, tension builds then releases to match the moods and flights of a musical composition. In his art, emotion can have a vague connection to the content, which Lynch seems to appreciate. He would argue intuition to be more important than musicality to his process, while other narrative artists, like Sam Shepard and Stephen Sondheim, mainly use music as an inspiration. Though we cannot dismiss the importance of scores to Lynch's work, usually those of collaborator Angelo Badalamenti.

Lynch is less concerned with the clarity of his works than how they affect us. Thus, interpretation of films like *Lost Highway* (1997) and *Mulholland Dr.* (2001) are boundless, though their intended emotional response is more direct. Lynch knows what his audience will be doing once it sees Laura Harring and Naomi Watts crying to Badalamenti's Spanish version of Orbison's "Crying." *Inland Empire* (2006) — a string of experimental shorts with little narrative cohesion — further shows the filmmaker's concern about the receiver's feeling. To discover the sender's unconscious motives is speculative mindplay.

The approach resulted in one of the most distinct of filmmaking styles, which Lynch has developed throughout his career. He used surrealism right away, in short films like *The Grandmother* (1970) and his first feature, *Eraserhead* (1977), their nightmarish tones a thematic continuation of Lynch's previous work in visual art.[3] After the latter film became an arthouse cult hit, producers asked him to adapt the life of John Merrick (*The Elephant Man*, 1980) and the Frank Herbert novel *Dune* (released in 1984) for the big screen. *Blue Velvet* (1986) was his first film to use narrative as a symphonic play-on-emotions and, not incidentally, the first by him to consider the classical Hollywood narrative's flexibility, as a shell for a surrealism. Thus, it was also his first to invoke the tradition of the American crime film, even if his style shares much with the European surreal tradition. Lynch's fusing of crime motifs, in films from *Blue Velvet* to the present, with his dreamlike style has been little explored.[4] The filmmaker realizes the vertiginous nature of film noir, a style using narrative clarity and closure on the surface, even if confusion lies in its moody visual approaches. Instead of Lynch's crime style working as a means of serving the other, more celebrated form (the surreal), his marriage of forms shows a symbiotic relationship between the two. Beginning as early as 1986, Lynch's approach is hardly new — though his 2001 film, *Mulholland Dr.*, would prove to be his finest statement on the crime film as American nightmare. Other notable entries came along the way.

Lynch's films reflect how the human dreamscape can veer toward nightmare. He aims to reach the unconscious, the territory of illusions appearing only at night. Lynch's dark worldview is the product of a subjective point of view aligned to a disturbed consciousness — if a main character isn't on the brink of madness, then he's in reach of some disturbing element. Classical American crime films approach some form of darkness, though it doesn't always overtake a given film's universe. The original gangsters had their freewheeling rise to power, which reflected the lure of crime while the viewer's perspective remained under the influence of morality, intended to judge the crime onscreen in lieu of aligning with it. Hence, the gangster's gradual downfall would reveal the film's guiding consciousness: a moralist's, contrary to the protagonist-gangster. While this film style used moral realism, the early films noir shrouded the entire narrative in darkness, even if the protagonist is in touch with a ray of hope (actual or imagined). The restoration to order at a film's climax was something bleak, as the (innocent) persons involved have discovered the darkness, or have succumbed to it. In this tradition, the viewer would become aligned with the morally compromised protagonist. Censorship has informed us that the protagonist — and all of us watching — have been bad, bad.

The perspective of the film noir, even if rooted in urban realism, borrowed much from the nightmarish. While its causal narration is steeped in realism, its content and conflicts come from our deepest fears of what we desire. While the finest examples of the style — *Double Indemnity, The Big Sleep, Out of the Past* — maintain such a tone, those that don't — *The Maltese Falcon, Kiss of Death* (Richard Widmark's psycho instigating the actions of the heroic Victor Mature) — align with a moralistic perspective. Such entries share more with the adventure yarn and the family melodrama, respectively. Neo-noirs like Polanski's *Chinatown* (1974), effective as they are at commenting on the tradition before them, focus less on the nightmarish than on creating pastiche of a tradition. In *Chinatown*, the dark worldview is social commentary.

A notable exception — a noir invoking surrealism — is John Boorman's *Point Blank* (1967). This victim-cum-avenger film features a hunter who's likely already perished. As Lee Marvin's character tracks down the man who double-crossed him, we know we're aligned with the cinematic equivalent of an unreliable narrator. Time abruptly shifts, and repeated flashbacks return us to the event (his attempted murder) which he aims to avenge. The film may reflect the "just-a-dream" fallacy, which expels a need for clarity and structure with the help of the most convenient of all narrative conclusions. (Think Lewis Carroll's ever-copied resolution to *Alice in Wonderland*, in which Alice awakens from her extended dream, and the approach to Ambrose Bierce's story, "An Occurrence at Owl Creek Bridge," the latter being *Point Blank*'s obvious predecessor.) But the style's heightened intensity makes the film all the more thrilling. It depicts an elegantly murky perspective that makes crime and retribution something dreaded and nightmarish.

Lynch takes surreal crime beyond the "is this real?" territory. His surrealism traps viewers in an extreme form of horror (see Lynch's early work). Yet, Lynch maximizes on the territory of terror while still using the suspense-ready noir motifs and style. Most crime films preceding his style work with realism, which are often as refined as they are gritty. Two of the most stylized would be Francis Ford Coppola's *The Godfather*, Parts I and II, essentially extending the realism no further than expressionist moments. It seems as if filmmakers relied on associations to "truth" when featuring crime and, hence, use verity and realism. Lynch found another universal truth: our fear of crime.

His first crime nightmare, *Blue Velvet*, fashions a traditional narrative as hyperrealism. Jeffrey Beaumont (Kyle MacLachlan), a college student, returns home to visit his father, just stricken with a heart attack. Jeffrey kills time by tossing rocks and jokes with the employees at his father's hardware store. Life in his small home town is mundane. Yet, before we meet Jeffrey, Lynch introduces his idyllic milieu as a distorted, overexposed rendition of a Norman Rockwell painting. An anachronistic 1950s firetruck rolls down a street in slow motion, a public servant upon it waving out in anti-realistic bliss, though we know it's all part of Lynch's dark theater, indicated by the film's bookended blue curtains. Sure enough, the nightmares rise: during his heart attack, Jeffrey's father's pulls a hose that spurts a leak, metonymy of the danger about to emerge. Then two images reflect absurdism: a child wanders toward the victim; then beneath the grass, in extreme close-up, insects rummage, tearing and consuming. This transition reveals the nightmarish depths that will synthesize a traditional, goal-oriented narrative.[5] Lynch uses the latter to reveal noir's hellish undercurrents. For this artist, tradition is a disarming means of delivering the nightmarish.

If traditional noir invokes a bleak worldview,[6] then Lynch maximizes its pitch by revealing the underside of *Blue Velvet*'s small town. His discovery of a severed ear turns him into an unofficial investigator[7] and leads him to a version of a criminal underworld. On one hand, the ear invokes the fragmentation of surrealism (with Luis Buñuel and Salvador Dalí's *Un Chien Andalou* as the obvious inspiration), while the body part becomes evidence, and a "lead" into the underworld. Jeffrey begins a relationship with a neighborhood blonde, Sandy (Laura Dern), a detective's daughter. She first appears glowing from a shadowy street, undoubtedly an ideal for Jeffrey, now realized. She ends partaking in Jeffrey's detection, learning of a lead (to Dorothy Vallens) by eavesdropping on her father.

Dorothy (Isabella Rossellini), with a name recalling Lynch's long obsession with *The Wizard of Oz*,[8] will be Jeffrey's anti-ideal, the embodiment of his sinister urges. When he stakes out her apartment, and ends up hiding in her closet, she pulls him out at knifepoint. His desire for sex and danger leads to this underworld, a Pandora's box, from which we expect absolute hell. Dorothy's apartment exists just off the edge of the real toward the nightmarish.[9] Curiously, her hold-up of Jeffrey turns into an arousal, as she takes down his pants and he admits, oddly without fear, that it feels good. The actual nightmare is about to come, in the form of Frank Booth's (Dennis Hopper) arrival. When he knocks on the door, she rushes Jeffrey back to his hiding spot, a primal voyeuristic scene about to begin.

Jeffrey Beaumont (Kyle MacLachlan) sees beneath the placid town of Lumberton in *Blue Velvet* (1986, Sony Pictures Home Entertainment).

This appearance of Frank, an ultimate villain, accentuates Jeffrey's encroachment. Frank is a hyperbolic, almost absurd, manifestation of evil. We know that Lynch creates from instinct, and that the emblematic characters in this film — the down-home Jeffrey and Sandy, the lustful masochist Dorothy, and Frank's flatly drawn cohorts (who we will meet later) — have umbilical cords trailing back to Lynch's unconscious. But the distinct Frank Booth must have coalesced in collaboration between Hopper and his director.[10] It's baffling how a filmmaker, even of Lynch's imaginative powers, could conceptualize such a vivid madman and find a performer able to realize it. Instead, it seems Lynch thought up this villain in vague terms and conceived his dialogue (all of his trademark lines are in the original script) before Hopper fleshed him out. Hopper's delivery of the loony, redundant line, "You fucker's fucker!" (as he's about to ritualistically ravish Dorothy while Jeffrey watches in hiding), grounds the absurd as menace. Even his ridiculously hilarious line, "Heineken! Fuck that shit — Pabst Blue Ribbon!" barked later at Jeffrey, reads as a conviction of Frank's, even if loony — an exclamation mirroring character. Frank lives a constant over-the-top performance, continuing his evil with forced rage. A slow-motion flashback of him ranting before the initial rape, and his maniacal inhaling of nitrous oxide (his face visible through a clear mask), show externalized traits embodying threat. On one hand, it's scenery chewing specific to Hopper; on the other, it's so realistic that we accept it as the film's reality. A monster of the id, he's still grounded in flesh and blood. Thus, Booth embodies the film's realistic-surreal duality — a well-balanced lunatic unifying this crime-nightmare.

When Frank enters Dorothy's apartment (with Jeffrey in hiding), he commands her to begin a routine performance. A cabaret singer, she embodies passion in her ability to perform, both on stage and for Frank. Frank's obsession with her had grown during her concerts, and hence he's kidnapped her husband (when he cut off his ear) and son to make her into his "performance" slave. His perversion — he calls out to Mommy when making Dorothy expose herself— asks the audience to psychoanalyze, leaving Frank a warped man gone wrong. Yet, he screams the word "fuck," the word indicating both the sex act and one of destruction. (When he later yells, "Let's fuck! I'll fuck anything that moves!" like a war-cry, he channels an urge to consume and destroy.) Feeling and tasting a swath of blue velvet, matching the title of the song Dorothy sings in her cabaret performance, he beats and quickly rapes her to quiet his rage. "Now it's dark," he says, confirming his words when he first arrived, a wish now fulfilled. He's extinguished his urges and exposed Jeffrey's.

Since Jeffrey wakes at home in the next scene, the vivid images at Dorothy's feel even more like moments of a dream. Just having escaped danger, he's still drawn to her. The previous night, after Frank leaves, Dorothy had enticed Jeffrey then asked him to hit her. Jeffrey desires this dark sphere of sexuality, and gets caught by its other source (Frank) when returning to the apartment. This leads to a carnivalesqe hell-ride in a car full of Frank's cohort freaks. Frank becomes the deeper id, the actual urges beneath the lovely, exotic appearance of Dorothy. Jeffrey's sexual education is to experience this darkness, which entails kidnapping, blackmail, and murder. As an (unofficial) investigator, he comes upfront to his counterpoint: the source of the sundry crimes.

This new reality brings a darkness hardly present in the investigational setup. Still seeing Sandy, Jeffrey grounds himself in the prelude to the American dream (a courtship), while his investigation continues. He learns that Frank is connected to the police. Jeffrey makes it back to Dorothy's apartment, where he finds Frank's detective cohort and Dorothy's husband, both appearing as still-life images of death (the ear-less husband), or near dead (the cop), graphically and uncannily invoking Lynch's first short film/sculpture, *Six Men Getting Sick* (1966). Lynch visualizes death as a frozen night-terror, while Jeffrey avenges the transgressions by shooting Frank through the head, filmed in excruciating slow motion. As Detective Williams, Sandy's father (we take note), arrives to tell Jeffrey it's all over, the film's traditional narrative mask

Frank Booth (Dennis Hopper) and Ben (Dean Stockwell), members of a mysterious criminal network in **Blue Velvet** (1986, Sony Pictures Home Entertainment).

concludes by affirming familial unity. We may be inclined to read Jeffrey's sexual education as a bachelor's last splash, the acquired knowledge helping him with his new journey, entering a family proper. When reunited with her son, Dorothy leaves the film restored to maternity. To Jeffrey, Frank is the Oedipal father, defeated, though haunting the young man.

Like *Blue Velvet*, Lynch's following films mix classicism and traditional crime motifs with surrealism (if not with the same success). The filmmaker's *Wild at Heart* (1990) — which also starred Laura Dern, opposite Nicolas Cage — uses the lovers-on-the-run motif to ground the film in a criminal's conscience. Hunting them is Dern's obsessive mother, who serves as the repressed (and seriously disturbed), now returning. Lynch's television series *Twin Peaks* (1990–1991) featured the continual investigation of a murdered young woman with plenty of strange occurrences, and no resolution in sight — until he made the series' prequel as a feature film, *Twin Peaks: Fire Walk with Me* (1992). This film presents Laura alive, her murder imminent and, in the process, the criminal revealed. Many fans of the television series were unimpressed with the film, since it clarified the former's ongoing, Mobius-strip absurdism. Yet, *Fire Walk with Me* works as Lynch's purest rendition of the victim film: about one too conscious of the offense against her.

Though approaching the hybrid surrealism of *Blue Velvet*, *Wild at Heart* remains a pulp exercise, while *Fire Walk with Me* reveals the powerful results of Lynch's surrealism, fully transforming his crime motifs. *Lost Highway* (1997) shows Lynch loosening his classical narrative boundaries further, developing a narrative shaped on character emotions more than events. The film depicts the subjective life of Los Angeles saxophone player Fred Madison (Bill Pullman). When he receives videotapes of surveillance footage of his own home, we know that Lynch has some tricks up his sleeve. The tapes represent a window into Fred's unconscious, implicating him as the murderer of his wife. As in *Blue Velvet*, Lynch doubles female characters: Fred's wife has dark hair during the second narrative movement, in which Fred's character transforms into an entirely new person. *Lost Highway* reflects character experience — mainly, a surreal interpretation of it — through the workings of a criminal-centered thriller. Lynch's perspective reads Fred's psychology with such detail that the work becomes something of a victim film (though about a self-persecuted one). Lynch hadn't worked with such subjectivity since his debut feature, *Eraserhead* (1977), which uses surrealism and absurdism to reflect the torment of one forced into parenthood.

Lynch's thematic follow up to *Lost Highway*, *Mulholland Dr.* (2001)[11] also employs the character experience/interpretation motif, with a more unified and kinetic result. Lynch has his two lead actors (Naomi Watts and Laura Elena Harring) double themselves, with a secondary character for each actress working as an interpretation of the first; and they eventually double each other. By doing so, the film enters extreme subjectivity, with the later actions of each performer working as commentary on what we've already seen. The film uses this doubling to reflect obsessive desire. While *Blue Velvet* makes its criminal underworld — Frank's actions as kidnapper, and ritualistic rapist to Dorothy, and his other gangsterism — into a netherworld between dream entering reality, *Mulholland Dr.* uses the dream life of working actor Diane (Naomi Watts, whose character dreams herself to be Betty, an aspiring actress) to fashion her subjective reality, how she copes with her disintegrating affair with her co-actor on a movie set, Camilla (Laura Elena Harring, whom Betty dreams to be an amnesiac calling herself Rita — after a Hayworth poster — then Diane, a revived fatale made for surrealism).

Commentators on *Mulholland* usually acknowledge the narrative's two movements, and each has been argued to be an interpretation of the other. The film's second narrative movement could be a realistic means of clarifying the dreamlike workings of the first half, as if Lynch comments on his own allusiveness by positing a suggested reading. This reading is hard to ignore but remains too simple an approach. Granted, Lynch has never been keen on allowing us to read his work and, hence, red herrings abound. Approaching the film's first narrative movement as a realization of Diane's desires reveals it to be a noir fantasy. This section works as a psychological profile of her character, as a window into her wish fulfillment in spite of the nightmarish associations. Considering the film's conclusion, her suicide, a Biercian "Occurrence at Owl Creek Bridge" dream-at-demise reading could apply — that the images/scenes of the first half unravel in her brain at the moment of death. The crime-film devices of the first movement serve Diane's wish fulfillment: to escape into a filmic dream better than the mundane reality of movie-making, and lost love. In *Mulholland*, noir is fantasy against impetuous crimes of reality.

The former movement — a chance meeting, mysterious investigation — is a titillating dream-wish, a mere longing after waking. Hence, her desired chance meeting develops into a noir murder mystery. As with most wish fulfillment, her fantasy helps her cope with waking life, the melodramatic letdown of seeing her girl fall into the arms of a film director. The dream-film, the first section of *Mulholland*, begins with Harring's role, getting held up by her own driver, at which point drag-racing teenagers collide with the car. This disruption brings her to the new home of Watts's character who, within her dream narrative, has arrived in a Los Angeles that's dewy sweet. When she arrives, an elderly couple helps her to her taxi (a couple who will serve as

Bette/Diane (Naomi Watts) and Rita (Laura Elena Harring) approach the mystery of *Mulholland Dr.* (2001, Universal Pictures).

tiny haunts later), and her cabbie gets her bags, right when she thinks them
stolen. She has arrived with hopes of realizing an acting career. And, as it
turns out, she finds another passion in the form of Harring's character. Harring
has found her way into Watts's apartment, which compels the latter to help
her solve the mystery of her lost identity. After a sexual union between the
two women, Harring dons a blonde wig, which has us considering the doubling motifs of Hitchcock's *Vertigo* and Bergman's *Persona*. Lynch stresses the
doubling by aligning the two women's faces in one shot, while in bed.

Meanwhile, in a parallel narrative intercut with the women's, a film director named Adam Kesher (Justin Theroux) watches his career and personal life
crumble. The results play as a blackly comic side narrative to the principal
one. Sinister film producers/moneymen force Kesher to recast the lead in his
1950s-era film, a connection that brings about the film's central number, Bal-
damenti's Spanish version of the Roy Orbison hit "Crying": when the two
women hear this rendition, it brings about the culmination of the dream,
which leads to the unfortunate second narrative movement. The change is
further urged by an id-borne figure called "Cowboy" (Lafayette Montgomery),
who absurdly resides in a ranch ... in Hollywood. (With characteristics of
both the avenging and bandit cowboy, he's a remnant of mythical and not
actual Hollywood — or perhaps a manifestation of a costumed man Watts happens to notice at a party late in the film's final narrative.) Miffed after learning about the fate of his film, Kesher returns home to find his wife cheating
with a caricatured, self-assured hunk, played by Billy Ray Cyrus, a doozy of
ironic casting by Lynch. Kesher takes revenge by covering his wife's jewelry
in pink paint, the actor's application of which looks like Lynch fooling around
on a piano (we can feel his direction of the actor as much as the scene's reference to the filmmaker's "orchestration"). Kesher's wife even gets the busi-
ness-end of the fist of a mountain-sized goon looking for the filmmaker. As
a figment of Watts's dream, Kesher, at this moment, reflects her wish for his
destruction, since he has, in real life, taken her beloved Camilla (Harring)
from her.

The latter narrative reveals Watts already as a working actress, but a mere
tag-along to her girlfriend, Harring. She's been seduced on the set by the
cocky Kesher, the film's addition to Lynch's young alter-egos (*Blue Velvet*'s
Jeffrey and *Lost Highway*'s Fred). Watts jealously urges her to hire a hitman
to kill Harring, the routine crime contrapuntal to the noirish dream investigation. Even in the reality-based second narrative movement, the nightmarish
haunts appear to Watts, keeping the film in her jeopardized perspective.

To reveal the subtext of *Mulholland* is to discover Lynch's new addition
to the crime film. Now surrealism is the principal form, with crime motifs as
a sublimated means of reaching the former end. (In *Blue Velvet*, we have the

reverse, more traditional though just as successful.) Many subscribe to the dreamlife-meets-nightmarish-reality interpretation discussed above, while some critics hesitate to over-analyze the film, preferring to let the tale's mystery remain enigmatic.[12] But understanding Lynch's relationship between crime motifs and surrealism shows the logic behind *Mulholland*. The film's hitman, in actuality, gives Watts the blue key, a motif that has appeared throughout the culture of Freudian analysis and surrealism on canvas and film.[13] Essentially a noirish fantasy-mystery in the film's first narrative movement — the hunt to uncover the truth of Harring's role — covers up a criminal's growing psychosis (that of Watts's actual character). Watts, in waking life, moves to vengeance, her attempt to right the injustice done to her. Her issues are pathological and compulsive, as she roughly masturbates to subdue her anger, which is progressing to psychosis. During Watts's dream life, the dead woman that the two find in the apartment of the real Diane Selwyn represents Watts's *dream thought*, a cross of both her death wish against Harring, and her own death instinct (leading to her suicide), as she knows Harring is lost to her forever.

To further explicate Lynch's subtext would demean the film's powerful, enigmatic style, which is, naturally, his greatest achievement. The worthy point is to remember how Lynch relies on genre to unravel the criminal mind. By addressing surrealism and genre together, and one's unique relationship to the other, we realize the full effects of Lynch's opposing but unified trademark works, *Blue Velvet* and *Mulholland Dr.* The nightmarish would be adequate, but clarifying his work as crime nightmares leads to the heart of his alluring darkness.

11

The Bloody Frontier
Tommy Lee Jones's *Weary Avenger*

The motion picture camera will always love the prairie, even if the Western genre has grown dated over time. In the form of purported true-life tales, dime novels, and "Wild West shows," the Western tradition grew popular while the American West was still being chartered. The Western novel and film tradition remained popular up through the mid–20th century, especially through the conservative Eisenhower era. A tradition that championed heroism and community became a mainstay on the big screen and the most popular television genre in the early days of the medium.

As cultural tones changed, and much of America began to distrust the war in Vietnam instead of championing the cause to fight communism, the avenging man of action grew darker, more criminal. Many historical accounts note John Ford's *The Searchers* (1956) as the popular Western to challenge the man of action archetype. Appearing when "adult" Westerns became popular (along with Howard Hawks's *Red River* [1948] and George Stevens's *Shane* [1953]), *The Searchers* approaches mature themes instead of continuing the "kiddie" style of the Saturday serials. Ford's film helped to solidify the tradition as a genre proper, though John Wayne's Ethan Edwards grows ruthless in his quest to save a kidnapped girl from natives. Eventually, his goal is not to save but to *kill* her, thus removing any chance for miscegenation. This character foreshadows the Vietnam-era reinvention of the Western, in which the heroes are ruthless (Sam Peckinpah's *The Wild Bunch* [1969]), or the quest and its characters are inverted to deconstruct an American mythos (Arthur Penn's *Little Big Man* [1970]). These revisions, aiming to depict violence more realistically, were much like Raymond Chandler's goal in devising his new crime story way back in the late 1930s through the '40s: to show cops and criminals as they actually were.[1] This early–20th-century example reflects popular fiction and film's constant reevaluation of its own myths, a tendency not really new to the 1960s cultural revolution, but a constant inclination since the movies established conventions.[2]

After the new Westerns of the late 1960s/early 1970s, the genre welcomed the ruthless avenger, whose violence reflected the increasing coverage of the Vietnam war. The moral avenger didn't return to popular films until Kevin Costner's *Dances with Wolves* (1990) and Clint Eastwood's *Unforgiven* (1992),[3] both of which concern redeemed avengers who triumph by the films' endings. These new avengers abandon the ruthless *Dirty Harry* ethos of the Vietnam/Watergate era[4]; their quest results from soul searching, even if Costner posits the white man as redeemer to the "savage," a form of the "magic negro."[5] In the 1980s, comic-book-type heroes prevailed (even touted by President Reagan, who likened national goals to Rambo's actions, and invoked *Dirty Harry*). These cartoonish heroes were more focused on their goals than the morality of achieving them. With Costner's and Eastwood's films appearing at the end of the Reagan and George H.W. Bush eras, the movie Western — and more broadly, crime-themed avenger tales onscreen — became more concerned with the nature of justice than its execution. It was the first step towards the modern Clint Eastwood of the 21st century who, along with Tommy Lee Jones, exemplifies a new avenger figure.

The reemergence of the classical avenger notwithstanding, the nihilist Western has maintained long after Peckinpah. The American politics of war during the George W. Bush years inspired Westerns like James Mangold's remake of *3:10 to Yuma* (2007; with an ending informed by Martin Scorsese's 2006 film, *The Departed*, as much as the Elmore Leonard source story[6]), the Australian film *The Proposition* (2005) by John Hillcoat, and the Coen brothers' *No Country for Old Men* (2007), adapted from Cormac McCarthy's novel set in the milieu of 1980s drug trafficking (see Chapter 16 on the Coen brothers). Though villainy now thrives, the rugged old-time avengers haven't faded in this shadow of the contemporary Western and crime film. Along with Eastwood, Tommy Lee Jones's recent roles depict a rugged wisdom inclined toward justice. And, like his acting counterpart, Jones has investigated the moral imperative beneath his avengers.

The 1990s was a late-career coming-of-age for Eastwood, as the following chapter will show. The same decade saw a maturation for Jones. The actor began the decade playing fierce, compelling lawmen, entertaining to watch even if they were less dimensional. As Samuel Gerard, who leads a team of United States Marshals in 1993's *The Fugitive* (based on the 1960s television series), Jones often drops gruff jokes to provide relief in the tense film. Yet on the quest, he's unflappable — when a pistol-aiming Richard Kimble (Harrison Ford), professes his innocence, Gerard shrugs, "I don't care." His concern is

Ed Tom Bell (Tommy Lee Jones) has quite a problem on his hands in *No Country for Old Men* (2007, Miramax Films).

the mission, not its morality. The film never depicts Gerard outside of his job, since he embodies Kimble's powerful counterforce, the former having been wrongfully accused of killing his wife. This intense victimization of Kimble, propelled by a committee-flavored script (reported to have been rewritten countless times[7]), and Gerard's relentless pursuit made the film a smash hit. This film offers little character development of Gerard: it is more dynamic in developing Kimble's character, who moves from victim to his own avenger. In time, he proves his innocence by exposing corporate fraud, when Gerard eventually helps the wrongfully accused Kimble.

The Fugitive proved that Jones was the best man for such roles. By the 1990s, Eastwood's avenger had already grown overly iconic; his maturation was happening behind the camera in his new, post–*Unforgiven* career as a director. Jones indirectly followed his lead, with his potential for age-strong conviction. His presence could serve up a take-no-shit brand of vengeance, even if the chase leads to the wrong man. Though it won him a Best Supporting Actor Academy Award, his flat role in *The Fugitive* only needed two scenes to develop: one showing his constant pursuit, and another delivering comic relief. It was his potential that earned him such attention — he has an ability to be real and to sell whatever he delivers. His avengers, as diverting as they were, had only to develop.

His gruffness was territory for self-reference, as in films like *U.S. Marshals* (1998)—in which he reprises the role of Gerard—the cartoonish *Men in Black* films (1997 and 2002), and *The Hunted* (2003). The Jones persona made for comic fodder in *Man of the House* (2005), in which he protects a sorority of cheerleaders, and *Space Cowboys* (2000), in which he gallops to the stars with fellow icon Eastwood, who co-starred and directed. Jones's avenger began to grow in between these two entries—specifically, in 2003's *The Missing*, directed by Ron Howard. This film brought Jones to the prairie proper, the ideal locale for him to ponder the ramifications of justice.

In this film, Jones's avenger tributes the classical Western archetype: the badman making good. Having abandoned his family years earlier, Samuel Jones (Jones) returns to daughter Magdalena Gilkeson (Cate Blanchett) and his two granddaughters. As a loner, he arrives by order of his spiritual guide, who said it was imperative to curing his infection of a snake bite. Director Ron Howard and cinematographer Salvatore Totino highlight the estrangement between he and his daughter through deep landscapes. As a white man who's taken up Native American culture, Samuel is more of an outsider than Ethan Edwards, who returns from serving in the Civil War only to head out again on a quest. Having become the "other," Samuel is even more estranged from the start, while a similar progression for Ethan Edwards requires the full narrative of *The Searchers*. (At the film's end, Edwards cannot return to the community.) Hence, with the avenger's estrangement more immediate, *The Missing* becomes a conscious revision of the Fordian badman who may be irredeemable.

Samuel is essential to the search, though he's an unavoidable choice for Magdalena, who has detested him since he abandoned the family. The raid has left Magdalena's partner, Brake Baldwin (Aaron Eckhart), mutilated, the screaming of which haunts the younger daughter and represents the terror of the kidnapped, older daughter, Lilly (Evan Rachel Wood). (Their intention, to sell her into white slavery to Mexicans just over the border, avoids posturing "the other" as villainous, and is therefore all the more harrowing.) As the village "healer," Magdalena performs a professional duty while raising a family. Her presence is a deliberate inversion of the schoolmarm/saloon gal binary motif of the genre's classics. In the film's backstory, Samuel's abandonment of his wife saddled her with hard work and led to her early death. This, in turn, resulted in Magdalena's hatred of her father and her empowered feminist character. She remains the most dynamic figure in this avenger's tale. (For more on Blanchett, see Chapter 3.) The other avenger, Samuel, rediscovers a need for family while on the hunt for his missing granddaughter. He possesses the initiative to reclaim the lost girl, while also possessing a native's approach to tracking. Further, he carries a "witch doctor's" knowledge, as seen when he halts Blanchett's growing sickness by blessing a lock of her hair. His "savage"-cum-frontiersman's knowledge blurs the lines between each. With such villains to deal with — we should take note that the kidnapping natives have been perverted by white mercenaries (having worked as trackers for jeopardized cavalrymen) — Samuel must face an extreme counterforce, a strain common in other recent avenger films. A lieutenant (Val Kilmer) and his cavalry offer little help, and members grow more threatening to Samuel when they judge him as "savage." In this sense, the film borrows from the noir tradition, in which the ineffectiveness of the law calls for an unofficial investigator, here embodied by Jones (the actor's Westerner, Ed Tom Bell in *No Country for Old Men*, faces another powerful villain [see Chapter 16]).

Jones's directorial debut, *The Three Burials of Melquiades Estrada* (2005), written by Guillermo Arriaga, also features an extreme counterforce.[8] This film's avenger takes on the American Border Patrol and border politics, and Jones's character is therefore one of his most personal and political. Pete Perkins (Jones) undertakes an absurdist quest, a nature surfacing in the film's tone. Vengeance cannot be had; the best he can achieve is a *protest* against the crimes of the Border Patrol.

Like *No Country for Old Men*, also starring Jones, the milieu of *Three Burials* revises the classical American Western into a contemporary setting. Frontier mentality — i.e., the American colonists self-imposed right to the land — has inspired border politics. The westward charter of white settlers is now the anxiety of affluent America against poverty-stricken Mexico. The Border Patrol — the modern "Texas Rangers," if you will — polices the division of white America and southern neighbors, while the law upholds it. Yet, our protagonist, the rancher Pete (Jones), honors the work of the dispossessed (an "illegal" Mexican immigrant) and makes a place for him. He welcomes the services of Melquiades (Julio Cedillo), who takes up ranch work with Pete, and the two become friends.

As a man of the land more than domesticity, Pete relates to the displaced Melquiades. The former has traces of the classical man of action, as a loner with no family; he finds kinship only on the prairies, where he works. His romantic connection is to a married waitress, who also sleeps with a local sheriff named Belmont (Dwight Yoakam). Yet, Pete is especially in tune with his duties — he recognizes Melquiades's work ethic and is fluent in his language. Having become a close friend to "Mel," Pete agrees to watch over him like a father figure, a common role for Jones in his other avenger films. Here, Jones sets up a romantic tryst between Mel and a young blonde — ironically, the wife of the Border Patrol officer who will accidentally shoot Melquiades. This sense of fate is characteristic of screenwriter Arriaga (*Amores Perros, 21 Grams,* and especially *The Burning Plain,* his directorial effort), who's also known for the fractured narrative style as seen in this film, which reveals Melquiades's murder through multiple perspectives. Melquiades never feels safe in a land that will use his cheap labor but never accept him. Should anything happen to him, he asks Pete to return his body to Mexico. He can't bear the thought of being buried among the land of "billboards" above the border.

A Border Patrol officer, Mike Norton (Barry Pepper), shoots Melquiades after the latter fires at a coyote. Though an accidental death, it happens while Mike goofs off on the job, out in the fields with a pornographic magazine. Jones and Arriaga depict Mike as a public servant without a conscience. Having relocated from Cincinnati, he has little sense of the complex situation near the border. He remains expressionless on and off the job, and provides little intimacy as a husband. He has "quickie" sex with his wife, Lou Ann (January Jones), in his kitchen when he impulsively bends her over. He gives a mock-intimate line only to get her ready for his rutting. On the job, he chases a Mexican woman, who tries to cross the border, as if running down a beast. After jumping onto her from a vantage point, he strikes her on the face, letting his own rage show in a mock man-of-action display. His superior doesn't tolerate it, yet we know such displays will continue.

Even if it has better intentions, the Border Patrol enforces policies without considering the morality behind them. Pete's brief investigation reveals bullets at the scene of Melquiades's death, and knowledge of who shot him from his lover, who overhears the police discussing it. Pete tries to take on the matter legally, when he demands that Mike be arrested. But the case has already been buried — a symbolic burial highlighting the eponymous triumvirate (the first is the shallow grave into which Mike buries Melquiades; the second, Mel-

Pete Perkins (Tommy Lee Jones), plagued by the death of his friend in *The Three Burials of Melquiades Estrada* (2005, Sony Pictures Classics).

quiades's re-burial by the police; and the third, his rightful interment by Pete in Mexico, with the unwilling help of Mike).

The Border Patrol's actions and the local police's cover-up urge the avenger to action. Pete takes on the criminal beyond the law by kidnapping him. His ruthless invasion of Mike's home recalls the man of action's imperative as realized by the revisionist Westerns of the New Hollywood era, wherein Machiavellian motives are in order. After entering the mobile home, Pete pistol-whips Mike into submission and threatens the life of his wife, whom he already knows through the double-date tryst with Melquiades. Pete's unlawful power swells against modern frontier politics. The invasion becomes more criminal when he ties up the wife and leads Mike away at gunpoint. Their first stop is to Mel's (wrongful) place of rest (his second burial), where Pete will force Mike to dig up the body.

The film mixes the actions of the avenger/mercenary Pete with absurdist humor — as stated above, such a tone suits a battle that cannot be won. Mike turns into a leashed captive on horse and foot, somewhat like Lucky to the slave-driving Pozzo in Samuel Beckett's *Waiting for Godot*. Pete's journey moves into rural territories of Mexico, visually pure as shown by Jones and Arriaga. Pete and Mike live within the elements, encountering only loners along the way. Pete shows himself as one with the raw desert, while Mike, a would-be man of action, withers. Their treatment of Mel's body, a comical piece of rotting flesh, shows the true nature of these "men of the plains." Pete honors life, even in its decomposed state, while the body is merely an annoyance to the guilty Mike. The true Westerner forges on, morally grounded in his duty to justice.

Pete has grown criminal in his kidnapping, but lets Mike go after they bury Melquiades and Pete forces Mike to beg for forgiveness. The crime Jones avenges in a more recent film also cannot be truly avenged — only justified. In the beginning of Paul Haggis's *In the Valley of Elah* (2007), co-written by Haggis and Mark Boal, Jones's character, Hank, instructs an immigrant school employee to reposition an upside-down American flag, noting that it flies as such only when America is under absolute attack. His comment about the flag proves ironic, since he will develop into an avenger against the military system. By the film's end, he will invert the flag again, knowing that war has left the land in peril. Like *The Three Burials*, this film is based, albeit loosely, on real events that took place in Fort Benning, Georgia.[9] By moving the story to New Mexico, the film reorients Jones's character to a Western setting; this change helps to create a subplot concerning possible drug dealing, while Jones's character investigates and attempts to avenge another kind of murder on the frontier.

In *Valley*, Jones's avenger, Hank Deerfield, investigates his missing son, Mike, an enlisted private who's just returned from Iraq. By the end, Hank has to face the unfortunate legacy of the Iraq War: its effects on returning soldiers. Now more of an investigator than in *The Three Burials* (in which Pete learns the truth fairly early and takes immediate action), Hank hunts through the hidden policies of the local police and the policing factions of Fort Rudd, the fictional base from which Mike goes missing.

Jones's avenger in *Valley* may be the purest man of action in all the films discussed in this chapter. When Hank, a former criminal investigator for the Army, learns of his son's disappearance, with little thought he prepares for the trip. When his wife, Joan (Susan Sarandon), tells him it's a two-day drive, he responds, "For some people." Throughout the film, he distances himself from his wife, communicating with her only about their missing son. Later, after their son's body has been found, she blames his way of life for Mike's enlistment and death. Still cold to his wife, he says that he cannot sit idly and listen to her cry. If there is an emotional core to Hank, it's buried beneath his cold, stoic imperative.[10]

When Mike's enlisted friends become suspects, Hank maintains an idealistic view of warfare: that it's impossible for one to fight alongside someone, then kill him. He suspects drug-related/Mexican gang involvement. When Mike's Mexican co-private becomes a lead suspect, Hank pushes for his arrest, and even crosses the line by getting involved in it. His latent racism arises when he calls this soldier with a record a "wetback," provincial ignorance as much as a trace of old-time frontier racism (see Eastwood at the beginning of *Gran Torino*). Director Paul Haggis even juxtaposes Jones's trademark weathered face with the computer on which he researches. The videos retrieved from Mike's camera (discussed below) show vivid but tough truths.

The old-time nature of Hank resurfaces when he tells a bedtime story to David (Devin Brochu), the son of local detective Emily Sanders (Charlize Theron). It's the tale of David and Goliath, and their meeting in the Valley of Elah. Briefly scorning the mother for not sharing the Biblical ancestry behind her son's name, he then tells the boy of the underdog's triumph, one that he wishes to achieve. The eponymous story, however, reveals the irony behind Hank's quest. The boy later asks his mother why a child was chosen to defend the city, and we know that, even if David has the ability to defeat the great enemy, he must take the experience with him. So it is for most of the contemporary soldiers, resulting in their post-traumatic stress disorder. Mike's murder occurred after PTSD led to Mike's breakdown while out one night; his similarly affected, enlisted friends reacted by stabbing him in a frenzy. The ordeal becomes a tragedy of PTSD's effects, all existing in the backstory but resurfacing in the film as a torment. While "David" in the parable represents young American warriors, Hank cannot defeat the enemy that has consumed his son. It is an institutional curse.

Hank Deerfield (Tommy Lee Jones) initially follows procedure to find his missing son in *In the Valley of Elah* (2007, Warner Independent Pictures).

Earlier, while still searching for the truth, Hank investigates the world of the base as much as he can. When talking to one of Mike's friends, later a suspect, the friend notes that Mike just wanted to help the good guys and defeat the bad — an echo of Hank's imperative as an avenger and descendant of the classical men of action. With little help from local or military police (except for Theron's rebellious investigator), Hank wants to reveal the workings of a criminal underworld, allegedly drug/gang-related, but actually the workings of a greater (military) institution. While investigating this modern frontier/wasteland, Hank sneaks an important piece of evidence from Mike's barrack: his video camera/cellphone. By bringing it to a technician, Hank receives downloaded video files from the damaged phone, one at a time. These videos arrive in his email at an interval. They reflect the slow-developing investigation, but also act like the slow-burn of truth revealing itself. In the noir tradition, an indomitable influence of the past — what Mike had experienced overseas — plagues the current narrative, and through this cellphone device Haggis and co-screenwriter Mark Boal show how the fatalism of past events have permanently altered the present. One video shows Mike growing desensitized to violence, putting a sticker of a popular skateboard logo on a charred body of an Iraqi, and even torturing a captive one. (It's revealed that an ironic nickname Mike had acquired, "Doc," referred to this practice.) When Mike's body is found, his status changing from missing to deceased, the footage is intercut with a video Hank receives, of Mike running over an Iraqi boy. And yet a flashback later in the film shows Mike solemnly documenting the image, perhaps just a wishful thought for Hank. Beyond his juvenile glee at war, military policy makes him an accomplice to crimes against humanity and a sure victim of PTSD. The crime against him is everlasting and omnipotent.

12

New Paths to Justice
Clint Eastwood's
Late-Career Crime Films

In 2008, rumors abounded that Walt Kowalski, the principal character in *Gran Torino*, would be Clint Eastwood's last starring role. At the film's end, Kowalski dies from numerous bullets, albeit ones that he's called forth in a moment of sacrifice. A gang continues to terrorize Kowalski's young Korean American neighbors; hence, he chooses to stage a crime (i.e., his own death) in front of many witnessing neighbors. Thus came the most selfless moment of any Eastwood character, and the actor's sign-off to a career onscreen. Having become a celebrated director, and one of the finest working in the classical Hollywood style, Eastwood still had many films ahead of him, if only behind the camera. Thankfully, he will help keep the tradition of plot-driven, character-based drama alive onscreen.

Kowalski sacrifices himself by upturning the star's iconic image: Eastwood as "man of action." Eastwood made his career in the 1960s/1970s by playing characters with solutions, those who weighed goals over the morality of achieving them. The personas of his early career—Sergio Leone's "The Man with No Name" and "Dirty Harry"—are surefire, rough, and effective even if their obstacles grow large. (His first onscreen persona, as Rowdy Yates on the 1959–1965 television series *Rawhide*, remained goal-centered, in a very Eastwood style: deliver the cattle in a rough, likable manner.) Eastwood's loner in Sergio Leone's Italian Westerns never resisted a call to action: in *A Fistful of Dollars* (1964), Eastwood's character takes down three men in a quick draw, with room for some pre-shooting trash-talk. His protagonist in *The Outlaw Josey Wales* (1976)—something of a commentary on "The Man with No Name," though operating in a similar spirit—explains his ability to shoot down many opponents in a matter of seconds (he comments on a quick analytical eye as a trait of the renegade hero). Harry Callahan, a character of few (yet iconic) words, doesn't have such grace. He pursues outsized villains (psycho killers, terrorists) until he can blast them away as the final step to justice.

Gran Torino's Kowalski shows traces of this ruthless avenger. The aged autoworker may embody such a mentality — not on the city streets tracking villains, but as a hard-headed solver of conflicts on the job or at home. We'd guess that Kowalski loved renegade cop flicks and shoot-'em-ups in the neighborhood movie house — before it was torn down and the reels were forwarded to the new multiplex. The aged viewers of *Gran Torino* receive a dual hit: by seeing the everyman (bigoted, yet likable) Walt perish, they witnessed the death of their icon, who's also a surrogate for the viewer. Perhaps the resurgence of liberalism contrary to Bush had urged Eastwood, the compassionate Republican, to kill off his avenger (likely hearsay, and hardly our purpose here).

By witnessing the death of an icon, Eastwood fans also witnessed the last rites of a film movement. As this book discusses throughout, the pure, old-time avenger is now obsolete: the new avenger films reconsider personal justice through politics (see *The Three Burials of Melquiades Estrada* [2005], Chapter 10) or through gender (see Jodie Foster's victim-cum-avenger in Neil Jordan's *The Brave One*). Otherwise, filmmakers deconstruct rogue cops as

Gran Torino's Walt Kowalski, the "last" avenger to be played by Clint Eastwood (2008, Warner Bros. Pictures).

absurdist figures (see Werner Herzog's *Bad Lieutenant* [2009], discussed in Chapter 17, which itself revised the 1992 Abel Ferrara/Harvey Keitel misfire). Eastwood, now principally a director, appears in films like a shadow among revised archetypes: he always moves to resolve problems, but with more consideration.

Since 2000, in interviews (which he's always been reticent to give) Eastwood has dismissed the idea that his films comment on the ruthless archetypes that made him.[1] At the end of *Gran Torino*, the filmmaker either admits his self-commentary, or drops a playful jest on his fans. The sincerity behind the cinematic moment would make the latter seem doubtful. Kowalski, in a cheeky recreation of the "The Man with No Name's" multi-villain shoot-out, pulls out a lighter in lieu of a pistol. The menace and actions of his opponents, Hmong American gangsters, have grown unmanageable for the oldschool avenger. To defeat the gangsters, Eastwood must submit — though his bloody coughs throughout the film have signaled him as terminally ill.[2] Nonetheless, his family has dismissed him as old-time, out-of-date. The death of Walt's wife begins the film and signals the beginning of his isolation. He continues to live in what was once a center of working-class laborers, of second-generation European stock. Now it's the home of minority immigrants, which Walt initially regards with crusty insensitivity. Yet, Walt finds a "family" among Hmong American immigrants, and thus becomes a mentor to two teenaged neighbors. For them, he becomes a *passive* avenger.

The old-time Eastwood would avenge on call (as in the *Dirty Harry* series), or would avenge after witnessing a devastating personal loss (as in *The Outlaw Josey Wales*). The contemporary Eastwood still avenges, though not from a knee-jerk urge; he now supports personal relationships and communities. Action-based storytelling serves the filmmaker's career-long aspirations, to find a satisfying directing style: simple, direct, yet human (intentions he had from the start). This mature style shows how Eastwood's films have grown from competent genre entries to innovative works of crime-themed drama. These include his recent treatments of the mentor-hero as avenger, the victim archetype (2007's *The Changeling*), and a synthesis of these two archetypes and the criminal figure in 2003's *Mystic River*, his finest rendition of the crime film. The genres never left Clint Eastwood; they have bloomed into a distinct form of humanism.

We can understand Eastwood's resistance to self-analysis. His filmmaking approach is so natural and immediate — he shoots very few takes — that it appears instinctual. (More concerned with storytelling than supporting an ideology, he shares much with predecessor John Ford.) Eastwood likes to work quickly and not belabor any moments in his films. When directing a scene, his primary focus is the people he is filming, as he looks for actions that reveal character. He captures their instincts, resulting in an actor-reliant filmmaking style. He has less interest in a shot's formal design, unlike Leone, whose visual style borrowed more from Hitchcock and John Ford's long shots. In fact, such a formal style would seem anti-human to Eastwood, who takes more from actors' directors like Howard Hawks and Preston Sturges.

By looking to Eastwood's early career, we could misread how his style developed. When working on projects for Leone, Eastwood grew uncharacteristically detached during one of the actor's trademark films, *The Good, The Bad, and the Ugly* (1966).[3] As the final entry in the "Dollars Trilogy," the film helped make him an icon, in Europe first, then in America after the film appeared in 1967, just a year after the U.S. release of *A Fistful of Dollars*. The year saw a new moment in Hollywood, when filmmakers began featuring antiheroes in lieu of the classical protagonist, and the classical myths began to be reevaluated (most notably in that year's *Bonnie and Clyde*, a revision of the gangster film inspired by the French New Wave). Similarly, Leone revised the classical Western to highlight the violent nature of the American mythos. Curiously enough, he came upon the conceit by adapting Akira Kurosawa's *Yojimbo* (1961), a Western set in medieval Japan.

Eastwood was at first thrilled to make Leone's Westerns, as a means of breaking into films and away from the small screen, though Leone's perfectionism soon grated on him. Perhaps Leone ironically inspired the fast-and-instinctual tendency in Eastwood, who would form his own production company, Malpaso, to launch his film career in the United States. Eastwood would create a film style through his approach to making them. He would keep control over the final product by hiring his own directors, craftsmen from whom he would learn the trade.

Even if Eastwood's filmmaking style differed from Leone's, he still worked off the Italian director's narrative trope: the loner who serves up ruthless vengeance. This revisionist style of the Western goes back to Howard Hawks's *Red River* (1948) but, more directly, to John Ford's *The Searchers* (1956), in which John Wayne's man of action goes from hero to mercenary.[4] The film's iconic final scene, in which he cannot enter the homestead, shows that the prototypical man of action may grow too ruthless to rejoin society after his mission. Similar commentary appears in George Stevens's *Shane* (1953), in which the eponymous hero must depart after saving a budding frontier community. After *The Searchers*, *Shane*, and the Westerns of Anthony Mann, men of action onscreen could not hide their renegade instincts, a tendency appearing in Leone's work and solidified by Sam Peckinpah in *The Wild Bunch* (1969). Eastwood returned to the United States as a deconstruction of its storytelling tradition began. The myth of taming the West revealed its bloody truths.

After bringing some of his *Rawhide*-era television directors to his film projects, Eastwood found Don Siegel, whose *Invasion of the Body Snatchers* (1956) the actor found impressive.[5] Eastwood's partnership with Siegel eventually led to the creation of Eastwood's most iconic American role, "Dirty Harry" Callahan. The first entry of a series that would run into the late 1980s, named for its character, is an urgent, street-smart, gritty tale, a major contribution to solidify the Vietnam-era renegade-cop genre, along with *The French Connection* (1971) and *Bullitt* (1968). This era of the New Hollywood welcomed sex and violence onscreen, as productions geared toward young audiences while reflecting the unpopularity of the Vietnam War. In such a mood, justice was dealt ruthlessly, with the surviving avengers hardly moral.

Eastwood returned to the Western, mostly playing variations of "The Man with No Name." His first Western in American post–Leone, *Hang 'Em High* (1968), posits Eastwood as pure avenger. In the opening minutes, his botched hanging sends him on a quest for revenge. *High Plains Drifter* (1973), the first Western directed by Eastwood and released the same year as the first *Dirty Harry* sequel, added an existential, somewhat supernatural flavor to the Eastwood avenger, while relying on the same motivation and mentality.

The Outlaw Josey Wales (1976), although showing renegade tendencies, plays as a human take on the avenger. Immediately, the family of Wales (Eastwood) is killed by a ravaging pro–Union posse. Wales embarks on an education of his own, as he becomes a protector/accomplice to Lone Watie (Chief Dan George), who offers some humorous wisdom. The film, which Eastwood took over from director Philip Kaufman,[6] shows intimate direction (especially regarding Eastwood's interaction with the character Lone Watie), which Eastwood would later trademark. And yet the film has shocking, impulsive images, in which spectacle is favored over character. In Wales's initial descent, when he cannot defend his family, a slash across his face appears like a curse of an ex-soldier who has chosen a life of passivity (farming). The bucolic life represents emasculation. We'd guess that the scene was helmed by Kaufman, whom Eastwood accused of exploitation of the narrative for such sensationalism. Kaufman wasn't fired until he filmed the attempted rape of Laura Lee (Sondra Locke) in a manner that Eastwood found intolerable.

Through the 1970s, Eastwood mastered his starpower by developing his three famous personas: "The Man with No Name," the avenging cop and, additionally — and most financially successful, as it turned out — his "redneck" rumbler. Through the variety of roles, Eastwood never ran out of acting work as he developed his style behind the camera. Through the 1980s and 1990s, Eastwood continued to direct adaptations of procedural novels, knowing his rogue cop wouldn't miss the mark. To see his filmmaking style grow, and his treatment of the avenger archetype, we come to 1985's *Pale Rider*, a loose remake of *Shane*. This film is a notable entry in the history of the Western, in which genre fiction grows into drama. In *Pale Rider*, the Eastwood avenger (who calls himself "preacher") arrives in a small California town in which a local banker is trying to seize territory belonging to miners.

After this rendition of the classical Western, the filmmaker moved to historical drama, through a biopic of Charlie Parker (*Bird* [1988]). Eastwood gave his lead, acting-powerhouse-in-the-making Forest Whitaker, room to realize a troubled jazz great. Yet, a problem that would return to Eastwood's direction appeared. His fast, instinctive approach — a minimum number of takes while letting the actors mold their own performances — resulted in self-conscious supporting performances, namely from Diane Venora as Parker's wife, Chan. With much conviction from Whitaker, we overlook the shortcoming, though misfire performances would come again in Eastwood's films. By this time, Eastwood aimed to be a filmmaker of few words — known to accept scripts, pare down the dialog to a minimum, and focus on action and the heart of the character. Realized by this filmmaker, the dialog-heavy *Bird* isn't always graceful.

Eastwood's mainstream films continued to please his parent company, Warner Bros., while he took on experiments in between each project. In *White Hunter Black Heart* (1990), a curious though forgotten entry, Eastwood performs and directs a revision of the life of John Huston, who gets distracted by Hemingwayesqe hunting while trying to make a film resembling *The African Queen*. The project, which interprets the preceding film and myth, led Eastwood towards a major breakthrough, a major step toward his maturation as a filmmaker. He would achieve it by revising a genre that whetted him.

His 1992 film, *Unforgiven*, captured success on many levels. Following Kevin Costner's revisionist Western, *Dances with Wolves* (1990), Eastwood's film appeared when the mainstream was ripe for a retelling of, or should we say truth-seeking beneath, the Western mythos. *Unforgiven* didn't deliver a visceral revenger's take, although the unlikely villain of the film, Sheriff Little Bill Daggett (Gene Hackman), is ruthless in his method of keeping his town "clean." The film works in the classical mold, with a noble hero, Eastwood's badman who has made good rising to protect a community in peril. A clever turn in the narrative has Eastwood's Bill Munny and his small posse aiding a group of prostitutes. The saloon girl, a remnant of the genre's Golden Age (when censorship bleached her duties into "dance hall girl"), had been an unexplored archetype — deployed mostly to color a story, unless she proved to have a heart of gold and was hence worthy of marriage (as is Dallas to John Wayne's Ringo Kid in *Stagecoach*). Here, Eastwood and writer David Webb Peoples depict the perils for such women in the old West.

At first, Munny just wants the bounty for the man who slashed a prostitute's face. Then Eastwood's avenger addresses the morality of his goal. In dialog-based scenes, when he comes to learn the motivation of his cohorts Ned Logan (Morgan Freeman), and the Schofield Kid (Jaimz Woolvett), Munny shows an understanding justice. Eastwood's eye and handling of actors captures action as well as human interaction, as does George Stevens in *Shane*. Through *Unforgiven*, Eastwood realized the figure that would shape has late-career crime films: the introspective avenger. It was Dirty Harry reborn, a wiser Phoenix rising from the ashes. In later films, other actors would play the role for Eastwood and show as much awareness.

The figure appears in Eastwood's *A Perfect World* (1993), *Absolute Power* (1997), *True Crime* (1999), and *Blood Work* (2002), though the films seem aimed to please their parent company. The reflection came to full bloom in 2003's *Mystic River* (discussed below). In the films in which he acts, Eastwood plays an old-time loner with glory days but no close family in the present. In early Eastwood vehicles, a love interest and/or family would give the heroes a weakness: hence, Dirty Harry operates as a loner, almost in the noir detective style, or one like Josey Wales would love only to have them taken from him. From *Unforgiven* onward, Eastwood's figures have remained loners: if he's a parent, his children are at a distance; if a widower or a bachelor, he is removed from other relations. Though in Eastwood's later work, an avenger lives in isolation but finds a new relationship that drives his action. While the widower Munny in *Unforgiven* has children, he must leave them to embark on his quest. In *True Crime*, Eastwood's character, Steve Everett, is married with children, but remains removed from them through extramarital affairs and work as a crime reporter. The late-career Eastwood hero must make a personal sacrifice to avenge and, in turn, find personal redemption through building relationships and at times entering a community. The plots have other spiritual strains, such as a crisis of religious faith and an attempt to resolve it through action. Regardless of a film's specific motifs, Eastwood's lead characters make decisions based on their conviction, while religious belief comes on the side. When facing obstacles, Eastwood's later heroes investigate their conscience: the antithesis of the old-time *act-now, consider-later* Eastwood (anti)philosophy.

This sense of justice shows up in the 2004 non-crime film, *Million Dollar Baby*, which furnishes a dilemma that, for Eastwood's character, Frankie Dunn, requires action. The film presents an unlikely mentorship story, as does *Gran Torino* and the early Eastwood projects. Frankie agrees to train a female boxer, Maggie (Hilary Swank), after his initial resistance to do so. Their relationship provides a salvation for the nearly dried-up manager. Her passion brings out a glow that seemed to have died in Frankie years earlier. Yet, his real chance for redemption comes when he must take action for Maggie, in a life-or-death situation for her. Left paralyzed after an accident in the boxing ring, Maggie has lost all the passion that motivated her boxing aspirations, along with her literal life source. Though she lives on, she has figuratively perished and is trapped by paralysis. For Eastwood, motivation is realized by action, and his mentee has lost the ability to achieve that for herself. By acting against this debilitation, Frankie avenges an injustice against her (a metaphorical crime that happened by chance) by taking her life. If this mercy killing seems a universe away from Eastwood's justice in *Unforgiven*, his decision works off the same duty. He deliberates to himself, and is inspired by poetry and talks with Eddie Dupris (Morgan Freeman), a former trainee to Frankie who works in the gym. Frankie's choice to let Maggie go makes him something of a Christ figure, sacrificing the person who had "revived" him, for her own good. Yet, to him her predicament is an injustice, even if the Fates were the criminals. Now, he can only free the victim.

In the final crisis of *Gran Torino*, we see a connection to *Million Dollar Baby*, which proved popular and controversial, bringing an Academy Award nomination for Eastwood as actor and Oscar statuettes for him as director, as well as Swank and Freeman. Eastwood's Walt Kowalski in *Gran Torino* sees a dilemma present itself, and he chooses to become a deliberate Christ figure. "The Man with No Name"/"Dirty Harry" shifts into a passive redeemer,[7] who atones by releasing his guilt for killing a young enemy soldier in the Korean War. The avenger triumphs over evil (though through sacrifice), as in countless Eastwood productions — a marked difference from the prevailing villainy of recent crime films. In the process, Kowalski seals his inheritance to his "new" family (i.e., his neighbors), by granting them the ultimate gift (safety, freedom) with the film's titular boon going to Thao (Bee Vang) who, under the gang's influence, had tried to steal the car earlier in the film. As Maggie dies, Frankie seals the same familial bond to her.

In *The Changeling*, written by J. Michael Straczynski and released the same year as *Gran Torino*, Eastwood turned the theme of mentorship inside-out. This weepie-turned-avenger tale opens with a solid parent-child relationship, in the form of the real-life Christine Collins (Academy Award nominee Angelina Jolie) and her son, Walter, in 1928. When the boy goes missing, and the Los Angeles Police Department drags its feet in their search, a single, working mother (a supervisor to phone operators) must endeavor to find her child. The fact that Collins is without a husband and has to meet her son at home after work brings some latent family-values guilt upon her — we can imagine Hollywood censors playing up this angle, were the story filmed in the 1920s. As a true-life story, we can only speculate about the forces that worked against Collins. The film makes clear that she's not widowed (a usual solution for sympathetic Golden Age weepies) but had been abandoned, a progressive film treatment. Though when Collins notes that the boy's father shirked responsibility, Eastwood's narrative places blame and sympathy where each belongs.

The greater condemnation, however, is upon the authorities: the 1920s LAPD, and the city mayor. The police officials take the role of the criminals (territory already explored onscreen in Curtis Hanson's deft *L.A. Confidential*). They show not only negligence to Collins, but corruption. When her dilemma goes public over the radio, the LAPD quiets the bad publicity by bringing a "changeling" child to her — a boy abandoned at a roadside diner. She insists that the child isn't hers, while they hush her protests as photojournalists capture the "reunion" at a train station. The film's eponymous motif recalls a tale from European folklore, which itself stemmed from parental fear over a child's safety. Invoking this archetype, the film reflects collective fear. In this Eastwood picture, the central figure is no longer an avenger, although one appears early and proves effective.

The avenger is the Rev. Gustav Briegleb (John Malkovich), a church pastor who, through the power of broadcasting, alerts the public about Collins's peril. In a radio address early in the film, he sends out a pious prayer for Collins, and then delivers a strong critique of the LAPD. Briegleb is characteristic of the Eastwood avenger: he works off moral principles and exists as an agent of action. He addresses large problems while focusing on personal ones, as do Frankie and Walt. Briegleb uses his status to become an unofficial avenger as powerful as any other. With awareness and support, he helps Collins to be released from a sanitarium, in which the police have committed her as she would not sign a document confirming the boy to be hers and burying the cover-up. Without the use of violence, Briegleb cannot force the alleged actual criminal, a serial child killer, into confessing that he took Walter's life along with the others, though he is convicted for it. His approaching execution is a filmic ticking clock that Briegleb cannot outrun. Justice only goes so far, even with such a powerful avenger.

The later Eastwood makes use of ambivalent justice. *Mystic River* (2003), his contemporary masterpiece in the crime film, delivers vengeance-cum-sacrifice. At the film's crisis point, childhood friends Jimmy Markum (Sean Penn) and Dave Boyle (Tim Robbins) — still living nearby, yet estranged — face each other. The former, with a weapon, wants a confession from the other before executing him, on the banks of the eponymous waterway. The vengeance is for the murder of Markum's daughter, and Markum thinks Boyle guilty, though he's really something of a victim.

Mystic River's strengths are its tight plot and all-around strong performances. But most unique is its treatment of the crime film's archetypal figures. The film begins in the past, with three childhood friends — Markum, Boyle,

Jimmy Markum (Sean Penn) with the suspect Dave Boyle (Tim Robbins) in *Mystic River* (2003, Warner Bros. Pictures).

and a third, Sean Devine (Kevin Bacon). Boyle is abducted and becomes a sacrifice that saves the two other boys, whose two initials remain scratched in sidewalk cement, with Boyle's having a ghostly absence. Somehow getting away after being repeatedly abused, Boyle lives on as proof of the horrors taken against the unfortunate. Markum and Devine grow to be successful, the former as an ex-con who's made good as a shop-owner, and Devine as a homicide investigator. Once the narrative's central crime appears — the murder of Markum's daughter — these two men take on the archetypal crime roles. Devine investigates the murder, and the uncanny resurfaces when Boyle becomes a suspect: as in modern proverbial thought, the abused is likely to become an abuser. In a similar vein, Markum feels his criminal instincts resurface to seek out Boyle and make him pay for the action. Markum's vengeance, working off his past, makes him a blurred criminal-victim-avenger, a dynamic crime archetype possible only in the current genre style.

Boyle, the *pseudo*-criminal-cum-victim (we soon learn he's innocent), remains like a curse that Markum, and even Devine, must kill away. Whether he committed the crime or not, fate swirls down upon him, and order is established once he is gone. Though the three main characters take on different dimensions, and the film grounds them in a victim-criminal-avenger triad, they take on deeper symbolism. For example, Devine, the putative avenger,

The "surviving consciences": Jimmy Markum (Sean Penn) and homicide detective Sean Devine (Kevin Bacon) in *Mystic River* (2003, Warner Bros. Pictures).

is estranged from his wife — she calls him throughout the film, only to hang up when hearing his voice. Devine is a Eastwood loner now mourning his situation, a victim trying to restore contact. He reunites with his wife, but *only after* Boyle's death. The community builds only when the putative guilty are gone. A notable character outside the triad suddenly disappears at this restored conclusion. Detective Whitey Powers (Laurence Fishburne) is a surrogate investigator partnered with the less-effective Devine. Powers disappears because the static "hunter" (though especially well drawn by Fishburne) has no place in this film's conclusion: the wrongful prey has been taken. Hence, *Mystic River* begs a Freudian reading, by looking at the three figures as one fractured consciousness, with Boyle as a fear returned from the repressed (in a lifetime fearing memories of abuse), and Markum's death instinct emerging to destroy the fear. When pain returns, the dark memory must be killed away, whence comes repression, and in turn, psychological violence if the fear re-emerges. Powers accentuates Devine's goals while the hunt is still on, but once the pain has been killed, there's no need for his surrogate. Reflected through crime conventions, this psychological dimension allows for a dynamic character piece. Through the plot's resolution we realize how dynamic and integral each player is.

To argue that Eastwood was aware of this dimension to Dennis Lehane's source novel would be fruitless. It's more appropriate to highlight the victimization of this crime film, how the anxiety to establish order necessitates an avenger's sacrifice of an innocent. Thus, *Mystic River* is a dark entry for Eastwood, one focused on the harm of vengeance, in lieu of his other humanist avenger films. Eastwood broke new ground by fashioning leading players into agents of action and emotion. In his best work, Eastwood masters conventions and, through them, finds drama.

13

Woody Allen's Match*(ed)* Point
The Crime of Class

Like many films analyzed in this book, *Match Point* came as a surprise. By the early 1990s, the film-going community expected Woody Allen to produce one new film per year. Once in a while a notable Allen film gets attention — such as the Jazz Age homage *Sweet and Lowdown* (1999), which earned star Sean Penn an Oscar nomination — or Allen's light-comedy, *Small Time Crooks* (2000), which set aside the filmmaker's usual attention to the anxieties and self-loathing of the upper-middle class. Many of his other late-career works seem to pop up just before they drop off, without much notice. Two of his recent films (as of this writing), *Whatever Works* (2009) and *Midnight in Paris* (2011), gained notice with their inclusion of Allen-inspired surrogates, Larry David and Owen Wilson, respectively. Such self-reverence is common in Allen's work, especially in Woody-ish roles like John Cusack's in *Bullets Over Broadway* (1994) and Kenneth Branaugh's in the little-seen *Celebrity* (1998).

Even as a rare, attention-getting Allen picture, *Match Point* (2005) is a standout. In a short time before its release, the film gained notice as a fresh project for the writer-director, even if it spawned from familiar territory. A synopsis of the newer film reflects the influence of Allen's 1989 work, *Crimes and Misdemeanors*, which puts moral relativism face-to-face with crime and its guilt.

Crimes concerns an affluent ophthalmologist named Judah (Martin Landau), whose convenient extramarital affair with Dolores Paley (Angelica Huston) is growing beyond his control. With the rest of his life following a clean moral code, his one fault could draw everything else down, especially when his lover threatens to reveal their affair. Hence, Allen's film questions if personal interest — of an achiever, we should note — can trump an absolute sense of morality. When Judah considers the ease with which he could silence his problem, through a contract killing, he benefits from his class status and the connections it can provide to him. The narrative is hardly concerned with the authorities addressing the film's unsolved murder — thus the film, hardly one in the crime genre tradition, veers back toward character-based drama. Considering the associations to his name (Judah proper meaning "praise" but also invoking Judas) he must accept his betrayal to his unofficial love, yet never quite can, as his choice remains an unmanageable psychological burden, according to the film's final scene. With the happiness of his family life restored — they enjoy a classy party in this last scene — Judah here ponders the scenario that his choices have created. By telling his ordeal to Cliff Stern (Allen, who here acts as an authorial voice connecting to his own main character), Judah attempts to unburden himself but realizes, in terms of the *other* Judeo-Christian tradition, he now has a lifelong cross to bear.

This resolution is one of the most profound in the Allen filmography. The film's power was so lasting that fans had it fresh in mind when seating themselves to view *Match Point*. For those who came into the film fresh, independent of having seen *Crimes, Match Point's* theme was so masterfully delivered that only a director experienced with such material could have made the film.

Match Point comes 20 years after *Crimes and Misdemeanors*— after countless other Allen projects; the Mia Farrow/Soon Yi media debacle; and post–*Deconstructing Harry* (1997), in which Allen opened his misanthropic vein completely as opposed to letting it dribble in earlier works. *Deconstructing's* antihero, Harry Block, may be the most authentic Allen alter ego. Block (Allen) suits his own name when trying to write his newest novel. He's more adept at destroying his relationships or hurting the feelings of those close to him. The products of Block's imagination, portrayed in sequences that realize his fictional works, either symbolize the frustrations of his life — i.e., Death showing up at the door of a character who's trying to cheat on his wife — or attempts to restore order in it — i.e., when an actor (Robin Williams) comes out of focus, literally, and asks his family to readjust themselves for his sake. Block manages his characters' lives much better than his own; his life is the one narrative he can't master. And, similarly, the film finds him blocked on his current project. The duality of Block's life suggests a misanthropic sense of paranoia, that the world is out to get him. In this sense, Larry David, *Seinfeld* co-creator and *Curb Your Enthusiasm* writer/star (and *Whatever Works* star), is Allen's and Block's immediate descendant.

If *Deconstructing Harry* is the Allen oeuvre laid bare, then *Match Point* is *Crimes* purified. In *Match Point*, Allen clears away the dramatic roots of the film's 1989 predecessor and boils up the suspense. He thus finds the heat to realize the crime genre that was latent, though admittedly not needed, in his earlier work. I don't intend to dismiss *Crimes*— it is indeed a fine drama in which character is at one with the well-made plot: action stems from emotions, and never strays from them. But as a crime story, *Crimes* doesn't create the suspense to satisfy: we're concerned more with the choices that Judah makes than with the crime(s) that occur and the aftereffects. By honing close to Judah and making Dolores an unrealized, remote menace, *Crimes* remains distant from the threatening relationship. Whereas *Match Point*, a film about infidelity that leads one to kill, fully realizes the subject affair and all its suspense that's perversely addictive to viewers and damning to the characters involved.

While the 1989 film deploys a crime to draw the drama to a crisis (and conclusion), *Match Point* leans back to the classical crime traditions to revise them. The film bends the film noir tradition — along with its offshoot, the erotic thriller — into direct social commentary.

Crimes would suggest that the crime film is alien territory to Allen, and that *Match Point* would be something of a genre breakthrough for a classical comic-dramatist. Yet Allen has his own occasional (if idiosyncratic) pedigree in the crime story. It was fodder for his comedy, yet this early use of the crime film reveals a genre expertise and was the filmmaker's exploratory grounds for his recent, and purest, crime film.

Questions fueled the early works of Woody Allen, both in his stand-up routines and his early storytelling on the stage and screen. His scenarios questioned normalcy by introducing forms of deviance, as if the status quo were asking to be disrupted. In his stand-up act, he often used a mock-autobiographical perspective, outlining stories that were fictional but are funny to imagine and hear. In this way he is interested in disrupting establishments that he depicts in "straw man" absurdity, much like his inspirations, Groucho Marx and Bob Hope. Both Marx and Hope worked in a heightened form of the fish-out-of-water scenario, i.e., in different situations not suitable for their characters, yet quite suitable grounds for their humorous iconoclasm. Similarly, Allen described cartoonish worlds in which his first-person alter-ego would wrack around, and thus deliver pure comedy from irony. Allen brought this style into full bloom in his narrative farces, beginning with his script for the film *What's New, Pussycat?* (1965) and running through his satires on dystopic fiction and Russian Literature/philosophy, the war film genre, *Sleeper* (1973) and *Love and Death* (1975), respectively.

The format of the narrative feature allowed room for Allen's wit. His earliest works — *Take the Money and Run* (1969), *Bananas* (1971), and even his script for *Pussycat*— play like modified stand-up routines, as do the films of the comics who inspired him. Allen's material was honed into "shaggy dog" narratives more dedicated to jokery than narrative arcs for story development.

In these films, each a series of set pieces, Allen's persona disrupts a system (lawful citizenship in *Take the Money*, a revolutionary group in *Bananas*), and *gets* disrupted by it (when law or revolution has its way with him). Essentially, Allen's early aesthetic emphasized the collision of normalcy and irreverence. Filmic storytelling in the American tradition is about causal relationships — conflicts rising, then concluding — while Woody Allen boiled such tendencies into a disruptive sensibility. Early Allen works use crime as an immediate means for this kind of disruption. Hence, we find the roots to Allen's tendency toward crime and his unique treatment of it.

The fond self-referential humor that begins *Take the Money and Run* — of a young Allen stand-in botching his theft of gumball machine contents — is more telling than it seems. The joke rests on the fact that the young character is a deliberately established presence (as a miniature version of the well-known comic, Allen) and a presence ironic to what we expect in this type of film: the caricatured youthful criminal, soon to be replaced by an adult character. The archetypal "baddie youth" has soiled hair, skin, and clothes: symbolically, Rousseauian purity fallen on hard times. Allen's young protagonist is Virgil Starkwell, a fair-skinned, bespectacled, and freckled nebbish, looking as though he were dropped into the situation by careless parents (the kind of self-deprecation of Allen's stand-up routines). He is an innocent, comically delivered into wrongdoing, where the crime leaves this perpetrator particularly dazed.

The other bits in the film play along the same logic and audience expectation. As unrelated bits at first, these routines nevertheless showed Allen's skill with language, timing, and verbal storytelling. As sequences in the early films, Allen deploys visual wit to nail the pun, which would become his trademark until he modified his comedy into a classical style. In another jest from *Take the Money*, Virgil Starkwell, now grown into the mature Allen, attempts to pull off a bank job. Incompetent before he even begins, Starkwell misspells a robbery note — by writing "gub" instead of "gun" — and, in another occurrence, he meets up with unexpected competition from another gang of robbers (a bit revised by the Monte Python troupe in 1979's *Life of Brian*). Crime is punishment to the Allen protagonist even before he can be caught and convicted.

Allen has always loved film and playing with genres; hence, after *Take the Money*, he didn't refrain from trying something outside the mockumentary. In *Bananas*, the satire on the politics of Central American revolutions, Allen is pushed into criminal acts, this time by the revolutionary gang which has captured him. (Curiously enough, it all happened because of a woman, a softened femme fatale in a cartoonish universe.) Again, the insecure Allen persona goes to the wrong side of the law.

The filmmaker changed genres again and again as he honed his farce aesthetic, becoming decidedly more highbrow with each outing. In *Love and Death* (1975), the mock-historical film stuffed with Bergmanesque soul-searching, the Allen persona is first employed by a noble side, the Russian resistance against the imperialistic French. (When his superior indicates the moves in battle that will lead to their win, Allen replies, "What do we win?") But later in the film, we see Allen further developing his comic crime treatment. By infiltrating Napoleon's castle, he has been assigned to assassinate the leader. It's an image of incompetence fashioned for comedy, and once again an image of insecurity made more inferior by a crime situation. Allen's character, Boris, gets in a mess to impress Sonja (Diane Keaton, an actor who became the [often unattainable] motivation for Allen's antiheroes). His quest ends in death, wrapping up the potential romance with the fatalism of the title's latter part. In death, he has a moment to ponder, before he follows the reaper (in a white sheet) to the beyond. The peril of unlawful acts offered only love's promise.

After *Love and Death* and *Sleeper*—another satire in which the Allen role joins another revolution, this one against an oppressive dystopic government—Allen realized his long-running filmmaking style. Instead of dropping characters into pure (if witty) farce, Allen let his literary sensibility inform his comedy. *Annie Hall* (1977), an undisputed classical romantic comedy, looks back to Allen's 1969 stage play, *Play It Again, Sam*, which flirted with such sentiment (a film version was later directed by Herbert Ross, from a script by Allen, and starring him). *Manhattan* (1979) also thrilled fans and gained new admirers, with a Bergman-inspired pastiche (*Interiors*, 1978) coming in between. In *Annie Hall* and *Manhattan*, Allen drops the crime story as a means for revealing his alter-ego's isolation. The new Woody Allen now belonged to the arthouse club he admired for years. The Allen role in these films has a legitimate go at romance, even if he ends up not winning the girl. Yet, this alter-ego remains a misfit of love, isolated by his attraction towards Hollywood beauties.

This late–1970s run may be the highlight of his career, and the one most studied, discussed, and revered. That *Annie Hall* and *Manhattan*, his most critically regarded films, will remain the prime source of Allen scholarship is obviously not our purpose here. Though, more importantly, these films were the first occasion he broke from crime film motifs. For the most part, the 1980s saw the filmmaker exploring his romantic drama, in the elite New York of the times (see the well-made scripts of 1986's *Hannah and Her Sisters* and 1988's *Another Woman*) or in period pieces (1987's *Radio Days*, 1985's *The Purple Rose of Cairo*), the exception being 1984's *Broadway Danny Rose* (about a literary agent chased by gangsters) and 1983's *Zelig*, Allen's impostor-hero once again subverting normalcy. After *Broadway*, Allen didn't pick up the crime film thread until the 1990s.

Bullets Over Broadway (1994), a notable entry between *Crimes* and *Match Point,* may be the most satisfying of the three, thanks to its excellent cast and constant laughs. (The Academy noticed Allen that year, giving Dianne Wiest a statuette, and Jennifer Tilly and Chazz Palminteri nominations for supporting roles.) In *Bullets,* Allen keeps things light and airy, suitable since he's looking to the 1930s gangland for his inspiration. Co-written by literary-adaptation director Douglas McGrath, the film is also a writer's tale concerning the immortal questions, "What is art?" (or, what if it is smothered by populism) and, "What makes an artist?" David Shane (John Cusack), the Allen counterpart, is a rising playwright who's tired of his work being butchered in production. Now that he insists on directing, he cannot find backing. Enter a mob boss, who insists that his dimwitted showgirl moll (Tilly) take the lead. The drama is light, somewhat literary, and high concept — promising conflict, ego flexing, and, naturally, some bullets.

But the clever turn is the goon brought in to watch over Tilly's Olive, the wanna-be actress moll. Cheech (Chazz Palminteri) is committed to his job as watchman, until he can no longer stand Shane's lofty dialog and begins rewriting it. (When helping Olive rehearse her lines, his reading of "how could you *concoct* a theory so *tenuous*" is a delight. The reading is both a comic rendering and commentary on literary language. Later, Cheech tells Shane flat out, "You got that problem: you don't write how people talk.")

Cheech is talent in the rough, one who's lived purely without artistic

Playwright David Shayne (John Cusack) gets helps from gangster Cheech (Chazz Palminteri) in *Bullets Over Broadway* (1994, Miramax Home Entertainment).

pretensions and therefore remains objective about the world. His bully-every-one attitude, whetted by his life of crime, has not perverted his talent — according to Allen and McGrath, the art runs deeper than morality. He nonetheless acts the criminal when knocking off Olive, a very moral decision in his eyes, since it will save his work of art. His action results in a mob hunt, a storyline told rather slightly, though it does bring the film's center, David, to his realization: that he is not an artist. Here, the crime narrative supports the development of the broader comic drama, and the character of Cheech makes *Bullets* into a revisionary genre work, beyond it being just a clever crime comedy. In fact, his personal moral imperative — to serve his own good over the well-being of others — echoes Judah's in *Crimes* and precedes *Match Point*.

Aside from *Crimes* and *Bullets*, to find *Match Point's* other predecessor we must look to a crime movement of the early 1980s, and the preceding decade that inspired it.

The early 1980s — the era following Allen's breakthrough — was marked by the influence of George Lucas and Steven Spielberg. Filmmakers reacted against the reactionary New Hollywood directors before them. From 1967 to 1969, films like *Bonnie and Clyde* (1967) and *Easy Rider* (1969) redefined Hollywood by breaking down the studio system and tapping into the power of younger audiences. The filmmakers brought independent producing to the mainstream with films featuring sex and violence. This model brought a new, personalized sensibility through the 1970s, until George Lucas's *Star Wars* (1977) brought Golden Age classicism back, through the reformatted adventure stories. The new fantastic journey was more knowing, with the filmmakers at times winking at their audience. Post–New Hollywood filmgoers were familiar with the conventions their favorite filmmakers tore down, and the new, movie-crazy filmmakers were ready to play the referential game. Lucas began in the New Hollywood style, as his *THX 1138* (1971) is a mod, anti-establishment take on dystopia. His next science fiction picture, of course, had another pedigree. Francis Ford Coppola, often mentioned in the same breath as Lucas and Spielberg, proves to be even more of a transitional figure, since his *Godfather* series was in line with New Hollywood but possessed the epic sensibility of the next film movement.

Classical motifs abound in *Stars Wars*, many of which recall the Western — from Luke Skywalker's return to his destroyed home on the planet Tatooine (Lucas has often mentioned the abduction scene in John Ford's *The Searchers* as an inspiration[1]) to a stagecoach chase reimagined, in the new film, as a ragtag bounty hunter's ship called the *Millennium Falcon* (which doubles as a "cavalry" coming to Skywalker's rescue near the end). The Lucas-produced and Spielberg-directed *Raiders of the Lost Ark* (1981), an often-comic adventure, was even more reflexive, with continual winks to Hawks and Golden Age swashbuckling which, like the *Star Wars* references, passed like a breeze over the heads of thrilled audience members.

George Lucas appears to have jump-started the era of genre pastiche, though it came before *Star Wars*. *Rocky* (1976), the film that had downbeat-ready audiences cheering unexpectedly (as would Lucas's film), was an old-time battler tale with an ironic hero. Spielberg brought back the classical quest in the 1975 sea-adventure-cum-horror film *Jaws*, which, along with *Star Wars*, created the 1970s blockbuster. Like the films by Buster Keaton and Harold Lloyd years earlier, new prankster filmmakers used genres to produce farce, as did Woody Allen in his early films (discussed earlier) and Mel Brooks (with the Western in 1974's *Blazing Saddles*, classical Universal Studios horror with *Young Frankenstein* [also 1974], pre-sound era in *Silent Movie* [1976] — a style that had worn out by the time Brooks made his mock space opera, *Spaceballs* [1987], long after the *Stars Wars* days).

With the return of classicism, it wouldn't take long for the crime genres to appear. Two years before *Rocky*, Roman Polanski's *Chinatown* (1974) appeared, the trademark New Hollywood neo-noir. This film redirected the path of the private eye noir archetype, who in the classical films investigates some repressed, underworld crime network. In *Chinatown*, the investigator reveals a broad-scale crime — i.e., one against an entire city, concerning fraudulent use of Los Angeles's water supply. *Taxi Driver* (1976) also brought noir sensibility to color film. The film's director, Martin Scorcese, revised the gangster mythos earlier in his *Mean Streets* (1973), a rough, episodic film that was largely improvised. Its irreverent take on the gangster was more in spirit with the New Hollywood's upending of genres. With *Taxi Driver*, Scorsese and Paul Schrader employ an avenger to right injustice in a modern, soiled noir landscape — Scorsese's home turf, New York City. This film makes its disaffected misfit into a hero, as did John Ford's *The Searchers*, which Schrader has noted was his inspiration. Yet, like *Mean Streets*, *Taxi Driver* is a holdover from the late '60s, while it reclaimed genre motifs. A more referential genre-fondness appeared in the Lucas/Spielberg age.

Yet, these allusions were scattered before *Star Wars*; afterwards they were expected. American mainstream film was about looking into the past, a postmodern sensibility that turned out to be hardly experimental in its streamlined form.

The re-emergence of crime conventions — namely, the noir style — brought about a new crime genre in the early 1980s. With the freedom to offer more sex and violence, thanks to the establishment of the ratings system, filmmakers employed convention to continue the tradition of neo-noir. Yet, the early 1980s neo-noirs were either conscious revisions of classical noirs —

Body Heat (1981) — or direct remakes reheated for the new times — i.e., Bob Rafelson's remake of *The Postman Always Rings Twice* (1981).

In these films the femme fatale figure becomes especially fatal. In *Body Heat*, like *Double Indemnity*, a woman lures an everyman, Ned Racine (William Hurt) to murder her husband. Her temptation doesn't come in flirtatious banter, as in Billy Wilder's 1944 classic, but in her outright sexual come-ons. But in the relationship, she takes full control, while Racine is a passive victim. In the remake of *The Postman Always Rings Twice*, a wanderer (Jack Nicholson) forces himself onto an unhappy wife of a gas-stop owner, Cora (Jessica Lange), as in the original. While Cora, the femme fatale, doesn't take the kind of control that the figure in *Body Heat* does, Rafelson invokes the vivid (and often brutal) sexuality of James M. Cain's original bestseller which was softened for the big screen 1946. (The other glaring example is in the film's ending, which, under the Motion Picture Production Code's influence, made Cain's antihero a blandly redemptive inmate heading for execution.)

This new, heated style of noir laid the groundwork for a budding crime genre, which turned out to have blockbuster potential: the erotic thriller. Popular crime films of the mid– to late–1980s used the femme fatale figure but, as did the neo-noirs previously discussed, made her into something beyond the portal into which a hero would fall. In 1987's *Fatal Attraction*, femme fatale Alex Forrest (Glenn Close) entices the hero, Dan Gallagher (Michael Douglas), into what seems like a casual encounter, until she continually stalks him, even re-establishing contact with him by feigning interest in buying his home. The one false move made by Dan, indulging in casual sex, turns into a full-blown nightmare in the hands of a psychotic fatale.

Similarly, the top-grossing *Basic Instinct* (1992) grabbed interest by promising a now-famous shot of Sharon Stone's undergarment-free crotch. Yet, the film redelivered the psycho-mistress premise we see in *Fatal Attraction* (the latter film also featuring Michael Douglas as the hero-victim). Thomas Leitch notes that these films show conflicting feelings toward sex, as equally alluring and treacherous.[2] The overpowering female figure reflects a fear of the liberated woman of the 1970s, much like the classical noir films do of the working women during World War II. Through the end of the 1990s, the fatale figure was again an accomplice to the hero more than a perpetrator (see John Dahl's *The Last Seduction*, 1994). In Woody Allen's *Match Point*, the male hero is once again given the blame he had been assigned prior to the late 1980s/early 1990s erotic thriller, partially because Allen's antihero is more developed than those in the preceding films.

Match Point concerns an aspiring outsider, a tennis instructor named Chris (Jonathan Rhys Meyers). He sees possessing a dreamy affair as a component to gaining wealth and prestige. The side-girl, Nola (Scarlett Johansson), is another material gain, and he treats it as such when it proves dangerous to his well-being. As in *Crimes*, Allen is intrigued by these dire matters, and offers a tone to match them in the newer film. Over the years, Allen has honed a long-take, multi-actor style of shooting. His camera frames all the players together, making them visually close, if not so emotionally, or he glides the camera to follow them. Often actors will walk out of frame while still holding the floor in speech, while Allen films an actor's reaction shot. Allen's approach recalls the foreign vérité works of the 1940s–1960s, of which the director has been fond, while maintaining his own style and personality.

But true to the classical noir tradition — and the broader American crime film, for that matter — Allen tightens his shooting style in *Match Point*. He tightens his usual room-wide style of shooting interiors. His shots are focused, his tone cold over the illicit passion heating up within. The camera resists following the players, as is Allen's habit — and if the camera does follow, it moves in nervy turns or jumps, the passions stifled by the cold framing.

Allen stays removed from the upper-class Hewett clan. To stay true to Chris's distant point of view, the filmmaker doesn't want us to know or even care about the family Chris wishes to join. Allen uses a similarly cold style when featuring the daughter, Chloe (Emily Mortimer) — on whom Chris

Match Point's Chris Wilton (Jonathan Rhys Meyers) finds temptation à la noir in the form of Nola Rice (Scarlett Johansson) (2005, DreamWorks).

cheats with Nola — an unusual choice, to be sure. In a more traditional crime narrative we'd care about her and root for justice, or be affected by her downfall. But such moral justice isn't Allen's concern. Chloe exists as a pawn, whom Chris toys with and manipulates — he is, after all, Allen's main interest. A moralistic critical approach would misdirect an understanding of Allen's modern crime study, as such a take would for Stanley Kubrick. It's subjective filmmaking, and in *Match Point*'s case, the player is a rather devious subject.

When looking back to the narrative archetype that Allen inherits (i.e., the James Cain film noir, centered on an outsider instead of a private eye), the tone suits the content. Noir is visually characterized by shadows with low-key lighting to accentuate them. Thus, the film casts the mood of the players' dark psyches into the objective filmic world. Working in modern color, Allen avoids noir pastiche and discards the now-clichéd shadows. His darkness appears as a visual chill — the camera placement and movement still, intent instead of darkened.

To match his tone to a setting, the New York–based filmmaker takes his tale to London. Using British culture thus may see trite, considering the very Americanized perspective in which Allen has operated over the years. Yet Allen's style avoids the usual bland, unfamiliar gaze that stateside films project onto London. *Match Point* does not strive to comment on British class, but on an outsider's desire to excel in it. The film also concerns obsessive love, and the repressed guilt that comes with it — the one-two punch behind the film noir tradition. Allen uses the genre to explore the psychology of an outsider, one who aspires to upper-class complacency. English class is a suitable means for Allen's criminal/(a)moral study, for, after all, English letters and drama have scrutinized class ever since the modern era.

It's hardly shocking to see Allen use class as a backdrop. The filmmaker, after all, has made a career of exploring the lives of the urban upper-middle class in America. Having grown up in a Brooklyn tenement, the filmmaker seems happy to have reached a milieu of slick apartments and pricey restaurants. The movie houses he visited in Manhattan provided his escape as a child — the high lifestyles of the residents depicted onscreen eventually became his goal. His success and cultural status have made him a spokesman for his class, beyond being just a member. His "mature" filmmaking style, from *Annie Hall* onward, showcases this population — their lifestyle, leisure, trappings — while working-class characters are either comic foils or newcomers to the more fabulous life. In *Hannah and Her Sisters*, an extramarital affair is a thing of hushed desire, undertaken when one steps away from the dinner party to embark on a flirtation.

In *Match Point*, however, the affair is repressed, boiling into a murder. After all, the cheaters of *Hannah* are members of the class; Chris is still aiming for a spot. We sense from the film's early scenes that he wants to ascend, but not until the fates serve him favorably does this potboiler produce a social critique. He submits when tempted by crime, but the new, comfortable world he's reached through crime alleviates him.

The narrative in *Match Point* uses the classical noir synthesis: a morally questionable man (Chris)—in this case, already romantically involved with a woman—meeting a seductress (Nola), who's engaged to Chris's brother-in-law, Tom (Matthew Goode). In the classical style, Nola is at first the darker of the two forces, pulling a morally gray man into bad deeds and moral descent (for she usually offers up the crime that will trap the man into trouble). Here, in this revised noir, she isn't solely culpable, even if Allen gives her a classically inspired introduction, in a femme fatale's white dress, back-lit with natural light from a large window. Though resistant at first, she embarks on the affair since she's disliked by his family and unstable as an aspiring actress. Chris sees her beauty—very American, in this film—as another thing winnable now that he has begun his social ascent. The two have disparate motivations but are compatriots—not in citizenship, but in the fact that both are outsiders coming in, she from the American West and he from Ireland. This husky-voiced American woman, as impetuous in her speech as she is sultry, has the seemingly impossible goal of becoming an actress in London. Chris wants to escape his role as tennis instructor—likely profitable, but still a role limited to serving the upper class.

In an early scene at a lounge, Allen marks the strong connection between the two. It appears while their affair is still as the flirtation stage, and still boiling below the surface. The two have recognized each other as variations of themselves; although they have different goals, they are both trying to marry into wealth. At this point, the two are worthy of a friendship, as Allen establishes a connection beyond the sexual. Chris and Nola are something real, after all—their affair holds more dramatic weight than just an impulse to fuck each other against all opposition.

By this time, Nola is already pegged as an outsider, disliked by Tom's mother and politely tolerated by his father. She's on her way out, and sure enough, Tom breaks their engagement. We read her attraction towards Chris as an act of desperation as much as passion, now that she is alone in London. She wants to assimilate and thus succeed, even if she's impulsive. His need for all the spoils is what moves the affair. Chris demands that they see each other when he spots her at an art gallery, months after they had separated. Such resistance may read as haughty flirtation in the classical noir, but here it is just confusion. At this point, Nola is less the fatale and more the victim.

Their affair doesn't develop into a criminal pact, as was the case for Walter and Phyllis in *Double Indemnity*. The crimes remain solely on Chris's side. By pursuing Nola in the first place, Chris commits a social crime, which coincides with the extramarital union in the classical Cainian noir archetype. He has violated the social contract of marriage and fidelity. If he were found out, his banishment would be as harsh as a painful demise. With his every move, he both relishes his new life and distresses over its volatility — not unlike *Double Indemnity*'s Walter Neff, who keeps his secret from Keyes, the brotherly boss he is trying to scam. Eventually, the social crime leads Chris to commit the actual one: the murder of Nola. The act would assure his comfortable lifestyle.

Chris's method of murder is alarming, in that he kills a landlady to set up Nola's murder. We realize the first murder helps to mask the crime as a robbery. Yet, Allen details Chris's painstaking moves to pull off the landlady's murder. His pull of the shotgun trigger elicits no guilt in him, only frustration in that he has to resort to such crude measures. He murders with his father-in-law's sportsman rifle; while this sets up tension over the motive, it also reminds us of the cushy place from which Chris operates. He even goes to a lavish sports room to claim the murder weapon.

The noir/Machiavellian protagonist: Chris Wilton (Jonathan Rhys Meyers) in *Match Point* (2005, DreamWorks).

After Chris returns to the family home and learns that he'll be a father, his mother-in-law quips that he "looks shell-shocked." While this may see like an exploitive jest (the kind that only Allen can pull off), it still reflects the absurdity found when power and wealth allow a cold-blooded killer to pass as status quo. The film's coda echoes this point: Tom wishes that Chris and Chloe's baby — now born — be lucky, while the baby itself appears nondescript, nothing worth noticing from Chris's perspective. He stares out the window, hardly having found the satisfaction he's desired.

Earlier in the film, after Chris has murdered Nola, a police hunt is on. Now Allen addresses the themes of chance and luck, realized by the barely referenced tennis motif. We know Chris's game is one of chance, and that he is in the hands of the Fates. In the film's slow-motion shot, when Chris tosses away a ring he took during the murder (to make it appear to be a robbery), it falls backward on a rail, like a tennis ball landing unfavorably for a player. The police have a great deal of evidence when they find Nola's diary. After all, a cheating boyfriend is always suspect number one, and often guilty, in a woman's murder case. But the cops call off the case when they find the ring on a drug dealer, the type upon whom Chris modeled his double murder. We could say that fate and luck are the central themes, but we can't forget that the case would lead to a different scenario were Chris not a member of the upper class. The cops fit the crime to the usual suspect, and the real criminal walks due to his (inherited) status.

14

David Mamet

Crime, Power, and Perspective

David Mamet's smooth transition from the stage to film in the late 1980s proved him to be a pure storyteller. Known for his distinctive form of drama, the author views writing for each as two very different acts: the former literary, an art of words, and the latter an act of writing for action onscreen.[1] As varied as he may be as a scriptwriter — having worked sporadically in television, he has recently left his stamp there by creating the series *The Unit* for CBS — Mamet's best work returns to common thematic territory. His early stage work depicts how various walks of life may turn villainous. His breakthrough 1977 play, *American Buffalo*, concerns a small business owner (of a resale shop) and his cohorts turning into small-time hoods, the eponymous collectible becoming the cause for robbery. In his 1992 two-character drama, *Oleanna*, a college student turns into a false accuser of sexual harassment against her professor. (In 1994, Mamet adapted and directed the play for the screen.) By focusing on menace and verbal assaults more than actual violence (as do most of Mamet's stage plays), *Oleanna* remains one of his most searing works, the implication being as damaging as an actual conviction would be. His best-known play, the Pulitzer Prize–winning *Glengarry Glen Ross* (1984), looks to the iconic-ironic figure of the American salesman, treating the subject as both tragic (as in F. Scott Fitzgerald's *The Great Gatsby* and Arthur Miller's *Death of a Salesman*) and melodramatic (*Double Indemnity*, both James M. Cain's novel and Billy Wilder and Raymond Chandler's film) to show the inclination toward criminality. Mamet's drama uses crime motifs to explore power relationships and how they profit from the weak. Through this synthesis, crime conventions-cum-character study, Mamet refined the crime drama, as did his predecessor Harold Pinter.[2] In this sense, by the 1980s Mamet as playwright had achieved what the current trends in crime movies have recently achieved:

genre work as concerned with motivation and character as it is with onscreen action.

Mamet has since written plays as varied as a Faust tale (*Faustus*, 2004), political and legal satires (2007's *November* and 2009's *Race*, respectively, with the latter treating the criminal accusation of rape), as well as experimental stints in between. Yet, his work for the screen (and often his stage work) returns to crime to fuel narrative. As a pure storyteller, Mamet has shown himself as comfortable with plot-driven narrative forms as he is with character-based studies. He has noted that television introduced him to his passion for storytelling, and that he stumbled across the theater accidentally.[3] From his first screenplay gig, adapting *The Postman Always Rings Twice* (1981) for filmmaker Bob Rafelson, to his writing-directing debut, *House of Games* (1987), Mamet has shown mastery — and through it, a fondness for genre territory. (Even his low-key, elegiac character study *Things Change* — co-scripted by Mamet and Shel Silverstein — is grounded in a gangland scenario.) At the same time, he hasn't lost the dramatic heft of his crime-oriented stage drama. In his films, crime and investigation build up the narrative, using tension to craft a mystery or interest for a thriller. The crime scenario, then, focuses on power struggles appearing throughout the ordeal, or after the crime's resolution. With a sharp, visual narrative style and an eye for entertaining fans of intellectual thrillers, Mamet's films capture the life behind the crimes. He began this filmmaking with a firm grip, already having mastered stage drama; his film work developed by using different approaches to the humanistic thriller.

With such a sure hand, Mamet has been dismissed as a filmmaker, notably by David Thomson, who reduces Mamet to a "cold mechanic."[4] Such reactions focus, probably too closely, on Mamet's mastery of plot, his ability to keep a narrative taught. Such crisp storytelling at times seems to upstage action and movement against character motivation; Mamet himself describes drama as "habitual action," showing Aristotle's argument that plot holds more importance than character scope.[5] Yet, to argue that Mamet's thrillers reduce character is to misread his use of fine plotting. Character development is always the end result of his plot work, even if the latter seems to be his goal during the narrative progression. Often, characters develop in relation to power struggles which they have instigated or through which they must navigate.

Interestingly, unlike his stage plays featuring criminals, most of Mamet's films focus on an investigator/avenger (or a victim turned investigator). (The Mamet film that immerses itself the most in crime is *Heist*, which gives the eponymous crime meticulous, and unfortunately cold, treatment — a case that best supports David Thomson's argument against the filmmaker.) Mamet's onscreen protagonists are removed from the criminal world (though they may participate in it or become victim to it), while the films' perspectives reveal a unique relationship between the crime and the non-criminal. Foster Hirsch posits that films told with a perspective removed from the crime are less dynamic, due to their lack of complexity associated with the crime.[6] Mamet's directing debut, *House of Games*, however, shows how Hirsch's compelling rule can be loosened. *Games*, like his other early crime films (and stage dramas), concerns an unusual crime but is more interested in the minds involved, both those creating the crime and the victim to it. Margaret (Lindsay Crouse), a noted author/psychiatrist, treats patients for compulsive behavior, until she learns of her limitations in understanding the criminal psyche. When she's almost conned by Mike (Joe Mantegna) through a mock poker game, she learns about a community of criminals playing off one another and working more intimately than any others Margaret has witnessed. As a victim now tempted into the world of criminality, she spans the boundaries of two archetypes; pulled into the fascinating world, she still teeters on the edge. Mamet uses crime motifs to unveil an underworld, one that will be familiar to most viewers; though here it concerns the crime as performance, itself reflecting the acts Margaret studies. Having a certain amount of power as a therapist, she desires the absolute control of a situation in the con game to learn about its masks and its deeper machinations. But her curiosity, in turn, is her weakness, allowing the group to con her again. It's as if the members realize her fixation with the shields they create, thus deciding to make her a "mark" in their larger scam, which creates in Margaret the need to avenge herself. The narrative is driven as Margaret morphs into different archetypes: victim-turned-pseudo-criminal, then victim to avenger. Mamet uses suspense to highlight the crossways between power and helplessness.

A con game also appears in *The Spanish Prisoner* (1998), though the protagonist remains removed from the scam and is always a victim in flight. Joe Ross (Campbell Scott), who has devised an industrial process yet to be patented, gets conned into losing it. He falls victim to an intricate scam: after realizing his new accomplice, Jimmy Dell (Steve Martin), may be deceiving him, Joe is then conned by another who's posing as an FBI agent to assist him in capturing Jimmy. Joe is then accused of murder and goes on the run, much like Hitchcock's Roger O. Thornhill. The allure of a new life — one with the power of handling such great material — had thrilled Joe and left him susceptible to the smooth players in the con. Add to this the promise of a direct, desirable woman (Rebecca Pidgeon) approaching Joe who proves to be in on the scam. The power is a bait which will lead to a switch — i.e., extreme loss of power. On the run, he makes his best attempt at avenging himself.

On paper, this layered ruse would intrigue, but Mamet's handling of it

A con revealed: Jimmy Dell (Steve Martin) and Joe Ross (Campbell Scott) in David Mamet's *The Spanish Prisoner* (1997, Sony Pictures Classics).

drives the suspense. As Joe is duped by the scam, so are we by Mamet's universe of illusion: Joe embarks into the high life, part of which proves to be manufactured for the crime against him. Unlike in *House of Games*, this protagonist has no relationship to the criminals, since the perspective remains restricted to Joe, the con men remaining behind their façades. Its suspense notwithstanding, *Prisoner* loses the unique perspective of *Games*. *Prisoner* treats the con with a less thematic payoff: we don't learn about the workings of such political trickery. In this case, Hirsch's arguments hold: Scott's character (i.e., the viewer's perspective) never reaches the power that can usurp his intellectual property and safety.

Character perspective is central to *Homicide*, Mamet's 1991 police procedural film. Bobby Gold (Joe Mantegna) is assigned to investigate the murder of a Jewish candy store owner. As a Jewish officer working with routine bigotry, Gold feels the assignment — and its distraction away from a hot drug dealer case — to be subtle hazing: he even hears his African American boss, during a verbal spat, refer to him using a slur. Later in the case, Gold's latent self-hatred shows itself during his anti–Semitic tirade over the phone when he notes that the Jews may have caused much of their own pain. But the investigation reveals the extent of anti–Semitism and triggers all of which Gold remained ignorant, or kept buried within himself. At the end of a neo-noirish investigation (full of tough-talking cops perhaps as seamy as Mamet's lowlifes of the stage), the film's third act is burdensome. Mamet positions Bobby's self-realization as the narrative payoff, though as a later development it lacks the swift momentum of the earlier narrative. The filmmaker reforms his investigator, leaving him discontent in a world he recently thought he had mastered (i.e., getting the baddies) and inverting the writer's *Edmond* (see Chapter 14). *Homicide* remains a unique, although not quite successful, experiment.

Mamet's 1999 adaptation of the Terence Rattigan drama *The Winslow Boy* is a traditional avenger's tale that works through the British legal system: a family must clear their 13-year-old boy charged of stealing a postal order, a charge which led to his being expelled from the Royal Naval College at Osbourne. *Spartan* (2004), putatively a political thriller though working mainly as a crime piece, brings the investigation into an underworld of sorts. Bobby Scott (Val Kilmer), a member of the Delta Force who trains candidates, is assigned to track down the president's missing daughter. In a film beginning with a winding chase through woods (part of the training) and a brutal battle between two recruits for the last opening, Mamet begins the investigation with ascendance to power into the faction which Bobby belongs. Scott learns that Laura, the president's daughter, had been drugged and abducted from a bar where college students are known to prostitute for rich businessmen. To gain information, Bobby pulls a con on a secret service agent who was assigned to watch Laura. By acting like another agent, Bobby gets him to confess, only to reveal the ruse a moment later (which will urge the agent putatively to kill himself). Later, after learning that Laura may be the victim of a Dubai-based white slavery ring, Bobby pulls a intricate con on Tariq Asani (Saïd Taghmaoui) by staging a gas station robbery, during which it appears as though he's killed everyone. He (disturbingly) makes good on the assumption by pretending to kill the guard who drives Tariq and actually killing the death-row inmate riding with him. Fearing for his life, Tariq admits his part in a slavery ring, also swearing to a means for their escape. The ruse proves to be only so tight when they stop at a convenience store (actually a stop for Bobby to make contact with his team) and Tariq spots an agent through a window. Thinking he and Bobby to be compromised, he grabs a shotgun from another car and fires into the store. When Bobby kills Tariq, their plan to infiltrate the ring dies. Not squeamish about killing to achieve his goal, Bobby also won't resist the need to torture to extract information, even breaking an arm to do so, thus as much in kind with *The Departed*'s Frank Costello.

Yet, Bobby's ruthless methods and deception are overshadowed by the government's con. A false news report describes Laura as having drowned along with one of her professors at Martha's Vineyard. Curtis (Derek Luke),

Bobby's trainee now working with him, finds Laura's earring at the beach house they had just staked out, proof that she did not drown as reported. It's soon revealed that the president took Laura's secret service protection with him to shield his affair, and that he'd rather sacrifice his daughter than commit political suicide. The ordeal reveals crime on the political scale, one that cannot be defeated even if the immediate victim can be saved.

The physicality of *Spartan*'s opening scenes, an approach continued throughout, returns in Mamet's 2008 film, *Redbelt*. This putative martial arts film begins with Jiu-Jitsu training in which one of two fighters must use a handicap, in this case an arm tied down. Also like the earlier film, *Redbelt* features a mentor who is moved to action. Mike (Chiwetel Ejiofor), a martial arts instructor, lives by strict warrior codes: he honors combat and resists bringing it to competitive sport, in spite of the alluring profits. Both films deliver early physical scenes featuring control and concentration, the means by which these mentor-warriors maintain their power.

But, like *Spartan*'s Bobby, Mike will find his power compromised — not in the fight ring, but by the machinations behind the competitive sport, and show business in general. Mamet's hyperactive plot brings Mike through numerous trials: he takes on life's curveballs with the same acumen he has on the mat. The countless oppressions reflect the emergence of a noir universe. Eventually, he becomes the victim of a scam by a network of promoters and an aging movie star, Chet Frank (played by Tim Allen). When Mike saves Chet during a bar fight, the latter gifts him with a watch, which Mike passes on to Joe (Max Martini), his student, to help him out with medical bills. When Joe tries to pawn the watch, it proves to be stolen, and he's suspended from his police job. Meanwhile, a sales deal made by Mike's wife, Sondra (Alice Braga), and the wife of Chet proves null, leaving Sondra in the red for $30,000. Even worse, when Mike learns that a promoter has stolen his method of drawing marbles to see who will be handicapped in a match, the promoter threatens blackmail concerning an accident early in the film, in which a shaken lawyer, Laura Black (Emily Mortimer), shot out his front window. Joe, in turn, takes his own life, the pressure of the theft accusation and this burden proving too much to bear. Mike's honor and stature make him victim on many levels, including the fact that he refused to fight competitively for the promoters. Yet, he does so to help Mike's widow with her finances.

The various ordeals lead him to a match where he sees his marble-drawing method used by a magician to fix a match. The public theft is the last of the affronts against him — the demeaning of his life's work, and the loss of his wife, whom Mike later learns revealed information about Laura shooting out the window to the fight promoters. Mamet's climax has Mike counteract to it all by engaging in an actual fight against Ricardo, Sondra's brother and a mixed martial arts champion scheduled to compete at the event. The unlikely staging of the showdown — no amount of resistance can halt Mike from the fight — captures the attention of the crowd and the television cameras, as well as the martial arts figures who share Mike's code: fighter Morisaki, who presents Mike with his ivory-studded belt, and the mentor of mentors, The Professor, who in the ring bestows to the "champion" the much-honored, eponymous belt. They honor Mike for the purity of his passion, and his ability to defend it. Hence, Mamet concludes with his beleaguered protagonist triumphant, even though the noir universe revealed will remain a pall over his personal and professional life. Mike's journey is a descent with a measure of vindication, albeit with a new perspective the injustice has served. As in the best of Mamet's films, crime is at the roots of *Redbelt*'s conflict. It is exploited by seamy elements, resulting in power struggles, and informs/reforms perspective.

15

New Ganglands
The Journey to *Public Enemies*
and *American Gangster*

As an archetype, the classical gangster mirrors today's viewer as much as he did in his heyday. Through his rise to power and fall from it, he reflects our thrills and our guilt which ensues from them. Moralistic in its original form, the 1930s story of the gangster is a contained unit, more so than the noir-style plots of the following decade. A noir antihero's descent comes about from a wrong step; fatalism sets in when the compromised character meets the femme fatale or is offered some form of a Faustian deal. His demise suggests turmoil extending beyond the plot's finish, should he survive. The gangster's rise to power is his maturation, if short-lived; he realizes his longtime wish, though the fulfillment will also lead to his end. In this rise-and-fall archetype, we have a truncated life story, the violent ending recalling his ruthless beginning.

When experiencing the classical gangster's demise, we find an ironic catharsis. We do not purge emotion in sympathy, as with many tragedies, but with a mix of pity and disgust. The narrative ends in moral judgment, a *deus ex machina* at the hands of censorship. In spite of the structure, viewers delight in the gangster's exploits. As an unlikely hero to Depression-era audiences, the gangster plays as celebratory, aside from his censorship-based origins. There's more behind the fandom of the early 1980s take on the classical gangster, Tony Montana—witness the youth of today wearing T-shirts and leather jackets bearing his face—than his memorable lines and trademark machismo.

The gangster's deliberate construction, devised to delight the audience and moralize as well, had no direction to go but to evolve. The gangster-hero's mid–1930s revision into a rough G-Man, under the influence of the Production Code Administration (solidified in 1934), became an early precursor to the renegade cops of the 1970s. This lawman, essentially a revised classical gangster, seemed entitled to his fierce actions, which are necessary responses to his opposition (see the discussion of *Dirty Harry* in Chapter 12). The 1940s gangsters in John Huston's *Key Largo* (1948) looked back to the old days; the pop-psychology and milieu of *White Heat*'s (1949) Cody Jarrett was of the times, even if the narrative looked to the past.

Yet, the gangster didn't experience a major revision until mainstream Hollywood could more accurately depict him. It was not until the 1960s, when the cultural revolution necessitated a loosening of censorship, that the gangster film became truly reflective. In the process, filmmakers reevaluated gangster films like other genres — *Psycho* (1960) and *Night of the Living Dead* (1968) being notable examples for horror; the pre-'60s Western *The Searchers* (1956) and *The Wild Bunch* (1969) for their own genre. In the benchmark year in American film, 1967, Arthur Penn's *Bonnie and Clyde* returned to the gangster myth — not by depicting big-time crime bosses, but rural bandits on the run (equally an inspiration to Depression-era citizens). On one hand, the film took up from an underground/B-movie trend of biopic exploitation films on such bandits, including Max Nosseck's *Dillinger* (1945) and Roger Corman's *Machine-Gun Kelly* (1958) while continuing the lovers-on-the-run motif (*You Only Live Once* [1937], *Gun Crazy* [1949]). Penn's film also borrowed techniques from the French New Wave to jar viewer expectations and better restrict the film's point of view to the criminal (even if an entry like Howard Hawks's *Scarface* [1932] mostly sticks to its title character, the moralistic tones indicate his ensuing downfall). After *Bonnie and Clyde*'s success, the bandit biopic would continue (1970's *Bloody Mama*, 1972's *Boxcar Bertha*). These films highlight gang crime as youthful (at times nihilistic) rebellion, an attack on the social norms opposing the cultural revolution. While the classical gangster took over society from the underbelly, the New Hollywood bandits stole — and ran — from it.

As compared to its predecessors, *Bonnie and Clyde* is known for its sympathetic portrayal of its characters. The actions of the classical gangsters work off sexual perversion (*Scarface*'s Tony Camonte is attached to his sister; *Little Caesar*'s Rico Bandello, to his buddy) and casual racism against immigrant European cultures. Penn's film points to Bonnie's sexual desires, and Clyde's inability to fulfill them, as instigators (if pop-psychology based) to crime. Clyde cannot complete intercourse until Bonnie's poem predicts their demise, when his fear crumbles as he grows into a legend. When they barely escape a chase that leaves them battered and Clyde's brother dead, the film grows even more sensitive to them, in lieu of coldly recounting their demise (as in *Scarface*). When they perish, execution-style amid a spray of bullets, we see the moment as an injustice, opposing the classical genre's "justice-served" conclusion.

If *Bonnie and Clyde* revises the myth, *The Godfather* makes it into an American legacy. It focuses on Michael Corleone's rise, while the requisite fall comes, ironically, in the form of the don's heart attack in a peaceful orchard. The coming-to of Michael takes up — and expands — the first half of the myth, while Sergio Leone's revised gangster film, 1984's *Once Upon a Time in America*, expands the latter half. The film starts with the beginnings of the gangster-protagonist's descent, the moment he sells out his accomplice/friend. In the classical genre, the gangster's turn against his buddy begins the former's demise; in *Bonnie and Clyde*, the father of gang-member C.W. Moss gives them up; in Scorsese's *Mean Streets* (1973), the rancorous actions of friend Johnny Boy bring about his own death, and an end-of-innocence moment for protagonist Charlie (the film's contemplative conscience). In *One Upon a Time*, the gangster's ensuing demise has him reflecting on his journey. He looks back to his early years, growing into his own criminal empire, to the end of his days in the business. While the film uses a 1940s opium den to begin Noodle's reflection, we soon realize that he looks back to this moment from his old age, in the late 1960s. The opium den reflection recalls the moment that Noodles turned against Max, and began his spiritual demise. Inspired by the New Hollywood–era revision of the gangster paradigm, Leone's film presents a meta-analysis of the archetype, by aligning with the myth and reflecting on it: a gangster who ended his own tenure of power. In *Bonnie and Clyde*, the downfall comments on the contemporary rebellion by referencing the original myth. In *Mean Streets*, the protagonist completes a moral education. In *Once Upon a Time*, the gangster's education is an inquiry about his own life and, in the process, the tradition of the American gangster.

Revisionary gangster films, those before and after Leone's, highlight either the rise or the fall. It's as if the full classical myth is too complete and requires a breakdown, to place either end under a microscope, with the tradition's structural influence remaining, nonetheless. Abel Ferrara's *The King of New York* (1990) features the fallen ironic hero. His departure from prison, at the film's beginning, shows he's lost what once was. His literal descent at the finale echoes his figurative one at the start of the film. Though it may appear to reflect the full classical plot, Scorsese's *Goodfellas* (also 1990) highlights the protagonist's fall, as he tells his story in retrospect in an ironic take on the noir-inspired voiceover — within the witness protection program. Gun-toting will always be flashy, but to remain vital the gangster film needs to refresh its tradition without betraying it. Leone's film — with its reflection on genre, unearthing the lives behind the gangster myth, and serving as social history — is the high point by staying true to its tradition and welcoming its reinvention.

Gangsters may be the stuff of legend, but they were always inspired by true events. A recent trend in the crime film, though certainly not the rule, has been the fictionalized true crime. This style cuts away the mythologizing done in many Hollywood adaptations — such as the early sound gangland films, borrowing from the headlines — to work with the source behind such narratives. David Fincher's *Zodiac* (see Chapter 6), while not a gangster film but a document of a true (and extensive) investigation, remains a standout in its commitment to truth and assessing a crime myth — here, the serial killer. Similarly, the recent gangster films document real-life criminals: Michael Mann's *Public Enemies* (2009) concerns the 1930s legend John Dillinger, while Ridley Scott's *American Gangster* (2007) features drug lord Frank Lucas. Interestingly, the pair covers both versions of the classical gangster: Mann's film, the rural bandit; Scott's, the urban gang leader. Taking up from Leone and the strongest modern gangster entries, both films assess the myth they inherit. Mann reveals how the gangster archetype inspired the original cinematic myth, and how this tale of glitz to a bloody downfall is elegiac throughout. Scott's film stays closer to the full classical myth by showing how the bootlegger archetype transformed into the drug boss of the 1970s. Both films develop the character of a hunter after the gangster, which was a cutout figure in the original tradition, a sounding board to accentuate the hero's exploits and deliver to viewers the necessary downfall. Each shows how reality creates myth, and how the latter, in turn, influences the former. In these films' concern for the (literal) past, they add to the growing legend.

Enemies is set at a time curious for the gangster film. The plot transpires in 1933, right when the classical Hollywood gangster was forced to evolve by the Motion Picture Production Code. It's also just prior to the Repeal of Prohibition, enacted with hopes of crippling organized crime. Nevertheless, the film opens with an effective Dillinger (Johnny Depp) at work. His prison escape unravels in an ordered fashion and defeats the authorities as it transpires. After his gang is free, he punishes a member for causing another's death. The entire enterprise adheres to a system of underlying rules, which define the gangster.[1] Dillinger follows such a tight code during his heists that he can brag to the press of how he always takes under two minutes. Indeed, he is living his own legend. His notoriety helps him intimidate the police during a jailbreak and bank employees during a robbery. Though he doesn't reveal his identity to Billie Frechette (Marion Cotillard) when picking her up — she will become more than a just a moll, but a partner — when he tells her his life story, it unravels like the introduction to a folk character:

> I was raised on a farm in Mooresville, Indiana. My mama died when I was three. My daddy beat the hell out of me because he didn't know no better way to raise me. I like baseball, movies, good clothes, fast cars, whiskey, and you.

Embracing his own legend helps to fuel his exploits, even if it signals his demise. While officially a narrative on true crime and the forming of the FBI (an adaptation of a 2004 book of the same title by Bryan Burrough), *Public Enemies* elegizes the gangster by concentrating on his fall. His twilight appears by the opening scene, once he realizes that the ordered systems of crime will fail. Dillinger's ballsy work had caught the attention of the crime syndicates, now focusing on bookmaking (with Prohibition coming to an end) and seeing his notoriety as a liability. The news is dispiriting to Dillinger, who had thought the organization's bosses to be his compatriots. When breaking from jail, Dillinger arrives at a bookmaking location to find that he will jeopardize their operation, which in one day makes as much cash as he does in one of his planned heists.

A driving force for Dillinger is the lady to whom he has promised himself. Hardly the trophy moll, she doesn't hide her "undesirable" Native-American ancestry from him, nor does she fall immediately for his approach. Dillinger loves "good clothes," while her job is to hang them, i.e., coats, at a nightclub. Countless "covers" pass through her hands, while Dillinger's becomes evidence in the Feds' possession. Her vulnerability — and lack of shame for it — draws her to him, while his vulnerability grows throughout the film.

Romance in the earlier tradition spells trouble. It's as if the gangster film cannot escape the tragic association of the lovers-on-the-run motif, which inherits its desperation-to-demise tone from *Romeo and Juliet*. Once a hood falls in love, it will detract from his life of crime, as it does for a young Noodles in *Once Upon a Time*. While trying to establish a relationship, Noodles's impetuousness leads him to rape, when he feels he must take possession of the girl as the classical gangsters perpetually have with their molls. The gangster must separate personal relationships from his career, or the former will risk all that has made him. For Dillinger, his ideal romance leads him to return to Billie, even if the action would result in his capture. Once those involved with the investigation hear his confession to return to her, in a tapped phone call, fate sets in. Agent Melvin Purvis (an unromanticized portrayal by Christian Bale) says, "She will come to him, or he'll go to her." As businesslike as the statement is, it spells out Dillinger's doomed path to his death at the Biograph Theater. His romantic reliance indicates that he is habitual, and able to trace — thus, another aspect of his ordered nature that, in the end, will ruin him.

After the film's opening jailbreak, the narrative counteracts with a sure capture: Agent Purvis hunting down Pretty Boy Floyd. The efforts of Purvis will not be futile. First calling off his men, Purvis aims through rows of apple trees as Floyd flees down a hill in the orchard. When Purvis's rifle shot takes him down, the event reflects the former's character and foreshadows Dillinger's

Agent Melvin Purvis (Christian Bale) awaits the appearance of John Dillinger outside the Biograph Theater in *Public Enemies* (2009, Universal Pictures).

fall. With such a name, the agent sounds as unheroic as Dillinger is legendary. "Purvis" may seem down-home, even nebbish, but he operates through close attention to procedure, a gangster's level of adherence to rules that are used against him. A man of small stature in real life, Purvis in the film provides even fewer words; a man of action taken not from popular culture but from history. All business, he assures the press that his department will catch Dillinger. When his target proves difficult, J. Edgar Hoover (Billy Crudup) orders him to bend the rules. When instructed to torture a captured, hospitalized gang member, Purvis sees crime perverting his moral imperative. The scene revises the hospital-hit of many gangster films, beginning with 1932's *Scarface*, by making the law culpable, even if the scene feels more like a critique of George W. Bush–era interrogation policies of terrorists. Even with policy against him, Purvis remains focused and highlights the elegiac nature of the doomed legend.

Scott's *Gangster* presents the complete rise-and-fall of its titular character. Like Mann's film, Scott's title refers back to a filmic tradition, and in the process, implies commentary of it. ("Public Enemies" both evokes the effort to end a crime spree, with the establishment of the Federal Bureau of Investigation, as well as a classical film in the genre, *The Public Enemy* [1931] directed

Frank Lucas (Denzel Washington) sits at the head of the table with his new criminal network in *American Gangster* (2007, Universal Pictures).

by William A. Wellman and starring James Cagney.) As powerful as the rise of Frank Lucas (Denzel Washington) may be, his capture is just as prominent. The avenger working against Lucas, Richie Roberts (Russell Crowe), is something of a lost soul. The source narrative compels Roberts to take down Lucas, but this result comes only by Robert's evolution: his character growing to meet his determination. Opposition to him awaits on more than one front. By working honestly, he refuses to steal a sizable amount of drug money found on the job. His action reads as a rejection — and hence, an affront — to the majority of police who would seize drug cash and take payoffs. This territory is extensively covered in Lumet's 1973 Al Pacino vehicle, *Serpico* (also based on a real case), though this is just one of many elements in *Gangster*.

The growing power of the opposition spells out the fate of Lucas, which dovetails with the classical archetype, even if it revises the character's motivations. Lucas himself rises to power in the spirit of *Scarface*'s Tony Camonte and *Little Caesar*'s Rico Bandello, though Lucas's motivations go beyond the classical mold. Lucas doesn't take down the current boss — he works for him, while the elder serves merely as an inspiration. In lieu of taking over, Lucas ascends by blending criminal ambition with capitalist ingenuity. He sees a method to overtake the drug market by selling a more effective product, pure heroin only slightly "cut down." For a means of acquiring it, he looks to the media and the cultural moment. Bodies returning from Vietnam come in a steady flow, and the constant death becomes a way for him to ship his product. The fact that his product is more dangerous, even fatal, creates irony: political turmoil — poverty, post–Equal Rights racism, the Draft — begets the same in the American city. This gangster's business sense clarifies the latent social history behind the original filmic myth: American bootlegging. This entrepreneur finds a new opportunity, as do the young gang members in Sergio Leone's *Once Upon a Time in America* (i.e., saving jettisoned goods by attaching salt to them, which will melt and help the goods rise to the surface), now drug sales (as in Brian De Palma's 1983 reworking of *Scarface*). Both practices show the American legacy of capitalism fueling the structure of the land's crime.

As compelling as Lucas's rise may be, his demise calls attention to the concept of the original filmic gangster, and his moralistic "fall." In Scott's film, after Richie infiltrates Lucas's base situated within a ghetto it oppresses, Lucas becomes a witness. The legal deal-making behind the scenes adds realism to what is often a cold demise. In the classical films, it's as if the avenger's power feeds off the gangster's, who gets more development and more credibility. Before we know it, the cops besiege the criminal as he turns chicken, now unarmed, his power gone. In this revision, the gangster maintains his power by turning against his own organization.

For years popular culture has followed the advice of John Ford's *The*

American Gangster's Frank Lucas (Denzel Washington, left) alters the prototypical gangster's demise by providing evidence to Richie Roberts (Russell Crowe, far right) (2007, Universal Pictures).

Man Who Shot Liberty Valance (1962): "When the legend becomes fact, print the legend." Yet Mann and Scott's films look past the legend to find the truths that inspired it. As high profile "public enemies" belonging to history (and, to an extent, the classical film tradition), both Dillinger and Lucas cannot escape the sights of their respective hunters. The organizational work behind their capture infuses history into the legend. The films recall how truth fashions original film myths, and how these traditions grow into cultural history by returning to the facts.

16

The Coen Uncanny
From *Blood Simple*
to *No Country for Old Men*

In November 2007, at the beginning of Oscar season, one film in release seemed so fresh, yet so familiar. It shared marquees with works of a similar taste: *Michael Clayton* (see Chapter 2), a paranoid thriller renewed for our age; familial deceit veering toward bloodshed in Sidney Lumet's taut but overblown *Before the Devil Knows You're Dead*; and another work (though not purportedly in the crime tradition) revealing a particular heart of darkness: P.T. Anderson's alternate Western, *There Will Be Blood*.

The film in question, *No Country for Old Men*, appeared in a new wave of American crime films, and like many others had an uncanny resemblance to earlier works. The irony of everyday folk caught up in violence has appeared throughout Joel and Ethan Coen's careers, most notably in their 1996 film *Fargo*, though as early as their 1984 debut, *Blood Simple*. In all three of these films, a protagonist instigates his own futile dance with death, and in each an antihero cannot overcome the conflict. In the filmmakers' debut, the involvement of Loren Visser (M. Emmet Walsh), a downright ironic hired killer (donning a ten-gallon hat and driving a Volkswagen Bug), still proves to be a threat to lovers Ray (a bartender, played by John Getz) and Abby (wife to the bar owner, played by future Coens' mainstay, Frances McDormand). In *Fargo*, the menace is a cold-blooded Swede named Gaear Grimsrud (Peter Stormare), the more effective (and menacing) half of a bumbling pair of crooks. Yet, the film's antihero is Jerry Lundegaard (William H. Macy), a car dealership manager who has his own wife kidnapped to collect ransom from his wealthy father-in-law, Wade Gustafson (Harve Presnell). While Grimsrud causes major damage (killing a policeman and passersby who witness the crime scene, later the kidnapped woman, and eventually his own partner, in one of the film's trademark scenes), Marge Gunderson (McDormand), the pregnant police chief/Earth Mother, becomes the true counterforce to Lundegaard. (Coming upon his location by accident, she also takes down Grimsrud.) In *No Country for Old Men*, a mobile-home dweller, Llewelyn Moss (Josh Brolin) discovers a bag of cash after a drug deal gone bad. His taking it results in being hunted by Chigurh (Javier Bardem), a villain almost too extreme for credibility.

Each film realizes the depths of evil consuming an overreaching innocent; the film following each seems to outdo the one before it. *Fargo* adds a note of hope with Marge's triumph at the end, though the evil she's uncovered proves devastating. *No Country*'s Chigurh seemed a distillation of *Fargo*'s Grimsrud, with both possessing a cold, otherworldly nature. Whereas Grimsrud proves faulty by the tale's end, caught while trying to "dispose of" the remains of his partner via a woodchipper,[1] Chigurh operates without any threat to his mission. He even flees a crippling car accident on foot at the film's conclusion. Throughout the film, Chigurh comes as close to the mythical shadow figure as an element of realism can. If Charles Laughton hadn't used "Night of the Hunter" for his haunting 1955 thriller, starring Robert Mitchum, the title would have embodied the Coens's film. Cormac McCarthy, author of the source novel, borrowed an opening line of the Yeats poem "Sailing to Byzantium," but if the poet's "The Second Coming" weren't already one of the most quoted poems in the English language, it would have captured the tone even better: with the introduction of Chigurh, the *blood-dimmed tide* has *certainly been loosed*, as the *hour of a rough beast* has come.

Those turned off by the Coens' *No Country* described it as bleak, or even hopeless. But even these critics acknowledged the film's construction to be strong enough for the gruesome content. Former *Washington Post* critic Stephen Hunter (also a crime/suspense novelist) struggled to justify his negative reactions: "I admire *No Country for Old Men* for the way it tightens its grip as it progresses ... [but] I just don't like it very much."[2] His impulse to evaluate the content (apparently the morality of it) outweighs his admiration for the film's technique. Even veteran critic Jonathan Rosenbaum admitted that the film was a "very well-made genre exercise" in the midst of his critique of our veneration for psycho killers.[3] He compellingly argues that our obsession with sensationalized murders places psycho killers in a godlike position. We cannot ignore that the serial killer is just a real-life, media-friendly version of the bogeyman, a time-worn archetype always inspiring our darker narratives.

These readings, especially in light of the Coens' career, highlight *No Country* as the extremity of their film cycle (consisting of *Blood Simple*, *Fargo*, and *No Country*). The Coens frequently use crime to shape their narrative; their script for Sam Raimi, *Crimewave* (1985), for example, features a pair of

Marge Gunderson (Frances McDormand) stumbles upon the truth in *Fargo* (1996, MGM Home Entertainment).

bumbling crooks. The Coens' 1990 film, *Miller's Crossing*, is a gangland tribute making frequent use of their treatment of the comic and brutal. *Raising Arizona* (1987) is their most outright version of the crime comedy, as it invokes slapstick style in an ironic caper plot of a working-class couple kidnapping a baby. The filmmakers' screwball comedy proper, *The Hudsucker Proxy* (1994), even concerns a *theft* of an idea. *Barton Fink*, the Coens' 1991 flirtation with surrealism, comes closest to the trilogy under discussion, since the film presents a serial murderer, as if released from the repression of this enigmatic film's psyche. The *Blood Simple–Fargo–No Country* cycle progresses with a common motif of the uncanny: an interrupted journey appearing as repressed horror. The Coens did not originate the filmic moment used in all three films, which is vital to storytelling, and especially the film noir tradition. True to the style, in each film by the Coens, the moment instigates a noirish descent.

   No Country begins with an halted journey: Chigurh is apprehended on a roadway and brought to a police station, where he murders the patrolman who escorted him. The haunting image of Bardem's face, as his handcuffed character strangles the officer, presents the blood-dimmed tide, loosed by the completion of this killing. It signals the onslaught that will be his character's continual action. The Coens have used such a moment to release counterforces in their films. Each moment begins on a roadway, when an already-growing force is challenged, then comes to fruition. In *Blood Simple*, it occurs when Ray attempts to bury his boss/lover's husband, Marty (Dan Hedaya); in *Fargo*, when two bumbling crooks (lacking proper tags on their car) are stopped by police, with a kidnapped woman tied and covered in their backseat. *Blood Simple* would seem to be the starting point of this discussion. Yet to begin our discussion, we must return to classical noir.

On film, the motif originates in the work that inspired *Blood Simple*: James M. Cain's *The Postman Always Rings Twice* (novel, 1934; film, 1946). Dashiell Hammett's novel, *Red Harvest*—often argued to be the prototypical detective noir—introduced the term the Coens borrowed for their title. But the narrative conceit, which they revised into a neo-noir motif, comes from Cain. In *Postman*, a cheating couple effectively disposes of a clueless husband, while *Blood Simple* inverts this motif for a comedy of (t)errors. In the Coens' take, the husband is already wise, and it is *he* who decides to *off* them, by hiring P.I. Visser. Insults from Marty to Visser, however, force the latter to kill the former, after he's doctored photos to make it appear that he held up his end of the deal. When Ray finds the remains, he thinks Abby is responsible for Marty's death, and buries the body to cover for her — this film's version of the uncanny moment. Soon, both lovers suspect the other to be culpable, their

The "new" Cainian couple: *Blood Simple*'s Ray (John Getz) and Abby (Frances McDormand) (1984, Circle Films).

respective fears fueled by miscommunication, the antithesis of the unholy union between *Postman*'s lovers.

In *Postman*, the husband's murder instigates the decline of Frank and Cora, two lovers meeting on a desolate, Depression-era California road. To escape their isolation, they drive Nick — Cora's husband, who's full of drink — to a lonely road, where Frank halts the car. This moment is prototypical of Cain — an ambush-murder by a lover, a motif of which also appears in *Double Indemnity*. In *Postman*, Frank and Cora plan to pull to the side of a cliff, with a deep echo, over which Nick sings. After Frank kills Nick with a wrench to the head, the echo of his voice returns, a portent of the curse the couple has brought upon themselves. The uncanny return of his voice also mirrors the frequent return this moment will have in the noir style. While *Postman* makes the murder a sure action, *Simple* makes the husband's death an alleged move, which fuels a noirish paranoia. Each lover suspects the other of having committed the crime, while the seamy Marty, who they tried to eliminate, haunts them. The "shape" behind Abby and Ray's fear is actually Visser, who hunts them and whose presence they sense in all ways but sight.

While inverting the noir narrative, the Coens revise the sure murder of Cain into a journey interrupted. Nick and Cora complete their task, while the darkness grows over them. In *Simple*, the pall chases Abby and Ray before they can even act against her husband. The Coens interrupt the lovers' path to a new life with a scene concerning just Ray and Marty. By this time, Abby remains in the background of the action, since Ray assumes she is already involved. After Ray cleans the crime scene, he takes Marty's body to a field — the scene replacing Cain's looming cliff— and digs a grave. When Marty suddenly awakens, Ray commits a spur-of-the-moment murder by burying him while still alive. A murder-after-the-fact like this recurs in Sam Raimi's *A Simple Plan* (the common word in the title capitalizing on the uncanny association to the Coens' film), when Hank (Bill Paxton) realizes that his brother Jacob's impulsive attempt to halt Dwight Stephanson (Tom Carey) with a wrench didn't work, and Hank finishes the job (see Chapter 19). In *Simple*, the moment Ray completes Marty's murder unifies the dual forces — i.e., paranoia and Visser — against his character.

Fargo begins with an eerie journey: a car emerging from a snowy haze in the film's opening shot. We learn it will be used in — and as payment for — a husband's kidnapping of his own wife. Lundegaard is driving to Fargo, North Dakota, to hire kidnappers. He even provides their transportation, in the form of a car he stole from his workplace. After they have kidnapped Lundegaard's wife, Jean (Kristin Rudrüd), they encounter the uncanny moment of interruption. With Jean making noise in the backseat — an incompetent Showalter tries to quiet her — the men are pulled over in the town of Brainerd

Kidnapper Carl Showalter (Steve Buscemi) caught in one of *Fargo*'s twists (1996, MGM Home Entertainment).

for not having proper tags. Showalter shows more incompetence when he tries to pay off the local patrolman for the violation, which results in Grimsrud grabbing the officer by his hair, pulling a pistol from the glove, and shooting him dead. The one-two action is a modern take on the quick draw, reflecting the film's death drive as instinctive. The crime snowballs when Grimsrud spies a passing car, its passengers witnessing the event. After a bloodless chase, during which Grimsrud tosses his cigarette as if he's pulling forth a scythe, he guns down a man from the car, who attempts to run off in a field. Grimsrud then casually shoots the woman passenger, who's pinned in the car. The wide expanse, over which Grimsrud speeds to catch the two, and then another, over which he shoots the man, is a contrast to the confined car interior, where this angel of death eyes his victim before her demise. As in *Blood Simple*, *Fargo*'s uncanny moment reveals that an attempt to check the growing darkness will be counteractive.

Blood Simple's barren field presents an unexpected murder during the burial, while *Fargo* presents a crime growing through absurd situations and decisions. While recalling Cain to a degree, *Fargo* more directly invokes *The Thin Blue Line*, a 1988 crime documentary about events which occurred in 1976. The correlation between the Coens' and Errol Morris's films helped sell

Fargo as a true-crime narrative, until the Coens later revealed their innocent hoax.[4] In 1976, while passing through the Dallas area, Randall Adams was arrested for the murder of police officer Robert W. Wood, occurring on the side of a highway. The abrupt crime is fresh material for hungry media and tabloid press, hence the Coens borrowed it to position their tale as ripped from the headlines. Morris's film highlights the nighttime gunfire as an element of mystery, since the truth of the perpetrator lies behind the press coverage and the conviction and life sentence of the wrongfully accused. More directly, the documentary looks to the injustice of the system, as it bypasses a likely suspect, David Harris (later proven guilty, who had been spending time with Adams), to avoid the lighter sentence that this teenager would get. Thus Adams, targeted as a "drifter," is assumed guilty and given a life sentence. *The Thin Blue Line* depicts how such a murder draws forth immediate fear, just as the real culprit worked off impulse and felt powerful. The quiet night of a patrolman is interrupted, and hence so is authority and the basis for citizens' stability. *Fargo*'s criminals create extreme terror, even if defeated by the resolution.

Not so in *No Country for Old Men*. This film marks Coens' departure from the uncanny force becoming re-repressed (i.e., defeated) by the film's finish. This turn shows the filmmakers' move to accepting the repressed as truly undeniable, and unconquerable. As it is freed, the noir darkness takes on its most punishingly effective presence. Though *No Country* is modeled on Western motifs, it essentially amounts to the darkest elements of noir.

Anton Chigurh (Javier Bardem) is a meta-generic presence. His continual hunting and killing invokes the serial killer film, though he works to reclaim money stolen from a drug deal gone bad. The caper elements grow to a noirish pall over Llewelyn, the man who took the cash, while the law's attempts to apprehend Chigurh (and Llewelyn), represented by Sheriff Ed Tom Bell (Tommy Lee Jones), reflect the Western genre's quest dying in modernity. The noir tradition has repressed a haunting force on the level of Chigurh, in favor of clear-cut, attainable villains. An earlier form of Chigurh appeared in *Fargo* as Grimsrud,[5] though the latter's captured (note, not killed) when Marge's bullet takes out his hamstring. *No Country*'s uncanny moment appears when Chigurh breaks away from police at the film's beginning, a sequence that results in two cold-blooded murders (one of the policeman and the other of a driver Chigurh pulls over to take his car). Chigurh kills the driver with an odd weapon — a gas-tank-fueled cattle gun. A cumbersome weapon — carrying it makes him appear to have a respiratory problem — it kills silently, with as little reaction from its user. The weapon makes Chigurh appear so odd he's both otherworldly and common, even a bit nerdy.[6] A villain of both the imagination and the headlines, he's a bogeyman and the mundane killer recurring in — and often worshipped (as Rosenbaum has claimed) by — the media and its recipients. Such a horror figure emerges from repression,[7] and in this case from repressed fears of sundry genres and non-fiction.

Thus, Chigurh is the virtual nightmare to Sheriff Bell, the latest (last?) in a line of Western lawmen who has met his match. Bell had begun his work under the influence of romantic, old-time Western ideals. His was a job of struggle and conquering, but overall one in which he would persist. The ideal comes largely from Western narrative motifs, in which true crimes/oppression were routinely defeated, though actually repressed only to re-emerge in revisionist takes on the tradition. Now, Bell discovers a product of such repression, a villain who's "the other," though not clearly Mexican, nor Native American. Chigurh is "unplaceable" because he embodies the repressed threat of the locale, otherworldly but damnable to the area he haunts. With Bell's imminent retirement, Western heroism is dying as he reluctantly pursues Chigurh.[8] Like his role in *In the Valley of Elah*, Jones's character aspires to feats suitable only to the past. The interrupted journey motif resounds for Bell, since his path to retirement is halted by an extreme threat, not letting his Western dream rest.

Though Moss thinks it very much alive, as he mocks Chigurh's attempt to be "the ultimate badass" and feels ready to take him on. Moss has a lofty

The silent hunter: Anton Chigurh (Javier Bardem) in *No Country for Old Men* (2007, Miramax Films).

self-concept, while living in a mobile home with a wife bewildered by his motivations. Posing as a rough, Moss is a foil. While hunting, he happens to spot the remains of a botched drug deal, gets the money, and sets Chigurh on a chase. A potential showdown proves a ruse for commentary on the myths of justice.

In 2010, the Coens released their adaptation of Charles Portis's novel *True Grit*, which abandons an unstoppable villain for a classical (yet renegade) avenger, Rooster Cogburn (Jeff Bridges). Yet, with their cycle completed, in which villainous forces bring noir to a self-reflective style, the Coens have made one of the finest contributions to the new American crime film.

17

From the Body Outward
The New Crimes of David Cronenberg

In his early career, David Cronenberg bridged two subgenres of the horror film: psychological horror, with his focus on fear of the human body's decay, and the gore film, by visually realizing this fear. This Canadian filmmaker entered horror in the 1970s, when the slasher film's success made realism routine, often mundane. While not ignoring realism with such detail, Cronenberg's characters were preternatural, even if created by humans. The results were demonic children (*The Brood* [1979]), human parasites (*Shivers* [1975], *Rabid* [1977]), and mass psychosis (*Videodrome* [1983]). Even when working with the fear of the unknown, Cronenberg reveals the weakness of our physical housing. It's as if realistic studies of sickness would have been too moralistic for the filmmaker,[1] while deep speculation would have made him lose interest. The viewers of his early works experience less of a catharsis while experiencing the terror of others: we are too concerned about our own body failing one day.

For this artist, horror is a strange and wonderful intellectual exercise, a unity of psychological terrors with blood and guts. The arthouse crowd prefers to see his career as realism with menacing supernatural MacGuffins, while the horror fanbase notes the reappearance of mad science behind the films' corporeal horrors. Cronenberg intends for his characters to remain painfully aware as their bodies fail, while the engines are (pseudo)scientific endeavors: a sexual virus in *Shivers*, an infected organ resulting from skin grafting in *Rabid*, physically externalizing negative emotions in *The Brood*, and a virus released through televised media in *Videodrome*. As strong as the argument is against his work as horror, his early films grow from conceits of the science fiction-horror subgenre. Hardly filmmaking masking itself with the speculative, early Cronenberg reaches the heights of genre revision. He continued this practice before bringing the same ingenuity to the contemporary crime film.

Upon returning to the same territory for a while,[2] Cronenberg broadened his commentary in *Videodrome*. The raging virus now traveled beyond the body to cable television signals, hence spreading through a source of voyeurism. The film adds to his usual theme — fear of sickness — but now with media commentary. Focusing on the new (at the time) media of cable television and videotape, *Videodrome* predicts the viral video phenomenon of the internet age. Soon to become an investigator, Max Renn (James Woods), a cable television programmer of sleazy material, learns his station is able to pirate foreign broadcasts. One found program features torture and murder footage. By investigating the program — which he learns originates in Pittsburgh, after realizing that Malaysia is a decoy — he uncovers a conspiracy, while the "programming" begins to mentally reprogram him. His mind, or the breakdown of it, becomes the perspective of Cronenberg's universe. Like in the 1919 breakthrough of German expressionism, *The Cabinet of Dr. Caligari*, an investigation reveals the machinations of a greater power. In Cronenberg's case, it leaves viewers of the "Videodrome" program susceptible to a brain tumor, hence, familiar territory for the filmmaker. While the finished version of *Caligari* reveals the narrative as the delusions of a madman, Cronenberg posits such a perspective as a transformed reality under "infectious" media, which creates a new thought system through external stimuli. The filmmaker makes the psychological horror film equally surreal, and more so a subjective tone poem. Nonetheless, his character/investigator falls in a series of steps reflecting both the slasher film — the innocents, taken down one by one, are transformed into one man, who breaks down slowly — and the detective film, in the noirish tradition of the investigator succumbing to the seamy world he investigates.

With *Videodrome*, the filmmaker further expanded his psychological dimensions, hence creating resistance for fans to think of him as a "genre" director. Yet, the film shows the power of genre commentary. His followup, *The Dead Zone* (1983), is a crisp Stephen King adaptation, with little of the director's sensibility.[3] Yet, in 1986, Cronenberg returned with a sharp undercut of an established horror property: the 1958 Vincent Price classic, *The Fly*. Originally a blend of menace and camp — best remembered for the immortal "Help me!" scene, a blip of comment on cloning — was refashioned by Cronenberg into a reflection on ambition and science. The mad scientist figure now investigates the psychology of deterioration by way of Dr. Moreau–style cloning. A strong presence of the science fiction/horror tradition appears, with a transformational device aiming at advancement but bringing descent. Still, *The Fly* is Cronenberg's finest comment on the psychology of suffering. As a man-beast, Seth Brundle (Jeff Goldblum) is hyper-aware of his own approaching collapse. The buggish transformation creeps us into awareness.

After Cronenberg turned to the disintegration of two mad twins (1988's *Dead Ringers*), he moved to literary properties — not the usual British 19th-century fodder, but modern, adaptation-resistant works. Daring as the filmmaker has been with his choice of content, his move to film William S. Burroughs's 1959 antinovel, *Naked Lunch*, and David Henry Hwang's 1988 meta-stage drama *M. Butterfly* were practically suicide missions. The filmmaker would never satisfy fans of Burroughs, who pieced together the semi-autobiographical riffs into one of the baggiest of postmodern novels. Cronenberg chose to streamline the narrative of William Lee (Peter Weller) killing his wife and then descending into a hallucinatory underworld. The film's second act (if we should call it that) takes off as a fugitive film, though soon dissolving any crime film motifs for surreal narrative play. With the point of view more subjective than *Videodrome*'s, Cronenberg folds in divergent plot developments to reflect the novel's disjointed spirit (and including other works by Burroughs). Fans would hardly call it faithful, yet Cronenberg finds the source's spirit while maintaining his own style. Here, the filmmaker again considers bodily decay by visualizing Burroughs's own preoccupation of it. This film develops the psyche's fear of bodily dissolution beyond the level of *Videodrome*, which, in comparison to *Naked Lunch*, plays like a sinister prelude.

In its stageplay form, *M. Butterfly* is one of the most transcendent works of contemporary drama. Based on a true story, the play has built-in sensational appeal, about a man purportedly duped by a cross-dressing male into thinking "she" was the real thing: a demure operetta singer from Peking. The torn-from-the-headlines premise is a flat-out MacGuffin, through which Hwang delves into the psychology of racism, sexism, and East-West relations. Rene Gallimard, the poor fool duped by a manifestation of the West's illusions of the East, is jailed for espionage, where the play begins. This setting also helps to construct the play's framing device, as the narrative employs flashback to depict Gallimard's gradual acceptance of his descent: the crossdressing singer led him into spying. In the end, Hwang uses the postmodern stage-awareness, an undercutting of a classical opera (*Madam Butterfly*), and memory play motifs popular at the time (see Arthur Miller's *The Ride Down Mt. Morgan*, John Guare's *Six Degrees of Separation*, Paula Vogel's *How I Learned to Drive*) to crack open Gallimard's psyche and, through his experience, channel a universal comment on illusion and identity.

Both the film version of *M. Butterfly* (1993) and *Naked Lunch* (1991) are properties of psychological depth — essentially, a familiar style for this filmmaker. Cronenberg approached literary adaptation as a challenge, not a convenience. The territories are dark, Cronenbergian, and quixotic, the material that Terry Gilliam would tackle while caring less about being faithful than capturing grandeur, even if his Icarus wings fall away in the sun's heat. Cronenberg, however, stayed faithful and delivered profound, if dense, films.

He returned to his bodily horror territory in 1996 by adapting a more workable novel by J.G. Ballard, *Crash*, which treats, with a strange veracity, the quirky premise of fetishists getting off on car crashes. Cronenberg's next entry, *eXistenZ* (1999), uses virtual reality for similar means, in a film that critic J. Hoberman described as a retread of the darker and more probing *Videodrome*.[4] Things got darker and more disturbing in 2002's *Spider*, an early entry in the recent trend of child abuse victim films, including *L.I.E, Mysterious Skin, Towelhead,* and *Precious*. These films seek the ultimate cinematic crime by seeking the most extreme of victims. In Cronenberg's take, the victimized surfaces as incoherence personified, played by Ralph Fiennes who makes Geoffrey Rush's character in *Shine* seem articulate. Regardless of the trying narrative (the broken title character defamiliarizes viewers), *Spider* transfers Cronenberg's theme of decay from the body to the mind, as it ails communication and sanity. It's one strange, deep turmoil: true rotting from the inside.

In retrospect, *Spider* is true to the filmmaker's oeuvre, but also its nadir. The film's title character lives through extensive trauma of witnessing his mother's murder by his father (who, in a Lynchian style, presented his mistress to the boy as his mother), all trauma directed at the mind. While slightly revising bodily horror, Cronenberg had worked the motif until, like the title character, it had (very) little to say. Only a new genre would make sense at this point in his career.

Wisely, Cronenberg decided to remove the torments from bodily ailments to the milieu one occupies. The conflict now concerns criminality, how the self inherits the devious. Cronenberg moved to the crime film with *A History of Violence* (2005), an adaptation of a graphic novel of the same name. The graphic novelized crime story proved promising grounds for Sam Mendes in *Road to Perdition* (2002), yet with *History* the film moves beyond an interactive comic text. Concerned with how the body progresses and transgresses in a deviant milieu, Cronenberg created a visceral take on the crime film. Not ignoring the body when depicting the resulting violence, he captures the psychological oppression of such a life.

As a Canadian, Cronenberg makes an odd resident for this study. Yet his *History* is one of America, in which an East Coast hood has escaped to the Midwest to begin a new, redeemed life. At the film's beginning, Tom Stall (Viggo Mortenson) seems the picture of the pure, simple life running a diner and heading a happy family. His genial greetings to customers while pouring coffee make him seem nothing but the captain of the wrestling team, 15 years on. It's an image of small-town America, fabricated in its crisp detail, much like the veneer of David Lynch's *Blue Velvet* that holds something darker, even more vivid (see Chapter 10). Tom's Norman Rockwell–inspired appearance is a sharp turn from his carnal relationship with his wife, Edie Stall (Maria Bello), which channels a base energy into his character. She appears turned on by both his stability as a provider, and his image as the homegrown high school athlete now applying his work ethic to business. She enacts a cheer-leader-jock sex fantasy to channel his past life, an ironic move preceding the revelation of his actual, dark past. This one early sex scene (more follow) spices up a pretty humdrum professional life. It also hints of deviance in Tom, enough that his criminal past, which will soon resurface, won't disorient the viewer.

Another scene (this one disturbing instead of titillating) sets the tone of the film: a roadside murder scene delivered after the fact, leading to a boy about to be killed. The villains are characterless monsters, the kind of human hunter that Chigurh in the Coen brothers' *No Country for Old Men* would have been, were he not realized with such sensitivity and detail. While Chigurh is a player central to that film, the killers opening up Cronenberg's *History* prove to be MacGuffins. Yet, when reaching Tom, the killers show his peaceful existence to be a veneer.

These killers bring about the first narrative turn and the steps toward the revelation of Tom's past. When the killers visit Tom's diner after closing, ready to attack a woman, he reacts with a criminal's survival instincts. This small-town diner man turns into a master killer: beyond warding off the crime, he violently extinguishes it. In this scene, we see the agility and presence of actor Viggo Mortenson that caught the filmmaker's attention and

The criminal "reemerges": Tom Stall (Viggo Mortensen) in *A History of Violence* (2005, New Line Cinema).

made him into his muse (he would appear in *Eastern Promises*, discussed later, and leads the cast in the filmmaker's 2011 film, *A Dangerous Method*). The community does not witness Tom's brutal efficiency during this night-time scene — it seems to be for our eyes only — but his moral imperative. Now a local hero, he makes the news, unknowingly opening the Pandora's Box of his past. We learn Tom is really Joey Cusack, a Philadelphia gangster in a self-made "witness protection" program by having relocated to the Midwest. Soon more villains arrive, this time directly looking for Joey. He is something of a loadstone, as if channeling demons from the netherworld for them to return a damned angel that has escaped into the heavens.

Joey doesn't see himself as an escaped Lucifer, but a redeemed soul; the film, however, doesn't have such a clear position. Joey must turn avenger to protect his family. In this sense, he serves as a revised man of action: the most effective were the baddies who turned to the right side of the law. The hoods in *History*, essentially, want Tom returned to his home back East, a journey that Cronenberg portrays as a descent to a primal state. Indiana features small downtowns and verdant fields, while Philadelphia is noirish territory. As an inverted Western, a frontiersman who had found tame land out West must return to the hellish urban territories of the East, the land abandoned for something better. In terms of Christian myth, it's a picture of the redeemed having to prove his redemption by confronting the Miltonic pandemonium from which he escaped.

Even if the city looks dark, the confrontation happens in a stately mansion, albeit the home of a career criminal, Tom's brother Richie (William Hurt). As the crime head in this realm, Richie is Lucifer, happy in his realm. The unofficial hero of *Paradise Lost* is, of course, Lucifer, and this film serves up two warring versions of him. In Milton, Lucifer (in the form of a serpent) seeks out the Christ/Adam figure in the Garden of Eden for vengeance, which leads to the Fall of Man. In Cronenberg, Joey is Lucifer who thinks himself to be Adam, in his own paradise, though summoned to hell by the alternate version of himself. The redeemed, in the end, must defeat the evil influence. In his final showdown with brother Richie, Joey triumphs through catlike speed and acumen in battle: violence as natural as the breath of life. Though his family members don't witness the results, his swift triumph suggests to them that evil, hence "violence," may still have him.

A History of Violence develops into a revelation of the main character's duality, his paradoxical self that is neither damned nor redeemed, equally criminal and avenger. Cronenberg continues the theme in his follow-up, the tonally similar *Eastern Promises* (2007). This film leaves the United States for London, and through the new setting focuses in on the eponymous criminal body, the Russian mafia. In both *History* and *Promises,* the East perverts of the West, with *History's* Midwestern tranquility invaded by the Eastern state's crime now moved to the mob invasion of London from Eastern Europe. *Promises* concerns a mob employee, Nikolai, played by Mortensen. In following the classical gangster motif, he rises in the boss's confidence by showing commitment and effectiveness, for him to earn his "stars" tattooed on both sides of his upper chest and upon his knees, symbolizing that he kneels to no one. The signs are forever worn, and earned through murder. The film's final turn, however, reveals him to be a secret agent for Scotland Yard, Russian by birth and an impostor to a dangerous element of his mother culture. The final set piece, a fight scene reflecting Nikolai's last battle with his brother in *History* (both violent acts result in a confused identity), takes place in a sauna. Having clothed himself in only a towel, a bonding element requested by a boss, Nikolai gets blind-sided by two mob hitmen with sickle knives. Nikolai manages to down both by blocking the slashes and mangling the arms that wield them. Like Joey Cusack, Nikolai kills better than he serves justice.

A girl in question is Tatiana, who has died while giving birth to her baby. This birth attracts the interest of midwife Anna (Naomi Watts), who cares for the baby and is curious about the diary left by the dead girl (written in Russian). The young woman, the diary reveals, was imprisoned by the Russian mob's sex trade. Later, we see the prominence of this white slavery: as well as the ways in which playthings, the women — from Russia and other Eastern European countries — are used as sex partners for mobsters who need to prove their allegiance through the act. Dominating the women proves they'll perform regardless of the innocents involved.

Another dual identity for Viggo Mortensen in *Eastern Promises* (2007, Focus Features).

Hence, Watts becomes an unofficial investigator, her search leading to Nikolai's syndicate, headed by Semyon (Armin Mueller-Stahl), whose sinister nature is hardly a secret. His son, Kirill (Vincent Cassel), operates as Nikolai's immediate boss, even though the two share more of a brotherhood. Kirill is a loose-cannon presence next to the calm, focused Nikolai. The criminal network is imposing to Watts,

The unofficial investigator confronted: Anna (Naomi Watts) and Nikolai (Viggo Mortensen) in *Eastern Promises* (2007, Focus Features).

until Nikolai is unmasked to the viewer. The film finishes with a voiceover, the words of a dead girl (read from her diary) who laments her loss of identity. The words echo Nikolai's own lost identity: as a spy, he's done well; but he's done too much as a contract killer for the Eastern Promises. Joey cannot dissolve his past criminality; Nikolai has entered into it, undercover.

Cronenberg reveals Nikolai's moral code more and more, until we acknowledge him as a reasoning criminal, or compromised avenger. *Eastern Promises'* final twist adds ambiguity à la Joey Cusack to Nikolai's character. Nikolai finishes the film as an impostor to the film's alluring criminality, even if he's been perverted by it. *A History of Violence* investigates the psychology of the criminal who attempts to redeem himself. To do this, he must turn himself into an avenger, even if his vengeance only highlights his criminality. Criminality has seeped in to Nikolai. He fears its effects long before he can think of overcoming it.

The crime film environment often shows the natural complexity of its archetypes — how victims or criminals can turn avenger — and some of the best have suggested such character change. Yet, in Cronenberg's fine films, the archetypes cannot shift so fluidly. Histories of violence remain.

18

Reclaiming the Renegade Cop
Werner Herzog's *Bad Lieutenant:*
Port of Call New Orleans

It's hard to pinpoint when the law began to go renegade in American movies, though the change was complete by the early 1970s. The coppers of gangster pics and noirs are mostly solid authority figures, positioned to overcome the criminals in question. An early ruthless avenger (of the plains, not the city) is Ethan Edwards, who in 1956's *The Searchers* becomes so obsessed with finding the kidnapped Debbie that he grows crazed, too condemned to enter the homestead after completing his quest. Today, the film is widely regarded as the beginnings of the new Western, and one of Hollywood's first steps toward redefining itself. By the late 1960s, more common than the avenger-gone-bad was the victim-turning-avenger: for example, Lee Marvin's double-crossed gangster in John Boorman's 1967 film, *Point Blank* (a case of criminal-cum-victim out for vengeance). This tradition would become popular in the post–New Hollywood 1970s, with the *Death Wish* avenger series (a murder victim's husband becoming an avenger). By this time, the renegade cop came around in the form of Dirty Harry, a neo-noir avenger plagued by what he must combat: in the first entry, a serial killer (see Chapter 6).

The renegade cops of the 1970s, Eastwood's along with *The French Connection*'s Popeye Doyle and the Blaxploitation super-bads, moved away from the offbeat anti-plots of the New Hollywood. If they resolved the immediate conflict (as does *Dirty Harry* but not *The French Connection*), a larger one — the omnipotence of evil — would still loom before them. In turn, the not-quite-vanquishing renegade cops preceded the surefire, Reagan-era, comic-book-style superheros of the 1980s (Sylvester Stallone's *Rambo* series, the roles of Arnold Schwarzenegger). By the 1990s, the renegade cop became an artifact to deconstruct, as did the classical myths of Hollywood to filmmakers of the late '60s (the gangster for *Bonnie and Clyde*, the idea of the horror film's monster — actually human — for *Night of the Living Dead*, etc.).

In the wake of the first renegade cops, the corrupt cop appeared on film (see *Serpico*), a real-life haunt borne from the headlines, earning his own place within the crime film genre. He hints toward a distrust in authority that rose from the New Hollywood era, which itself worked off the enforced paranoia of the 1950s "Red Scare"/McCarthy movement. Hence, many viewers saw Abel Ferrara's *Bad Lieutenant* (1992) as an unmasking from a filmmaker who rethought the American Gangster (in the elegiac *The King of New York* [1990]) and the science fiction mythos (in *Body Snatchers* [1994], the popular motif realized in the literal darkness of a military base). Ferrara's *Bad Lieutenant* ponders what obsesses a cop, how violence can unravel him, and how the crime he sees breeds corruption. It would seem a modern social problem film, if it had an everyman — an audience surrogate — working beside him. Instead, the film offers only darkness, a far cry to what most of us could relate: a work of psychological anti-realism.

The film's many disturbing scenes helped it to earn a cult following and a rating of "NC-17" in America (though an edited rated "R" version exists).

Harvey Keitel (left) on the job as the *Bad Lieutenant* (2009, Artisan Entertainment).

It stars a face familiar to gritty New York crime stories, Harvey Keitel; Scorsese's early-career muse. After dropping his sons off at school, he breaks out his cocaine, and Ferrara lays out his approach by the first scene: fast-and-loose defamiliarization. Played by Keitel, the lieutenant recalls the actor's role of Charlie in 1973's *Mean Streets*. A Catholic with a crisis of faith, Charlie ponders the pains of hell when holding his hand over a church candle. Hence, we can even read the bad lieutenant as Charlie grown, having traveled a really bad road and sending himself straight to hell. Even with a relationship to the Church, the lieutenant hates its rule and icons. He desires redemption, even if unable to submit to it. Ferrara and his co-writers intend for the rape of a nun — the investigation of which makes for the film's story arc — to be a counterpart to the lieutenant's own torment, a connection submerged beneath his habitual deviance. The lieutenant's addictions are to drugs, gambling, and exploiting teen girls.

Like Travis Bickle of Scorsese's *Taxi Driver*, Keitel's lieutenant is a survivor of the urban wasteland. His attempt to maintain control through drug use (self medicating fails to describe his actions) are fractured by the nun's rape. It is as if the crime has unmasked the lieutenant's own faults, making him both criminal and internalized victim. Ferrara stays with gritty realism, informed by Scorsese though not as attentive to urban setting and design. *Bad Lieutenant* remains subjective to its eponymous character, save for a brief point-of-view reaction shot of one of the lieutenant's victims watching him. Ferrara utilizes expressionism during some drug use scenes, and then the surreal when Christ himself appears to condemn the fallen cop. Overall, the film lingers over mundane details — of how he shoots up; how he sneaks drugs from a crime scene; and how he opportunistically pulls over two young girls.

With a film so subjective, we desire a window into the lieutenant's being, how he feels during these unsavory events. The tone remains somber and seamy because it can be. Perhaps the lieutenant lives from one hellish moment to the next. His life may be a depressive hell from which he wants an escape. But we struggle to reconcile this feeling with any sense of jubilation in his better moments. Even if the film suggests Scorsese's Charlie gone bad, the lieutenant ends the film by turning into *Mean Streets'* Johnny Boy (the Robert De Niro character), the financially troubled loose cannon who gets a barrel to his head (in a film style reflecting to its characters' mentality). *Bad Lieutenant* isn't a morality play, though Ferrara tries to make it one. Only darkness comes from the sexual and chemical stimulants.

As unredeemingly dark as the film is, it seems to wear a moral veil, reminding us — in case we hadn't noticed — that said lieutenant is indeed bad. Even when getting off, he cannot find succor. This element suits the project's pedigree: Ferrara has created a 1990s exploitation picture. The original circa–

1960s style spawned from a moral rebellion, with many of its sex-ploitation films spending every inch of film flouting the authority that restricted them to the grindhouse or drive-in. But Ferrara fails to match his style with the character's perspective. Being bad is never fun for the lieutenant: the claustrophobic film condemns its own actions. Were we removed from his view, Ferrara might have an excuse for this approach. But as tooth-and-nail a filmmaker he is, he remains moralistic: his character may hate the Church, but we wonder about the film's higher conscience, and why Ferrara embraces a world removed from the lieutenant's. A film that could certify the protagonist's violent glee, and not stay removed from it, is worth the effort. Ferrara's film doesn't take us there.

In an era of aimless remakes — the horror genre may murder itself soon — filmmaker Werner Herzog and screenwriter William M. Finkelstein understand such a character. We cannot speak of Herzog's feelings towards Ferrara's film, since the former asserts he made his film independently from the first version.[1] Finkelstein, who took on the name of an infamous cult item, appears to have wanted to rework the original, looking at it as a mechanic who knows the gears can run at a higher performance. His lieutenant may go to the dark side, but clouds never obscure him. He really lives as a bad cop, and we know it's true because the film, remaining aligned to his perspective, is so much fun. Herzog's *The Bad Lieutenant: Port of Call, New Orleans* (2009; hereafter referred to as *BLPOCNO*) is a thrill ride, no schizoid punishment like Ferrara's. The film has many devices to launch a black comedy: a best-of-all-worlds script, an able performer (Nicolas Cage), and a director not fazed by such a madman.

Whereas Ferrara has attempted descents into madness, Herzog has mastered them. The former uses a steep fall in his earlier films, like *Driller Killer* and *Ms. 45*, and we look, in terror, at an experience far removed from our own. Herzog uses similar experiences, though tapping into our personal fears of taking such a fall. Ferrara never welcomes viewer relationship to his characters — he'd rather we watch them as if espying odd urban dwellers, and deal in the netherworld. Herzog likes the strange but universal, through his sense of the mythical. Herzog's *Aguirre: The Wrath of God*, is an expressionism-meets-vérité study of obsession consuming the self. The film concerns colonial discovery, but the central player consuming his mission and compatriots (as the self-proclaimed "wrath of god") transforms into complete destruction. The visual apocalypse correlates to his psychological breakdown, the film uniting experience with perspective. The Herzogian take on insanity can become actual — *Rescue Dawn* — or absurdist — *Fitzcarraldo* — creating an auteurist range that grants Herzog control of a universe of pathos. The script of *BLPOCNO* was ideal for Herzog. This lieutenant's desire for control creates sharp irony: a tragic realization that's comical. This character continually serves as an authority while committing crimes. On an objective scale, his self indulgence would mortify; in subjective mood (Herzog's approach), it's a grand ride.

Finkelstein makes the immoral yet conscience-stricken source material by Ferrara into an amoral narrative. A bad lieutenant needs no superego; his superior's experience is nowhere near his own. This project required a performer who can humanize the title role while making it diverting. Working independent of each other, these contributors would not have such a fine recipe. Integral to Herzog's rendition of Finkelstein's script is actor Nicolas Cage.

In the filmgoing community, Cage's name raises red flags. After a brilliant early career, with distinctive roles in *Raising Arizona* (1987) and *Moonstruck* (1987), the actor was offered showy projects that, ironically, were too limiting for his high-energy style. Able to channel dread and fear as much as jubilation, Cage overtaxes a character restricted to just madness, or sadness. (See *Face/Off* [1997] or *Snake Eyes* [1998].) In *Raising Arizona*, the Coens' cartoonish take on the caper genre, Cage channels so much excitement that we think he has little else. Yet, he also finds fear when he is the target, the comedy transforming into a far cry for help. In Mike Figgis's *Leaving Las Vegas* (1995), Cage (in an Oscar-winning performance) goes to the depths of malaise; he shows that a life iced over with inebriation can often seem blissful, if essentially empty. Many have seen his recent works as similar to those of Al Pacino, a late-career turn towards overacting. But *BLPOCNO* offers a palette broad enough for Cage, while previous roles — *The Wicker Man* (2006), *Knowing* (2009) — aren't scaled large enough for him. In *BLPOCNO*, he delivers some of his highest energy work in recent films (and that means quite a bit). Yet, he realizes scattered dimensions in his character's struggle to maintain power.

Cage seems a loose cannon in the film's first scene. Hurricane Katrina has come, and many law officers have fled, even though the prisons haven't been evacuated. A water snake slides through the bars of a prison cell, noting that evil now lurks, even if the animal imagery will prove a red herring (to be discussed later). A drowning prisoner begs for his life, while McDonough (Cage) scoffs with Stevie (Val Kilmer). McDonough's decision to jump into the water and save him is as much a stunt as an act of kindness. The jump leaves him with a back injury, and relying on prescription drugs. Morality has little motive, though action results in (physical) damage.

The passing time shows McDonough earning the rank of lieutenant for his bravery, and likely more self-inflicted injury in the process. The time shift shows him already going beyond his prescriptions of Vicodin for pain management. When he finds a connection to the properties room, full of drugs taken in as evidence, he also shakes down clubgoers for their goods. One couple is leaving a club called Gator's when McDonough accosts them. His blind accusation comes up true: they are holding crack. To avoid punishment, the girl offers him a hit, and a sexual favor in the process. The moment turns into a bestial flexing of power for McDonough, making himself king of the urban jungle he patrols — especially when he forces the girl's escort to watch.

This is carnal nature turns into a humorous motif: McDonough begins to see iguanas. First seeing two on a table during a stakeout (unseen by partner Stevie), the animals reflect McDonough's disassociation with reality as his power rises. The whimsical surrealism by Herzog opens viewers to McDonough's perspective. The filmmaker allows this to inform the rest of McDonough's more realistic actions. Through a brief, recurring animal motif, the film opens the kind of porthole to the lieutenant missing in Ferrara.

Herzog matches a subjective point of view with urban detail. Examples of the kind of realism are inherent to the cop film, though also create McDonough's milieu. Following the skewed photography of the iguana, Herzog could have infused the film with many such moments, making it safely distorted like an unreliable narrator's in fiction. But Herzog steeps the film in reality, making the milieu far from the claustrophobic disassociation of Ferrara. With Herzog's lack of knowledge of the original, we cannot speak of a conscious reactionary approach. But the new take on a revised script is like Otis Redding bringing the lyrics of the Rolling Stones' "(I Can't Get No) Satisfaction" into his own territory. It's a personal rendering, making content into aesthetics.

That said, Cage's character does share the same preoccupations as Keitel's. Needing to maintain his control that is disappearing, McDonough incurs gambling debts, and is assigned a heavy case: in this film, a drug-related multiple murder of Senegalese immigrants. He seems dedicated to the case, though questionable once he threatens the mother of a witness and the elderly women in her cares. Described by his boss as someone who always works, McDonough grows an addiction that turns him into a shell of a man. Never faltering in his performance, Cage is like a withering Klaus Kinski in an early Herzog film, a man whose need for power expands beyond his physical capabilities. It's as if McDonough's lack of sanity won't affect his determination. He is a lawman immersed in the post-frontier milieu, where drug trafficking fuels an overwhelming crime network. In this sense, his ordeal looms like Sheriff Ed Tom Bell's in *No Country for Old Men* (see Chapter 16).

While declining, McDonough continues to exert his power (even if barely registered by others at times) to cartoonish effects. To relieve his girlfriend, a prostitute, from her john, McDonough rises in exaggerated stiffness, saying, "I'm the last person in the world you want me to be," as if parodying the ruthless cops of yore. Remarks like "We don't hit girls down South," and his mock-gangster nasality when in a pickle, offer more comic moments, and may convince Cage-phobics that *BLPOCNO* is another scenery-chew for the actor. But all these moments show McDonough's disregard for reality, his commitment to realizing his own dream of power. His shakedowns result in his own probation, at which point his character transforms into the true bad lieutenant. He seeks out Big Fate (Xzibit), a drug dealer and leading suspect in the murder investigation, and offers him backup. Here, the lieutenant goes to the authority *on the other side*— the head of crime syndicate — in his continual struggle for power. His imperative reaches beyond morality, making this crime film into an absurdist statement. When Big Fate questions McDonough's motivation, asking him why he lacks care for the murdered family, the latter delivers his purest amoral sentiment: he "never did" care. The film has no concern for the moral boundaries of a traditional crime story. *BLPOCNO* lets its title character live beyond such plot restrictions.

With Big Fate, McDonough turns up his performance, now as the corrupt cop, with phrases like, "I'll kill all of you ... to the break of dawn!" — the kind of mock-gangster-rap sentiment that's dismissible from a wanna-be badass but worrisome from a lunatic. The phrase, aimed at his new criminal compatriots, reflects a carefree nihilism, making the crooks feel that his power

Hope in spite of it all: Terence McDonagh (Nicolas Cage) and Frankie Donnenfield (Eva Mendes) in *Bad Lieutenant: Port of Call New Orleans* (2009, First Look Pictures).

looms beyond theirs. Herzog returns to hyper-subjectivity after Big Fate's gang takes down a pack of mobsters tailing McDonough. After the gang enters Big Fate's office, they get shot down by the latter's posse, at which point McDonough tells Big Fate to shoot him again, since his "soul is still dancing." Herzog shows the dead man (through a skilled stunt double) spinning away in a break dance. This kinesis is McDonough's mind cracked wide open, deliriously happy now that he has defeated his threat and gained more power. Folk harmonica on the soundtrack, like in other scenes, reminds us we are aligned with the lieutenant, and not in a morally infused objectivity. The man whom McDonough had slighted, who sent his father's gang after McDonough—due to an incident with his girlfriend, a prostitute named Frankie (Eva Mendes)—further fuels McDonough's power after the attack. The gangster visits the precinct, swearing, in fear, that he has no more beef with the badass cop.

With McDonough going completely criminal, we now await his fall. McDonough makes good with his bookie (Brad Dourif), from funds he took through Big Fate's drug deals. To resolve the narrative, the film can either claim the lieutenant, have him turn yellow and go against the film's inspiration, or it can stick to its guns. The move is abrupt, almost smelling like a *deus ex machina*: evidence against Big Fate turns up in possession of the police, making them able to arrest him. This kills McDonough's new plan, and he must veer back toward the law to maintain his power.

He ends up as an extreme ironic antihero, almost a redefined one: he uses his inside information with Big Fate to lead to his arrest. While Stevie wants to knock him off, by faking a disruption of some kind, McDonough insists that they cuff him properly, holding some allegiance to the wrong side of his mock double-agency. From this comes a promotion to captain and evidence he's going clean: along with Frankie, pregnant with his child, his father, and Dad's significant other, McDonough avoids the wine during the ceremony, though we leave the film with the lieutenant self-medicating, when discovered by the prisoner he saved in the film's first scene. "Sometimes I have bad days," he tells him. But his megalomania leads to the final image: psychic removal to a surreal aquarium, where McDonough wonders if "fish have dreams." He swims aloof, removed from reality, having maintained his power, as the director maintains perspective.

19

Sam Raimi's A Simple Plan
A Triumph of Classicism

It may seem odd to end this book with a discussion of one of the oldest films featured. We come to *A Simple Plan* (1998) now because it is a transitional crime film in that it rejects the postmodern time-play in the popular Tarantino style prevalent during its release. At the same time, it's a film steeped in tradition, with a structure reflecting Aristotle's cause-and-effect, linear plot structure. A chapter on this film could, in fact, have opened this book. But appearing near the beginning of the crime film's recent revival, it proves to be one of the finest renderings of the theme's development of character. From the outside, *A Simple Plan* shows how simplicity can make for the finest in genre storytelling. It also shows the depths that such an approach can reveal.

The film is a successful adaptation by the author of the source novel, Scott B. Smith. In translating his story for film, he condensed the plot into its tight structure without sacrificing any of the tale's intrigue. The film has two other obvious predecessors: the Coen brothers' *Fargo*, released two years' prior, and Carl Franklin's *One False Move*, going back to 1991. *Fargo* (see Chapter 16), aside from its ironic humor, uses a minimalist narrative, which the snow-barren landscape accentuates. The events let loose characters that couldn't inhabit any other film. Their comic sensibility was one shared by Raimi in his earlier films (though not to be found in *A Simple Plan*). Having used Joel Coen as an assistant editor on his debut, *The Evil Dead* (1981), Raimi also co-authored *Crimewave* (1985) with Joel and Ethan Coen. *A Simple Plan*'s characters are more archetypal than the Coens', but just as relevant. *One False Move* shares affinity with *Plan* in its cast — both star Bill Paxton and Billy Bob Thornton, the latter of whom co-wrote the script for the former film.[1] Noteworthy as an early example of tight-plotted, ruthless crime, *One False Move* sets up character types as starting points for their development.

Raimi's association with a controlled film like *A Simple Plan* seemed odd at the time. Many critics and reviewers thought of him as the creator of madcap visuals for cartoonish movies, with the *Evil Dead* series culminating in the especially goofy *Army of Darkness* (1993). In *A Simple Plan*, Raimi looks to the ethos of Midwestern small-town life and uses a style to match it. The only loose-cannon elements — and they are brief— are the humor of Billy Bob's character, Jacob, earlier in the film, and an eye-popping shotgun killing that throws its victim to a wall (as a cartoonish moment unlike the rest of the film, the latter element must be an in-joke to fans recalling Raimi's earlier career). Through a new venture in style for Raimi, his success here shouldn't be a surprise. The filmmaker has been a genre workman throughout his career, taking on tradition with a new sensibility and vigor. His contributions to the 1980s horror-comedy, through his *Evil Dead* series, are sizable, as he capitalizes on horror fans' predisposition for laughs, a factor minimally explored before him. (Raimi's debut feature, *The Evil Dead* (1983), helped start a horror-comedy subgenre in the 1980s.) Later in his career, Raimi revised the Western (in *The Quick and the Dead*, 1995) and took on romance, with less success (*For Love of the Game*, 1999). His recent horror-parody, *Drag Me to Hell* (2009)— at once recalling his *Evil Dead* films and the antithesis to recent "torture porn" horror — seemed like a getaway from his *Spider-Man* series, an occasion for fun. While recalling the filmmaker's own origins, *Drag Me* shows his handling genre material with ease.

Nevertheless, *A Simple Plan* marks the most special occasion, one showing Raimi having come a long way from his beginnings, as do his principal characters and plot device. The film begins with Hank (Bill Paxton), speaking in morosely voiceover, musing on his lost happiness, while onscreen he works in a feed mill, anticipating the end of the workday. His words invoke the tradition of classical noir: an obsession with the past that has sealed his fate.[2] Like the title of the film, Hank leads a simple life, in a small town with a steady, modest job. Likely set in the present, the film channels innocence and nostalgia through small town life. Hank walks home in the snow, with holiday time in the air (Christmas has just passed). He plays with children passing by, and jokes with a policeman, Carl (Chelcie Ross), jump-starting a car. The simplicity of the moment will be disrupted when Hank discovers money in a crashed airplane.

The discovery reveals a primal myth in the narrative, invoking the Christian Bible (Luke 10:36) and the adage that there is "no honor among thieves." The motif of greed sinking a triad of men mirrors a morality play, especially with the Christian resonance of the number three. A recurring plot motif, it appears in Chaucer's "The Pardoner's Tale." The author's narrative, told through the framing device of the Pardoner (hardly a decent man), is simplified into a moral allegory. The three bandits (who meet an old wanderer who predicts their fatal distrust amongst each other after finding gold) are intentionally vague for symbolic relevance. It was the aim of Chaucer, and the tellers before him, to have the greed resonate on a universal scale. The motif came to film in the form of John Huston's *The Treasure of the Sierra Madre* (1948), in which a bag of gold consumes its finders, a trio of prospectors. By moving the motif to a contemporary setting, Raimi and Smith ground it as a human narrative, with the everymen of today reflecting the universal. *Plan* appears to deploy static character types who will experience a series of suspenseful plot turns. Yet, the narrative develops the characters to show that their original, typecast appearances are premises of irony. In the best service that the genre can offer, the crime motif reveals true character.

Jacob (Billy Bob Thornton), Hank's brother, at first appears to be the latter's foil. He's introduced as a clown when joking with Lou (Brent Briscoe), obviously a drinking buddy, while Hank maintains a feeling of superiority. By having Jacob deliver humor, Raimi and Smith trick the audience into signing him off as comic relief. Such a role would lighten a crime narrative, especially one as stark and taught as this film. Thornton's character functions in the capacity until he transforms into a heart of darkness, one unable to bear

The prize appears for Jacob (Billy Bob Thornton), Hank (Bill Paxton), and Lou (Brent Briscoe) in *A Simple Plan* (1998, Paramount Pictures).

the evil that has surrounded him. As the plot reaches its climax, Jacob has seen the death of many near to him, including his best friend, Lou. In spiritual pain, Jacob asks his brother to mercy-kill him, thus creating a woodland-set allusion to John Steinbeck's *Of Mice and Men.* In the original narrative, the Depression-era migrant laborer George puts Lenny, his simple-minded friend, down because he has accidentally killed a woman. Essentially, George knows Lenny is not strong enough for their harsh environs, the embodiment of Steinbeck's naturalistic conceit. *Plan* evokes Steinbeck, with irony. The mercy killer doesn't instigate the act, but responds to Jacob's frenzied urging. Hank hasn't come to a realization on the level of George; the former thinks he can cover up the crime so he and his brother can continue their plan. It is Jacob, initially the simpler brother, who urges his own death. Now the Lenny figure has the realization, all too knowing. The original Lenny listens to his brother's description of happiness as his life is ended. Jacob dies in torment, seeing nothing but hell around him.

It takes Hank's own action, his pulling of the trigger, for him to discover the hell that Jacob has seen. His opening voiceover, describing his previous happiness, highlights his ignorance of the problems around him. Jacob's careless good times had masked his sadness. He's the only one of the two brothers to understand that their father lost their homestead farm by over-mortgaging it to pay for Hank's college, which led to his suicide, also unknown to Hank (who thought he died in an accident). In the film's most moving scene — one of the rare moments that doesn't directly drive the plot, though still develops character — Jacob, in a car outside Lou's home, reveals his lifelong feeling of loneliness. More than ignorant to certain facts, Hank now seems to have been ignorant about his brother; he was too busy being the fortunate son.

The narrative introduces his wife, Sarah (Bridget Fonda), as the female counterpart to her husband. She also works a simple job in a library to complete their simple life. Now pregnant, she promises a completed family to Hank and the viewer. (Considering she is with child, and the film's kinship to the Coen brothers' *Fargo*, Sarah undercuts the Earth Mother promise that we see in Sheriff Marge Gunderson. It takes complications in the plot for Sarah to transform into Lady Macbeth). She first urges Hank to return some of the money the three had found, to protect them against the criminals looking for it. This plan leads to the death of Dwight Stephanson (Tom Carey), when he is about to ride his snowmobile into the woods looking for a fox that got his chickens. Jacob hits Dwight out of desperation, but Hank finishes the job, in cold blood, by smothering him, leaving the old farmer with his toothless-appearing jaws hanging open, looking as if the life's been sucked out of him. (Hence, the titular "Simple" recalls the Coens' 1984 debut, *Blood Simple,* in which a supposedly murdered husband arises during his burial.) Sarah also

Crime changing character: Billy Bob Thornton, Bridget Fonda, and Bill Paxton in *A Simple Plan* (1998, Paramount Pictures).

urges Hank to tape-record Lou making a fake confession, with which Hank can blackmail him. This results in Lou, who goes for his rifle at the betrayal, dying as a result of the gunshot wounds caused by Jacob, now an unwilling killer twice over. Blackmail comes in a one-two punch: before his death, Lou tries to blackmail Hank for money before their agreed-upon time to split it up. With Lou as a threat, Sarah reacts with her own blackmail. Hence, the plot runs off both unity (dual blackmailing) and Lady Macbeth behind the scenes. The Lady Macbeth motif may seem dated here, with its inherent misogyny, as it positions Sarah as the agent behind much of the misfortune. Yet, this woman fueling the action indicates more than her removal from prominence, but her latent unhappiness. While Jacob shielded his discontent, Sarah's was hidden behind her June Cleaver–ish embodiment of the ideal housewife/mother-to-be. This Lady Macbeth's actions swell into Machiavellian plans. By revealing the truth of Jacob and Sarah, the film unveils its latent noir milieu.

Naturally, the truth of Hank's character also adds to the darkness. At the central conscience, Hank is our window into the film. Through him, we see this Midwestern milieu as one in which simple work and values are a means of reaching contentment, if only modest success. Sarah lives by the same values, until the greed peels them away. When their actions turn evil, they work in cold calculation: Sarah, while breastfeeding her newborn, details the plot to blackmail Lou, her weary face now looking sinister; Hank, while killing Dwight, looks away when covering the elderly man's mouth, pinching his nose to cut off his oxygen; and Hank when plotting out an alibi to a shaken Jacob after the two have killed Lou and his wife, respectively. The cold acts of evil further channel a latent noir universe. Frank Capra's *It's a Wonderful Life* (1946) makes an ideal small town the absolute reality, with George Bailey's nightmarish vision as the alternate reality, one from which he will eventually awaken. *Plan* inverts Capra's moral framework, by making the ideal small town an imaginary milieu. The truth appears in the snowy, empty field — the childhood home his father mortgaged away — in front of which, at the film's end, Hank finds himself, grief-stricken.

Age-old wisdom asserts that greed leads us astray, and that we must return to the right path once we've overcome our desires. The tragedy of *Plan* brings the film beyond the morality play origins, in which characters *represent* in lieu of existing. After Lou's death, when Carl finds Jacob outside of Lou's home, Jacob tells his brother he feels evil. While the direct address highlights the moral theme, veering the narrative back to the classical origins, Jacob's suffering — embodied in his close-up, with Hank in the background — reflects the fall of a man consumed with overwhelming Blakean experience. Greed merely reveals an innate opportunism that, for some, shadows out morality. The film offers an example of pure evil, in Gary Cole's character, though he works as a mere shadow to our principal player, Hank. The good, Jacob, dies young, and the evil lives on.

The film's effects are no surprise: hardly a moralistic treatise, *A Simple Plan* executes classical tragedy. The future of the genre is that of a refreshed tradition.

Chapter Notes

Introduction

1. Thomas Leitch, *Crime Films* (Cambridge: Cambridge University Press, 2002 [Reprint 2007]).
2. Foster Hirsch, *Film Noir: The Dark Side of the Screen* (New York: De Capo, 1983).
3. Robert Warshow, "The Gangster as Tragic Hero," in *The Immediate Experience* (New York: Atheneum, 1970), 127–133.
4. Richard Schickel, *Double Indemnity* (London: British Film Institute, 1992).
5. Hirsch, *Film Noir.*
6. Stanley Kauffmann, "Odd Surprises: Review of Lorna's Silence and My Fuhrer: The Truly Truest Truth About Adolf Hitler," in *The New Republic*, August 29, 2009, http://www.tnr.com/article/books-and-arts/odd-surprises (accessed 6/26/2010).
7. Manny Farber, "Underground Films," in *Negative Space* (New York: Da Capo Press, 1971 [Reprint 1998]), 12–24.

Chapter 1

1. Leitch, *Crime Films*, 103.
2. A cough by Martin Balsam's character, Mr. Green, accidentally gives him away to Lieutenant Garber (Walter Matthau) — the same cough Garber heard a number of times during his radio communication with the hijackers.
3. David Bordwell, Janet Staiger, and Kristin Thompson, *The Classical Hollywood Cinema: Film Style and Mode of Production to 1960* (New York: Columbia University Press, 1985).
4. This brief monologue, filmed in close-up, refers to the "bard," and thus recalls the opening invocation of *Henry V*, even the script quotes a line from the more familiar *Hamlet*.
5. "The Ultimate Heist: Making *Inside Man*," DVD, directed by Simon Sleap (Universal City: Universal Studios, 2006).
6. Roger Ebert, "Review of *Inside Man*," RogerEbert.com, http://rogerebert.suntimes.com/apps/pbcs.dll/article?AID=/20060323/REVIEWS/60314002 (accessed 6/3/2010).

Chapter 2

1. Russ Douthat, "The Return of the Paranoid Style," *Atlantic Monthly,* April 2008, http://www.theatlantic.com/magazine/archive/2008/04/the-return-of-the-paranoid-style/6733/ (accessed 6/3/2010).
2. Michael Guillén, "Tony Gilroy and His 'Parallel Universe Thriller,'" *GreenCine Daily*, https://www.greencine.com/central/tonygilroy (accessed 6/3/2010).

3. Paul Schrader, "Notes on Film Noir," *Film Comment* 8.1 (Spring 1972).
4. While Michael is Gilroy's creation, Clooney's fine performance realizes the suffering.
5. Jeffrey M. Anderson, "Interview: Tony Gilroy on 'Michael Clayton,'" *Cinematical*, <https://www.cinematical.com/blog/tony-gilroy> (accessed 6/3/2010).
6. Tony Gilroy, DVD commentary for *Michael Clayton* (Burbank: Warner Bros. Entertainment, 2007).
7. Gerard T. Koeppel, *Water for Gotham: A History* (Princeton: Princeton University Press, 2001).
8. Guillén, "Tony Gilroy."
9. Ibid.
10. Giorgio Agamben, *Homo Sacer: Sovereign Power and Bare Life.* Trans. Daniel Heller-Roazen (Stanford: Stanford University Press, 2001).

Chapter 3

1. Bordwell, et al., *The Classical Hollywood Cinema,* 5.
2. See Karen Hollinger, "Film Noir, Voiceover, and the Femme Fatale," *Film Noir Reader,* edited by Alain Silver and James Ursini (New York: Limelight, 1996 [Reprint 2005]) for a discussion of sexual roles and culpability in film noir.
3. For the definitive assessment of what makes a noir actor, see Chapter 6 in Hirsch, *Film Noir.*
4. For more on women in noir, see Chapter 4.
5. Schrader, "Notes on Film Noir."
6. Deborah J. Mustard, "Spinster: An Evolving Stereotype Revealed Through Film," *Journal of Media Psychology,* Volume 4, Winter 2000, http://www.calstatela.edu/faculty/sfischo/spinster.html (accessed 9/30/09).
7. Molly Haskell, "Paying Homage to the Spinster," *New York Times Magazine,* May 8, 1988, 18–20.
8. Richard Eyre, DVD commentary for *Notes on a Scandal* (Beverly Hills: 20th Century–Fox, 2007).

Chapter 4

1. Robert Porfirio, "No Way Out: Existential Motifs in the Film Noir," *Film Noir Reader,* edited by Alain Silver and James Ursini (New York: Limelight, 1996, 2005), 78.
2. Ella Taylor, "A Director Ever in Search of Survivors," *New York Times,* http://www.nytimes.com/2010/05/02/movies/02granik.html (accessed 1/18/2011).
3. Ibid.
4. In a scene from Lewis Milestone's *All Quiet on the Western Front* (1930), a soldier is blown apart while his hands, clinging to a wire fence, are all that remain of him.

Chapter 5

1. Exploitation films, like *Massacre at Central High* (1976), have played on the sensationalism of such conflicts.
2. Judith Hess Wright, "Genre Films and the Status Quo," in *Film Genre Reader III,* ed. Barry Keith Grant (Austin: University Press of Texas, 2003), 43.
3. While noting a connection between *Elephant* and *Paranoid Park,* critic J. Hoberman addressed *Paranoid's* "circularity," that its style returns to Van Sant's offbeat debut, *Mala Noche.* "Paranoid Park Returns Gus Van Sant to His Roots," *The Village Voice,* March 4, 2008, http://www.villagevoice.com/2008-03-04/film/sk8ter-boi/ (accessed 9/12/10).
4. On August 19, 2011, the "West Memphis Three" were freed after entering Alford pleas and being sentenced to time they already served.

Chapter 6

1. Vivian Sobchack, *Screening Space: The American Science Fiction Film*, 2d ed. (New York: Ungar, 1987), 17–63.
2. Since the term "serial killer" was not coined until the mid–1970s by the FBI's Robert Ressler, I will use serial murderer when referring to prior films.
3. The other influence from myth/folklore is Bluebeard (from the 1697 French folktale by Charles Perrault), who's been the subject of many early films. Charles Chaplin reworked the premise to make his black comedy *Monsieur Verdoux* (1947), starring Chaplin in the title role, that of a man who marries then kills widows to support his family.
4. Eddie Muller, DVD Commentary for *The Sniper*, on *Columbia Pictures Film Noir Classics, Vol. 1* (Culver City: Sony Entertainment, 2007).
5. Burt Topper's *The Strangler*, starring Victor Buono and also inspired by the DeSalvo case, appeared prior, in 1964.
6. Pauline Kael, *5001 Nights at the Movies* (New York: Henry Holt, 1991), 191. Also note that the masochistic "Scorpio" appears like a hippie affected by too many substances.
7. Nicole Rafter, *Shots in the Mirror: Crime Films and Society*, 2d ed. (Oxford: Oxford University Press, 2006), 93.
8. Pitt played a serial killer previously in *Kalifornia* (1993).
9. Robert Graysmith, *Zodiac* (New York: Berkeley, 1986 [2007]), 55.

Chapter 7

1. Rick Worland, *The Horror Film: An Introduction* (Malden: Blackwell, 2007), 243.
2. William Paul, *Laughing, Screaming: Modern Hollywood Horror and Comedy* (New York: Columbia University Press, 1994).
3. Kael, *5001 Nights at the Movies*, 618; Roger Ebert, Review of *Re-Animator*, *Chicago Sun Times*, October 18, 1985, http://rogerebert.suntimes.com/apps/pbcs.dll/article?AID=/19851018/ REVIEWS/510180303/1023 (accessed August 12, 2010).
4. The play premiered at the Goodman Theatre in Chicago on June 4, 1982. For more on Mamet, see Chapter 14.
5. Mamet has described *Edmond* as a commentary on the white race's long-time racial privilege that's now falling apart. Mimi Leahey, "David Mamet: The American Dream Gone Bad," *Other Stages* (November 4, 1982), 3. Edmond endorses the conservative political theories of Thorstein Veblen which claim that the leisure class sets the rules for the rest of society to follow. Richard Brucher, "Prophecy and Parody in *Edmond*," in *Gender and Genre: Essays on David Mamet*, ed. Christopher C. Hudgins and Leslie Kane (New York: Palgrave, 2001), 62.
6. In the play, this scene appears before the waitress's murder.
7. The film is based on the murder of Gregory Glenn Biggs by Chante Mallard. <http:// www.cnn.com/2003/LAW/06/27/windshield.death/> (accessed June 14, 2010).
8. Matthew Sorrento, "Object in Mirror May Be Closer Than It Appears: Stuart Gordon Talks About Horror, the Absurd, and *Stuck*," *Bright Lights Film Journal* 61 (August 2008), <http://www.brightlightsfilm.com/61/61stuartgordoniv.php> (accessed June 16, 2010).

Chapter 8

1. Eric Schlosser, *Fast Food Nation* (New York: Harper Perennial, 1998 [2005]), 120.
2. Kyle Smith, "Bean There, Bun That: Review of *Food, Inc.*," *New York Post*, June 11, 2009, <http://www.nypost.com/p/entertainment/movies/item_MzisT9ExiKm8XF4nwWzdYM; jsessionid=7EF1E3E3856E6B4FD8BD573902C78A55> (accessed 8/3/2010).
3. Something Weird Video releases these films on DVD and streams them specifically for cult film fans.
4. As the result of bad publicity from the film and other sources, McDonald's dropped their "supersizing" option at the end of 2004.
5. Critic Robert Sietsema aligned the film with science fiction/horror: "Some of the film's

scariest moments fall in *X-Files* territory." "Dying to Eat in *Food, Inc.*," *The Village Voice*, June 10, 2009, http://www.villagevoice.com/2009-06-10/film/dying-to-eat-in-food-inc/ (accessed 8/3/2010).

6. Howard Phillips Lovecraft, *Supernatural Horror in Literature* (New York: Dover, 1973), 12.

7. Karin Luisa Badt, "What's Wrong with Fast Food?: A Conversation with Richard Linklater and Eric Schlosser on *Fast Food Nation*," *Bright Lights Film Journal* 54 (November 2006), <http://www.brightlightsfilm.com/54/fastfood.php> (accessed 8/3/2010).

8. An exception would be critic Derek Hill, who astutely describes *FFN* as similar to "the best crime films" in which "there are no easy roads to the truth and no exit strategies once we get there." Derek Hill, *Charlie Kaufman and Hollywood's Merry Band of Pranksters, Fabulists, and Dreamers: An Excursion into the American New Wave* (London: Kamera Books, 2008), 57.

9. Brian Tallerico, "Richard Linklater, Fast Food Nation Interview," *Ugo Entertainment*, <http://www.ugo.com/ugo/html/article/?id=16019> (accessed 8/3/2010).

10. Dave Hoskin, "Dissent with Fries: 'Fast Food Nation,'" *Screen Education* 44 (2006): 24–28.

11. Gregory Stephens, "Cord Fed Culture: Living Large and 'Eating Shit' in *King Corn* and *Fast Food Nation*," *Bright Lights Film Journal* 68 (May 2010), <http://www.brightlightsfilm.com/68/68cornfedculture.php> (accessed 8/7/2010).

12. K.M. Jones, "Review of *Fast Food Nation*," *Film Comment* (November-December 2007), 73–74.

13. Stephens, "Cord Fed Culture."

14. Richard Linklater, DVD Commentary for *Fast Food Nation* (Beverly Hills: 20th Century–Fox, 2007).

15. Rob Nelson, "Grazed and Abused (Interview with Richard Linklater)," *Mother Jones* (November-December 2006), <http://motherjones.com/media/2006/10/grazed-and-abused> (accessed 8/7/2010).

16. Nelson, "Grazed and Abused."

17. Linklater, DVD Commentary.

18. In Chapter 10 of the autobiography *The Narrative of the Life of Frederick Douglass*, the author discusses the habit of slave owners supplying alcohol to their slaves.

19. Stephens, "Cord Fed Culture."

Chapter 9

1. The Friedman case was widely reported by the media. For a concise synopsis of the events, see case chronology at http://www.freejesse.net/Addendum.htm (accessed 4/20/2011).

2. See http://articles.nydailynews.com/2010-08-17/news/27072783_1_jesse-friedman-federal-judges-sensational-case (accessed 2/2/2011).

3. Susan Albert Loewenberg, "Interview with Dr. David Glaser, forensic psychiatrist," accompanying the radio broadcast of Bryon Lavery's play *Frozen* for L.A. Theatre Works, November 17, 2007, http://legacy.scpr.org/programs/latw/ (accessed 6/10/2010).

4. Hirsch, *Film Noir*, 172.

Chapter 10

1. Aside from frequently mentioning this practice in interviews, Lynch published *Catching the Big Fish* (New York: Tarcher, 2006), which collects his ruminations on meditation, intuition, and creativity.

2. Archive Interviews, *Blue Velvet: Special Edition DVD* (Century City: MGM, 2002).

3. Video Introduction to *Six Men Getting Sick: The Short Films of David Lynch* (Beverly Hills: Absurda, 2007).

4. Leitch, *Crime Films*, 184–191.

5. Bordwell, et al., *The Classical Hollywood Cinema*, 5.

6. Leitch, *Crime Films*, 184–191.

7. Ibid.

8. Allusions to the film have appeared in Lynch's *Wild at Heart* (1990), his television series *Twin Peaks*, and many of his later works.

9. *The Pervert's Guide to Cinema*, presented by and featuring Slavoj Žižek and directed by Sophie Fiennes (San Francisco: Microcinema International, 2009).

10. The filmmaker's original choice for the role of Frank, Robert Loggia, would have been a misfire — that growling-voiced performer would have been too mundane, too realistic.

11. Though Lynch did direct the moving and visually arresting *The Straight Story*, the film was from a script not originated by him. Thus, the narrative sits outside the filmmaker's usual sensibility.

12. Roger Ebert, "Review of *Mulholland Dr.*" RogerEbert.com, <http://rogerebert.suntimes.com/apps/pbcs.dll/article?AID=/20011012/REVIEWS/110120304/1023> (accessed 6/7/2010).

13. In Maya Deren's early surreal short film *Meshes of an Afternoon*, a key, along with a knife and other objects, serve as psychoanalytic symbols. This film set the course for many to follow.

Chapter 11

1. Raymond Chandler, "The Simple Art of Murder," in *The Simple Art of Murder* (New York: Ballantine, 1939), 1–22.

2. Tag Gallagher, "Shootout at the Genre Corral: Problems in the Evolution of the Western," in *Genre Reader III* (Austin: University of Texas University Press, 2003), 262–276.

3. See Chapter 12 for more on Eastwood.

4. See Chapters 6 and 12 for more on *Dirty Harry*.

5. For more on this archetypal stereotype, see Marvin D. Jones, *Race, Sex, and Suspicion: The Myth of the Black Male* (Westport, CT: Praeger, 2005).

6. *The Departed* is also a remake, of the 2002 Hong Kong film *Infernal Affairs*, and is loosely based on the Boston-area gangster Whitey Bulger.

7. DVD Featurettes, *Derailed: Anatomy of a Train Wreck* and *On the Run: The Fugitive* (Burbank: Warner Home Video, 2001).

8. The film was inspired by the killing of Esequiel Hernández, Jr. (May 14, 1979–May 20, 1997) in Texas, a mile from the United States–Mexico border. The shooting is also the subject of the 2007 documentary *The Ballad of Esequiel Hernandez*.

9. The film is based on the murder of U.S. Army specialist Richard T. Davis (March 14, 1978–July 15, 2003) and the investigation by his father, Lanny. The story was reported by Mark Boal in a 2004 *Playboy* article, "Death and Dishonor." Boal co-wrote the film with Haggis and eventually won an Academy Award for Best Original Screenplay for *The Hurt Locker* (2009), based on his experiences reporting in Iraq.

10. Roger Ebert perfectly describes Jones's face onscreen: "He doesn't smile a lot, but when he does, it's like clouds are lifting." Roger Ebert, "Review of *In the Valley of Elah*," RogerEbert.com, <http://rogerebert.suntimes.com/apps/pbcs.dll/article?AID=/20070913/REVIEWS/70913 0304> (accessed 6/3/2010).

Chapter 12

1. Selections from *The Charlie Rose Show*, *Mystic River Three DVD Set* (Burbank: Warner Home Video, 2004).

2. See the "Cough of Death" in Roger Ebert, *Ebert's Bigger Little Movie Glossary* (Kansas City, MO: Andrews McMeel, 1999), 215.

3. Mark Eliot, *American Rebel: The Life of Clint Eastwood* (New York: Harmony, 2009), 81–82.

4. For more on the development of the Western, see Chapter 11.

5. Eliot, *American Rebel*, 96–97.

6. Ironically, Kaufman would later direct the 1978 remake of *Invasion of the Body Snatchers*.

7. Viewers cannot escape the connection to Eastwood's roles, when Kowalski delivers to street gang members a line embodying "The Man with No Name"/"Dirty Harry" ethos: "Ever notice how you come across somebody once in a while you shouldn't have fucked with? That's me."

Chapter 13

1. Though Ebert has noted that *The Searchers* inspired *Star Wars* (see his November 25, 2001, Great Movies entry on Ford's film: <http://rogerebert.suntimes.com/apps/pbcs.dll/article?AID=/20011125/REVIEWS08/111250301/1023> [accessed 10/21/2010]), the latter film is based mainly on Akira Kurosawa's *The Hidden Fortress* (1958).

2. Leitch, *Crime Films*, 152.

Chapter 14

1. Featurette on *Redbelt* (Culver City, CA: Sony Pictures Home Entertainment, 2008).

2. Mamet dedicated *Glengarry Glen Ross* to Harold Pinter, who was instrumental in its being first staged at the Royal National Theatre (London) in 1983, and whom Mamet has acknowledged as an influence on its success, and on his other work.

3. David Mamet, introduction to *Five Television Plays* (New York: Grove Press, 1988).

4. David Thomson, *The New Biographical Dictionary of Film* (New York: Knopf, 2004), 569.

5. David Mamet, *On Directing Film* (New York: Penguin, 1992).

6. Hirsch, *Film Noir*, 172.

Chapter 15

1. Leitch, *Crime Films*, 103.

Chapter 16

1. Though the scene's quirkiness seemed completely fresh, murder/disposal of a body via a wood chipper–like device has a tradition: a suicide seemingly happens in a trash shredder at the end of *Once Upon a Time in America*.

2. Stephen Hunter, "Review: *No Country for Old Men* Chases Its Literary Tale," *Washington Post*, November 9, 2007, http://www.washingtonpost.com/wp-dyn/content/article/2007/11/08/AR2007110802476.html (accessed 6/10/2010).

3. Jonathan Rosenbaum, "All the Pretty Carnage: Review of *No Country for Old Men*," *Chicago Reader*, November 8, 2007, http://www.chicagoreader.com/chicago/all-the-pretty-carnage/Content?oid=997421 (accessed 6/10/2010).

4. Though the film begins with the text, "This is a true story," it finishes with a standard disclaimer that all persons depicted within are fictitious.

5. While in kind with the auteurs' work, Chigurh descends from author Cormac McCarthy's Judge Holden (from 1985's *Blood Meridan*), the otherworldly hunter of the mid–19th-century U.S.–Mexico border.

6. Stuart Covell, "Devil with a Bad Haircut: Postmodern Villainy Rides the Range in *No Country for Old Men*," in *No Country for Old Men: From Novel to Film*, ed. Lynnea Chapman King, Rick Wallach, and Jim Walsh (Lanham, MD: Scarecrow Press, 2009), 97.

7. Robin Wood, "The American Nightmare: Horror in the 1970s," in *Hollywood from Vietnam to Reagan* (New York: Columbia University Press, 1986), 70–94.

8. Pat Tyrer and Pat Nickell, "Of what is past, or passing, or to come": Characters as Relics in *No Country for Old Men*," in *No Country for Old Men: From Novel to Film*, 88.

Chapter 17

1. Though, in his later career, Cronenberg moved to more realistic depictions of sickness in *Crash*, about auto(motive) eroticism, and *Spider*, about memories of, and psychosis related to, child abuse.

2. The exception is his 1979 drag-racing film, *Fast Company*.

3. King had already claimed control over the filming of his stories, after Stanley Kubrick's *The Shining* deviated far from the King's sensibility and narrative.

4. J. Hoberman, "Trip Teases: Review of *eXistenZ*," *Village Voice*, April 20, 1999, http://www.villagevoice.com/1999-04-20/film/trip-teases/1/ (accessed 6/10/2010).

Chapter 18

1. Herzog originally wanted to change the title of the film, to avoid associations to the previous version. Barry Hertz, "TIFF Press Conference Diaries: Nicolas Cage and Werner Herzog on *Bad Lieutenant*'s unfortunate title and imaginary iguanas," *National Post*, September 15, 2009, http://network.nationalpost.com/np/blogs/theampersand/archive/2009/09/15/tiff-press-conference-diaries-nicolas-cage-and-werner-herzog-on-bad-lieutenant-s-unfortunate-title-and-imaginary-iguanas.aspx. (accessed 6/10/2010).

Chapter 19

1. Director Sam Raimi would film *The Gift* (2000), another script by the writing team, and a vehicle for Cate Blanchett.

2. Schrader, "Notes on Film Noir."

Bibliography

Agamben, Giorgio. *Homo Sacer: Sovereign Power and Bare Life*. Translated by Daniel Heller-Roazen. Stanford: Stanford University Press, 2001.

Anderson, Jeffrey M. "Interview: Tony Gilroy on 'Michael Clayton.'" *Cinematical*, <https://www.cinematical.com/blog/tony-gilroy>.

Badt, Karin Luisa. "What's Wrong with Fast Food?: A Conversation with Richard Linklater and Eric Schlosser on *Fast Food Nation*." *Bright Lights Film Journal* 54 (November 2006).

Bordwell, David, Janet Staiger, and Kristin Thompson. *The Classical Hollywood Cinema: Film Style and Mode of Production to 1960*. New York: Columbia University Press, 1985.

Brucher, Richard. "Prophecy and Parody in *Edmond*." In *Gender and Genre: Essays on David Mamet*. Edited by Christopher C. Hudgins and Leslie Kane. New York: Palgrave, 2001.

Chandler, Raymond. "The Simple Art of Murder." In *The Simple Art of Murder*. New York: Ballantine, 1939.

Covell, Stuart. "Devil with a Bad Haircut: Postmodern Villainy Rides the Range in *No Country for Old Men*." In *No Country for Old Men: From Novel to Film*. Edited by Lynnea Chapman King, Rick Wallach, and Jim Walsh. Lanham, MD: Scarecrow Press, 2009.

Douthat, Russ. "The Return of the Paranoid Style." *Atlantic Monthly*, April 2008, <http://www.theatlantic.com/magazine/archive/2008/04/the-return-of-the-paranoid-style/6733/>.

Ebert, Roger. *Ebert's Bigger Little Movie Glossary*. Kansas City, MO: Andrews McMeel, 1999.

Eliot, Mark. *American Rebel: The Life of Clint Eastwood*. New York: Harmony, 2009.

Farber, Manny. "Underground Films." In *Negative Space*. New York: De Capo Press, 1971 (Reprint 1998).

Gallagher, Tag. "Shootout at the Genre Corral: Problems in the Evolution of the Western." In *Genre Reader III*. Edited by Barry Keith Grant. Austin: University of Texas University Press, 2003.

Graysmith, Robert. *Zodiac*. New York: Berkeley, 1986 (Reprint 2007).

Guillén, Michael. "Tony Gilroy and His 'Parallel Universe Thriller.'" *GreenCine Daily*, <https://www.greencine.com/central/tonygilroy>.

Haskell, Molly. "Paying Homage to the Spinster." *New York Times Magazine*, May 8, 1988.

Hess Wright, Judith. "Genre Films and the Status Quo." In *Film Genre Reader III*. Edited by Barry Keith Grant. Austin: University of Texas Press, 2003.

Hill, Derek. *Charlie Kaufman and Hollywood's Merry Band of Pranksters, Fabulists, and Dreamers: An Excursion into the American New Wave*. London: Kamera Books, 2008.

Hirsch, Foster. *Film Noir: The Dark Side of the Screen*. New York: De Capo, 1983.

Hollinger, Karen. "Film Noir, Voiceover, and the Femme Fatale." In *Film Noir Reader*. Edited by Alain Silver and James Ursini. New York: Limelight, 1996 (Reprint 2005).

Hoskin, Dave. "Dissent with Fries: 'Fast Food Nation.'" *Screen Education* 44 (2006): 24–28.

Jones, D. Marvin. *Race, Sex, and Suspicion: The Myth of the Black Male*. Westport: Praeger, 2005.

Jones, K. M. "Review of *Fast Food Nation*." *Film Comment* (November–December 2007): 73–74.

Kael, Pauline. *5001 Nights at the Movies.* New York: Henry Holt, 1991.

Kane, Leslie. *The Art of Crime: The Plays and Films of Harold Pinter and David Mamet.* New York: Routledge, 2004.

Kitses, Jim. *Horizon's West: Directing the Western from John Ford to Clint Eastwood* (New Edition). London: British Film Institute, 2004.

Leahey, Mimi. "David Mamet: The American Dream Gone Bad." *Other Stages*, November 4, 1982.

Leitch, Thomas. *Crime Films.* Cambridge: Cambridge University Press, 2002.

Lovecraft, Howard Phillips. *Supernatural Horror in Literature.* New York: Dover, 1973.

Loewenberg, Susan Albert. "Interview with Dr. David Glaser, forensic psychiatrist," accompanying the radio broadcast of Bryon Lavery's play *Frozen* for L.A. Theatre Works. (November 17, 2007), <http://legacy.scpr.org/programs/latw/>.

Mamet, David. Introduction to *Five Television Plays.* New York: Grove Press, 1988.

_____. *On Directing Film.* New York: Penguin, 1992.

Muller, Eddie. *Dark City: The Lost World of Film Noir.* New York: St. Martin's Griffin, 1998.

Mustard, Deborah J. "Spinster: An Evolving Stereotype Revealed Through Film." *Journal of Media Psychology*, Volume 4, Winter 2000, <http://www.calstatela.edu/faculty/sfischo/spin ster.html>.

Naremore, James. *More Than Night: Film Noir in Its Contexts.* Berkeley: University of California Press, 1998 (2008).

Nelson, Rob. "Grazed and Abused (Interview with Richard Linklater)." *Mother Jones* (November-December 2006), <http://motherjones.com/media/2006/10/grazed-and-abused>.

Paul, William. *Laughing, Screaming: Modern Hollywood Horror and Comedy.* New York: Columbia University Press, 1994.

Porfirio, Robert. "No Way Out: Existential Motifs in the Film Noir." In *Film Noir Reader.* Edited by Alain Silver and James Ursini. New York: Limelight, 1996 (2005).

Rafter, Nicole. *Shots in the Mirror: Crime Films and Society.* 2nd ed. Oxford: Oxford University Press, 2006.

Robinson, David. *Das Cabinet des Dr. Caligari.* London: British Film Institute, 1997.

Schickel, Richard. *Double Indemnity.* London: British Film Institute, 1992.

Schlosser, Eric. *Fast Food Nation.* New York: Harper Perennial, 1998 (Reprint 2005).

Schrader, Paul. "Notes on Film Noir," *Film Comment* 8.1 (Spring 1972).

Silver, Alain, Elizabeth Ward, James Ursini, and Robert Porfirio. *Film Noir: The Encyclopedia.* New York: Overlook Duckworth, 2010.

Silver, Alain, and James Ursini, ed. *Film Noir Reader.* New York: Limelight, 1996 (Reprint 2005).

Sobchack, Vivian. *Screening Space: The American Science Fiction Film*, 2d ed. New York: Ungar, 1987.

Sorrento, Matthew. "Object in Mirror May Be Closer Than It Appears: Stuart Gordon Talks About Horror, the Absurd, and *Stuck*." *Bright Lights Film Journal* 61 (August 2008).

Stephens, Gregory. "Cord Fed Culture: Living Large and 'Eating Shit' in *King Corn* and *Fast Food Nation*." *Bright Lights Film Journal* 68 (May 2010).

Tallerico, Brian. "Richard Linklater, Fast Food Nation Interview." *Ugo Entertainment*, <http://www.ugo.com/ugo/html/article/?id=16019>.

Telotte, J.P. *Voices in the Dark: The Narrative Patterns of Film Noir.* Urbana: University of Illinois Press, 1989.

Thomson, David. *The New Biographical Dictionary of Film.* New York: Knopf, 2004.

Thompson, Kirsten Moana. *Crime Films: Investigating the Scene.* London: Wallflower, 2007.

Tyrer, Pat, and Pat Nickell. "Of what is past, or passing, or to come": Characters as Relics in *No Country for Old Men*." In *No Country for Old Men: From Novel to Film.* Edited by Lynnea Chapman King, Rick Wallach, and Jim Walsh. Lanham, MD: Scarecrow Press, 2009.

Warshow, Robert. "The Gangster as Tragic Hero." In *The Immediate Experience.* New York: Atheneum, 1970.

Wood, Robin. "The American Nightmare: Horror in the 1970s." In *Hollywood from Vietnam to Reagan*, 70–94. New York: Columbia University Press, 1986.

Worland, Rick. *The Horror Film: An Introduction.* Malden: Blackwell, 2007.

Index

203